Folded Selves

Reencounters with Colonialism:
New Perspectives on the Americas

Dartmouth College Series Editors

Marysa Navarro
Donald E. Pease
Ivy Schweitzer
Silvia Spitta

For the complete list of books in this series, please see www.upne.com and www.upne.com/series/RECS.html

Michelle Burnham, *Folded Selves: Colonial New England Writing in the World System*

Jennifer L. French, *Nature, Neo-Colonialism, and the Spanish American Writers*

Dan Moos, *Outside America: Race, Ethnicity, and the Role of the American West in National Belonging*

Hershini Bhana Young, *Haunting Capital: Memory, Text, and the Black Diasporic Body*

John R. Eperjesi, *The Imperialist Imaginary: Visions of Asia and the Pacific in American Culture*

John J. Kucich, *Ghostly Communion: Cross-Cultural Spiritualism in Nineteenth-Century American Literature*

Ruth Mayer, *Artificial Africas: Colonial Images in the Times of Globalization*

Irene Ramalho Santos, *Atlantic Poets: Fernando Pessoa's Turn in Anglo-American Modernism*

C. L. R. James, *Mariners, Renegades and Castaways: The Story of Herman Melville and the World We Live In*, with an introduction by Donald E. Pease

Renée L. Bergland, *The National Uncanny: Indian Ghosts and American Subjects*

Susana Rotker, *The American Chronicles of José Martí: Journalism and Modernity in Spanish America*

Carlton Smith, *Coyote Kills John Wayne: Postmodernism and Contemporary Fictions of the Transcultural Frontier*

Carla Gardina Pestana and Sharon V. Salinger, *Inequality in Early America*

Frances R. Aparicio and Susana Chávez-Silverman, eds., *Tropicalizations: Transcultural Representations of Latinidad*

Michelle Burnham, *Captivity and Sentiment: Cultural Exchange in American Literature, 1682–1861*

Folded Selves

Colonial New England Writing in the World System

Michelle Burnham

Dartmouth College Press
Hanover, New Hampshire
PUBLISHED BY
UNIVERSITY PRESS OF NEW ENGLAND
HANOVER AND LONDON

Dartmouth College Press
Published by University Press of New England,
One Court Street, Lebanon, NH 03766

www.upne.com

Printed in the United States of America

5 4 3 2 1

Library of Congress Cataloging-in-Publication Data

Burnham, Michelle.
Folded selves : colonial New England writing in the world system / Michelle Burnham.
p. cm. — (Reencounters with colonialism—new perspectives on the Americas)
Includes bibliographical references and index.
ISBN-13: 978-1-58465-617-3 (cloth : alk. paper) ISBN-10: 1-58465-617-4 (cloth : alk. paper)
ISBN-13: 978-1-58465-618-0 (pbk : alk. paper) ISBN-10: 1-58465-618-2 (pbk : alk. paper)
1. American literature—Colonial period, ca. 1600–1775—History and criticism.
2. American literature—New England—History and criticism.
3. Economics and literature—United States—History—17th century.
4. Colonies in literature. 5. Economics in literature.
6. Travel writing—History—17th century.
7. New England—Civilization—17th century. I. Title.
PS191.B87 2007
810.9'3553—dc22 2006023983

Contents

Figures

Acknowledgments

This book's final chapter concerns debt, and I end this project with my own profound sense of indebtedness to the network of institutional, collegial, and familial relationships that has made this book possible. I am grateful to the John Carter Brown Library for a fellowship that supported my initial research in early travel and economic writing, and for providing stimulating discussion through its lunch seminars. Santa Clara University provided a Thomas Terry research grant that allowed me to conduct final research in the Department of Rare Books and Special Collections at Princeton University's Firestone Library. I thank the staffs at Princeton University Library and at Cambridge University Library for their assistance with supplying photographs and permissions for the images contained in this book. I delivered talks based on sections of this book at the University of Oregon, the University of Miami, the University of California at Berkeley, and the University of Massachusetts at Amherst. I thank Gordon Sayre, Peter Bellis, Len Morzé, and Laura Doyle, as well as the audiences at those talks, for their helpful comments and conversation.

For their readings of and responses to various portions of this project at its various stages of completion, I would like to thank Dwight Atkinson, Jennifer Jordan Baker, Marc Bousquet, Petra Dierkes-Thrun, Jim Egan, Philip Gould, Jennifer Greeson, Jim Holstun, Bob Senkewicz, and Laura Stevens. Many of these chapters were fostered along by the feedback of my interdisciplinary writing group colleagues at Santa Clara; my thanks to Bridget Cooks, Marilyn Edelstein, Eileen Razzari Elrod, Andrea Pappas, and especially Juliana Chang, who organized us and kept us going, and Diane Jonte-Pace, Associate Provost for Faculty Development, whose office continues to support the group. Neil Schmitz, who has guided me since graduate school at SUNY–Buffalo, reappeared just in time to make me realize I needed a better title and to read a chapter draft. Ivy Schweitzer and Tim Sweet read this manuscript for UPNE, and I could not have asked for better readers. I am grateful to Ivy for her astute and insightful reading of the manuscript, and also for her terrific advocacy for this project. My thanks to Tim for sharing his generous intelligence and perceptive suggestions. At UPNE, John Landrigan was a most helpful and patient editor, and Jessica Stevens provided thorough production support.

I have been fortunate to have the help of two terrific student research assistants. Elizabeth Ricardo assisted me with initial bibliographic work; Stefanie Silva continued and completed that work, and helped with additional research. I am grateful for their speedy, careful, and cheerful efforts. My thanks to Helen Moritz for last-minute help with Latin. Phyllis Brown provided continued support for this project as English Department chair. Carolee Bird and Cindy Bradley in the Bronco Express Office at Santa Clara University's Orradre Library have dealt patiently and efficiently with the multitude of interlibrary loan requests that have helped sustain my research over the past years. An earlier version of chapter 2 first appeared in *American Literature*, and I am grateful to Duke University Press for permission to reproduce that material here. Chapter 3 appears in condensed form in *Early American Literature*, and the University of North Carolina Press has granted permission to reprint that material here. An earlier version of chapter 4 appeared in *Criticism*, which Wayne State University Press has given me permission to reproduce. All three chapters appear here in revised form.

My parents, Dick and Ulla Burnham, have provided me with books and occasions for inquiry for as long as I can remember. Finally, and most of all, for their indispensable perspective and indefatigable support, their laughter and their love, I thank Chip Hebert Cassin, Mara Alice Burnham Cassin, and Jana Ursula Burnham Cassin–who has waited very patiently for this book to get dedicated to her.

Folded Selves

INTRODUCTION: COLONIAL FOLDS AND THE SPACE OF DISSENT

> The modern world-system was born in the long sixteenth century. The Americas as a geosocial construct were born in the long sixteenth century. The creation of this geosocial entity, the Americas, was the constitutive act of the modern world-system. The Americas were not incorporated into an already existing capitalist world-economy. There could not have been a capitalist world-economy without the Americas. (Quijano and Wallerstein 549)

> The multiple is not only what has many parts but also what is folded in many ways. (Deleuze 3)

IN 1638 THE ENGLISH merchant Lewes Roberts published the first edition of a book that would be reprinted and updated constantly throughout the seventeenth century. *The Merchants Mappe of Commerce* was the first English guidebook to world trade, an enormous compendium of advice, explanation, description, and calculation designed to assist all those engaged in travel to and trade with the four corners of the world. The book's commitment is commercial, its scope global, and its imagination spatial: it is organized according to the four markets represented by the continents of America, Africa, Asia, and Europe. I begin this study with Roberts' book because it illuminates a transcontinental early modern financial geography in which I situate seventeenth-century New England writing—writing that has long been positioned instead within a predominantly national, temporal, and religious framework. Books on trade and travel like *The Merchants Mappe of Commerce* are every bit as critical to understanding the politics and aesthetics of colonial New England literary culture, I maintain, as are the sermons of Puritan divines—and they provide a far more revealing context for the study of colonial materials than any later American texts or events might.

But the illustrated title page of *The Merchants Mappe of Commerce* (see fig. 1), with its radiating eye of divine providence looking over and down upon the worldly architecture of commerce and navigation, makes clear just how interwoven religious and commercial sensibilities were for seventeenth-century English traders and travelers. Reminders of the divine might be said to bisect the page, from the providential eye at the top, to the reassuring words "Deo Ducente Nil Nocet / Deo Reipub. Et Amicis [When God leads, no harm comes / For God, for the Republic, and for friends]" that surround the ship that appears at the base of the page. These religious references hold up a page, however, that overwhelmingly celebrates the human achievements of trade and travel. The two columns on the left side of the page, named "Pondera [weight]" and "Mensura [measure]," hold up a sphere of the heavens and its constellations. At the base of this pair of columns is the image of an encircled anchor labeled "ad hoc [to this]." The two columns on the right, called "Nummi [money]" and "Cambia [exchange]," hold up a sphere of the earth and its four continents. An encircled compass beneath the phrase "Per hoc [by this]" decorates the base of these columns.[1] Navigational knowledge, the illustration indicates, is necessary to arrive and anchor at the distant regions where one might engage in profitable trade. Moreover, the crisscrossed alignment of the four circular images on this title page represents the intertwining of navigation with global commerce.

Roberts' book offers commercial, not navigational, knowledge, however. The words carved across the top and base of the four columns attest that the four tools represented by the columns (weights, measures, money, and exchange) assist in bringing closer together the four regions of the world ("Quatuor Mundi plagae / hic quatuor Instrumentis") and that the wares of the earth are the foundation of trade ("Orbis terrarum merces / Fundamenta Mercaturae)." Framed within a white and arched central panel

FIG. I. Illustrated title page of Lewes Roberts' *Merchants Mappe of Commerce* (London, 1638). Courtesy of Princeton University Library. Orlando F. Weber Collection of Economic History. Rare Books Division. Department of Rare Books and Special Collections.

in the very center of the page are the book's title and publication information. The panel is shaped very much like an open doorway or window, suggesting that the book itself is an entryway into the mercantile knowledge necessary for trade. The title page not only celebrates global merchant-travelers and the coordination of worldly skills and spiritual fortune that makes their voyages and exchanges a success, but invites readers into the world of calculation and exchange that enables world commerce.

In its own way, *The Merchants Mappe of Commerce* shares with the contemporary work of Immanuel Wallerstein and other world-systems theorists an explicit recognition of the global dimensions of the early modern economy. In *Folded Selves*, I bring these very different historical and theoretical traditions of writing and thinking into dialogue with each other, and locate in early English writings on travel and trade the emergence of an investment sensibility fashioned through transatlantic mercantile credit relations. These relations, I argue, produced reader-investors whose increasing implication in the world economy encouraged them to fold over the long distances and delays of transatlantic travel and commerce, and in the process to usher in a new representational economy that helped to transform dominant conceptions of language, money, and self. Positioning seventeenth-century New England literature and culture within this spatio-economic context also adds new meaning to the politics and aesthetics of New England dissent, which emerges here as episodes in which colonial selves struggle to resist, accommodate, or negotiate their own position within the folded terms of a developing world economy.[2]

Piety and Prices

The same interweaving of the spiritual and the commercial that characterizes Lewes Roberts' 1638 title page can be found in the language of contemporaneous New England writers. In his sermon series *Christ the Fountaine of Life*, for example, the Puritan New England minister John Cotton describes the experience of grace in the rather surprising terms of shopping. Among the many ways of "having Christ," Cotton notes, is "to purchase him, to buy him" (15). He goes on to clarify, however, that "sometimes for want of spending of money in a right way, many a man looses the Lord Jesus; so that though Christ cannot be had for money, yet sometimes without expence of mony he cannot be had" (16). This sermon, which speaks of the spiritual rewards of financial risk, was delivered in England during the years when many were deciding whether or not to join the Puritan migration to New England and surely spoke indirectly to the economic concerns of potential emigrants. Cotton's words clearly would have encouraged hesitant Puritans to imagine the high costs of colonial emigration as a kind of religious investment.[3] The collection was not published, however, until 1651, at a historical moment when prosperity was beginning to return to Massachusetts after a decade of economic depression.[4] This economic recovery, Darrett Rutman notes, resulted predominantly from mercantile investment and participation in "an elaborate Atlantic commercial world, a criss-crossing network of affiliated merchants and agents" (*Winthrop's* 186–87) that often confused and alienated nonmerchants by the complexity of its exchanges and the unpredictability of the commodity values that resulted from them. Like the goods subject to such market fluctuations, Christ too trades at variable rates, according to Cotton, since "in case of persecution the market of Christ goes at so high a rate, that a man cannot have Christ . . . unlesse he hazzard all his estate, or a good part of it: In buying and selling of a precious commodity, a good Chapman wil [*sic*] have it what ever it cost him: So Christ is sometimes at an higher, and sometimes at a lower rate" (17). In these passages Cotton not only represents the possession of Christ in the *language* of investment spending but suggests that such possession sometimes *literally* requires monetary expense.

Cotton's conflation of spiritual with economic language here puts him in good colonial New England company. Roger Williams—despite his strongly felt theological differences and debates with Cotton—often turned to the same language of the market. In arguing for the separation of church and state, for instance, Williams compared the church to "a *Corporation, Society, or Company* of *East-Indie* or *Turkie-Merchants*" (*Bloudy Tenent* 73) whose success or failure should not impact the stability of the civil government. In a published letter to Cotton, Williams refers to the selling practices of "the common civill Market" (*Mr. Cottons Letter* 46) to describe the duties of a minister, and in a private letter to Cotton's son he describes the ministry as one of "the worst trades in the world" (*Correspondence* 2:630). Economics again enters Puritan writing in simultaneously literal and figurative dimensions in John Winthrop's famous lay sermon "A Modell of Christian Charity," which, as much as his earlier "Reasons to be Considered," fully integrates the financial with the religious dimensions of colonization. Even while constructing his projected "Citty upon a Hill" on a broad vision of Christian love, Winthrop dispenses numerous and detailed instructions about spending and gaining money, forgiving loans, and respecting the hierarchy of social status.[5] By recognizing the sermon's audience as simultaneously those on board the departing ship, those already settled in Massachusetts, and those who were staying behind in England, Hugh Dawson brings to Winthrop's imagery of knitting and binding a decidedly transatlantic and interdiscursive stretch. He acknowledges that Winthrop's message in the sermon applies equally to the institutions of the church, the civil government, and the commercial joint-stock corporation that was the Massachusetts Bay Company (127).[6] On the same occasion of the *Arbella*'s 1630 departure from Southampton to Massachusetts Bay, John Cotton mixed biblical with bookkeeping advice in *Gods Promise to His Plantation*. He reminds his audience that among the reasons that justify removing to New England are the "opportunity to discharge their debts, and to satisfy their Creditors. I *Sam* 22.1,2" (10), as well as to "travaile for merchandize and gaine-sake," which is approved by "our Saviour" in Matthew 13:45–46 "when he compareth a Christian to a Merchantman seeking pearles" (8).

In selecting such passages, my point is not to reopen the old debate about whether the Puritans' religious or economic goals dominated their departure from Old to New England, nor is it to suggest that Puritan religiosity somehow screened, or was otherwise undermined by, monetary incentives. T. H. Breen and Stephen Foster wisely reject the "ferocious debate over the primacy of economic as against religious" motives for migration when they insist that "the whole attempt to separate one cause from another appears not merely hopeless but unhistorical" (53).[7] It would be equally unhistorical, of course, to separate such motivations—whether individual or collective—from the arrangements of colonial investment, joint-stock purchase, and commodity export that made migration for whatever reasons possible. Whatever the specific *motives* of early emigrants to New England might have been, the *arrangements* that made it possible for them to emigrate at all were largely economic. It is worth remembering, for instance, that the first English colonizers financed their projects through the creation of colonial joint-stock companies that depended primarily on the participation of merchants, and it is equally meaningful that "[e]very seventeenth-century colony was founded during a depression" (Kulikoff, *From* 53). Much colonial writing was produced and published in the first place by New World settlers for an audience of investors and others who remained in England, and these material conditions inevitably fashioned its rhetoric in a reciprocal and informing rather than determinative way.[8] I highlight the passages by Cotton, Williams, and Winthrop above because their very language exposes the profound interpenetration of economic and religious discourse characteristic of early New England writing, Puritan or otherwise.

That writing is also characterized by often intense debates about the economy of language itself, about the spiritual or political implications, for example, of competing seventeenth-century aesthetics of elaborate or restrained prose styles. Despite their shared pairing of economic and religious language, for example, the "orthodox" John Cotton and the radical dissenter Roger Williams are generally cast as dramatically different literary stylists.[9] Cotton is well known for his opposition to figurative language, expressed in the preface to the *Bay Psalm Book* and elsewhere, and his sermons are characterized by Perry Miller as "perfect examples of the Puritan ideal of the plain style" that "use hardly any metaphors or figures but those supplied by the Bible itself" (Miller and Johnson 314).[10] The work of Williams, on the other hand, is described by John Winthrop as full of "figures and flourishes" (*Winthrop Papers* 3:147) and "written in very obscure and implicative phrases" that "might well admit of doubtful interpretation" (*History* 1:147). Philip Gura has characterized the writing of most all radical New Englanders, Williams included, as "gnarled prose" (*A Glimpse* ix). The Anglican Thomas Morton meanwhile scoffed at the Plymouth Separatists' inability to decipher his densely allusive poetry (a conflict I take up in chapter 3). And Edward Winslow insists, in his 1646 official response to the religious radical Samuel Gorton, that Gorton and his allies "could not write true english, no not in common words" (7). For a group of people generally characterized by their commitment to interpreting signs, it is indeed striking just how often colonial New Englanders appeared unreadable to each other, their very selves often as dense and undecipherable as their texts.

Cotton and Williams—like Winslow and Gorton, or Winthrop and Anne Hutchinson—are largely remembered as theological opponents who battled each other in a series of confrontations that mark New England's first decades of settlement. Yet when one looks closely at the language of the most explosive moments of conflict or dissent in seventeenth-century New England—including Plymouth's dispute with Ma-re Mount, the Antinomian Controversy, the exile of Roger Williams, and the Salem witchcraft affair—one finds debates about the aesthetics of literary style virtually inseparable from debates about theology and politics. As Philip Gura notes, it was often the manner even more than the content or fact of religious dissent that troubled orthodox magistrates and ministers like Winslow and Thomas Shepard (202, 245). And folded together with those worries about religion and aesthetics are, I suggest, economic anxieties that are embedded in the language used by and about dissenters and their opinions. It is time to abandon our tendency to define dissent in the colonial New England context exclusively in terms of religious forms of difference, and instead to accommodate the variegated geopolitical and socioeconomic terrain on which dissensus erupts and through which it is disciplined.

Folded Selves thus brings together concerns with the economics of colonial investment, the aesthetics of prose style, and the ideas of dissenters in seventeenth-century English writing in and about America. How might we make sense of the economic figures and terms used in seventeenth-century writing by Puritans and others? When and where do the material contexts of global and local economic exchange enter into writing in and about the colonial periphery of New England? In what ways might matters of class/status, property, and profit speak from within putatively religious writing? How might we describe and understand the stylistic economies operating in early New England prose? What is the relationship between economic ideology, religious identity, and aesthetic sensibility in the early modern circumatlantic world?

Beyond Declension

Despite the persistence of both figurative and literal references to economics in seventeenth-century New England literature, students and scholars alike often find it difficult to imagine the writers anywhere other than in church, and harder yet to imagine them engaged in the comparatively mundane and worldly practices of buying and selling goods, trading in the marketplace, investing in ships and cargo, compiling or receiving bills of exchange, and exchanging money or commodities in shops. Even historians of the colonial American economy such as John J. McCusker and Russell R. Menard bemoan the fact that "[e]conomic issues have seldom commanded center stage in New England studies," which has "focused instead on religious and intellectual issues and on the search for the origins of an elusive 'national character,' for the transformation of 'Puritan' into 'Yankee'" (91).

This scholarly bias might seem the logical result of the archive: in contrast to the seemingly countless descriptions of the spiritual status and inner devotional life of Puritan settlers, there appear to be relatively few written accounts of their trading activity or financial practices. Or it may reflect the assumption that when financial references do appear in Puritan writing, they are merely figural terms that stand in for more meaningful theological referents. *Folded Selves* urges a reconsideration of both these assumptions by recalibrating the values assigned to metaphorical and literal language, as well as to economic and religious genres. And of course, the conventional picture of Puritan New England is the result both of which archives we read and of how we read them. As Stephen Innes has ably pointed out, once account books are given as much attention as church records in historical studies of New England towns, "[i]t appears that many, if not most, seventeenth-century New Englanders lived in acquisitive, market-oriented societies" (*Labor* 172). It also seems to be the case that churches and countinghouses were in dialogue more than they were in tension with each other in early New England, for Puritans did talk about material economic concerns in church (in sermons, for example) and contemplate their spiritual estates while recording their financial ones (in account books, for instance). When they used what Andrew Delbanco calls "the imagery of finance" (*Puritan* 61) to describe and discuss theological ideas, their very words reveal that these two realms depended on and sustained each other, that religious matters are also, at the same time, socioeconomic ones.[11] In this study, I aim to take the economic import of early New England writing just as seriously as its spiritual import, to recognize that these texts are simultaneously economic and religious documents, to pay close attention to the materiality of seventeenth-century aesthetics, and to ask how our perception and understanding of the Puritans and colonial America in general might change as a result.

Of course, it was not only in language that commercial and spiritual ventures overlapped. It is well known that the meetinghouse and the marketplace were located across from each other on King Street in Boston, and attending church and visiting the market were officially linked together in that city as early as 1634, when the town's weekly market day was explicitly chosen to coincide with John Cotton's popular Thursday lectures (Rutman, *Winthrop's* 181).[12] In 1639, Boston's First Church declined John Winthrop's offer of land on which to build a new meetinghouse, persuaded by Cotton's argument that moving it away from the market would unfairly disadvantage the tradesmen who resided near it and that "the fittest place" for the church "would be near the market" (Winthrop, *History* 1:383). By the time the Third Church, founded largely by a group of merchants who had split off from the First Church, later built their meetinghouse on this same plot of land, the commercial district had grown enough that the new church was located near its very heart and on the same road that local produce traveled on its way to market—a location that helped to ensure the new church's vitality and growth (Peterson 43, 163). Meanwhile, though the Separatist leaders of Plymouth Plantation, the Anglican Thomas Morton, and the idiosyncratic seeker Roger Williams held markedly different religious positions from each other, they all operated trading posts where they advanced credit to Native Americans in anticipation of receiving from them furs that were subsequently shipped and sold in a European fur trade that extended as far as Russia.

Thus the practices and geographic districts of market and worship frequently overlapped in New England just as the linguistic registers of commerce and piety did. Likewise, the distinction between and within the genres of economic and religious writing also collapsed—or, more accurately, never obtained for seventeenth-century New Englanders in the way we often assume it did. As Robert Blair St. George insists, the worlds of "markets" and "metaphysics" were for colonial Puritans "never separate, their historical progress never linear" (380). Just as the sermons of Winthrop and Cotton delivered prior to the *Arbella*'s departure from Southampton include reminders about the emigrants' economic goals and identity, for example, so is William Bradford's *Of Plymouth Plantation* a record both of the colony's special providences and of its complicated financial arrangements with various London merchants (an argument I develop in chapter 2). Like Bradford, John Hull, Massachusetts' first mint-master and one of the founders of Boston's Third Church, kept diaries that simultaneously record gains and losses in his economic estate as a result of ongoing investments in Atlantic shipping ventures, and gains and losses in his spiritual estate such as illnesses and recoveries, births and deaths, and successful or failed appointments to public office. Hull's diary resembles, in this sense, the account books that he kept as treasurer for Boston and as private merchant: it records an ongoing series of debits and credits that he hopes and trusts will ultimately reconcile. After losing his investment in a ship and its cargo, for example, Hull hopes that "[t]he Lord give me spiritual and heavenly treasure, when he taketh from me earthly! and that will be a good exchange" (161). A letter from an accountant near the beginning of Richard Dafforne's 1651 instructor's manual on bookkeeping ends with the poetic reminder that "Our life and understanding given is / By God, to use (as mony) not amiss; / How long't enjoy it none knowes better, / Then he that made us first his debtor" (A6r). There is for seventeenth-century Englishmen on both sides of the Atlantic world a constant traffic between spiritual and economic accounts; rather than being sharply demarcated from each other, the languages of profit and piety overlap and intersect.

This intersection occurs not only within individual texts but in the types of books produced by various writers. In addition to a number of explicitly theological tracts and pamphlets, for example, Roger Williams also wrote the 1643 *Key into the Language of America*, a volume designed in large part to help potential merchants and missionaries negotiate with native Algonquin-speaking traders (and the subject of chapter 5). Thomas Prince, minister and colleague of Joseph Sewall in the Third Church, not only wrote sermons but *The Vade Mecum for America; or, A Companion for Traders and Travelers*, which collected information such as currency values, exchange rates, and commodity price lists (Peterson 139). William Pynchon, founder of Springfield and wealthy fur-trading merchant, wrote in 1650 a theological critique of Boston's Puritan orthodoxy whose title—*The Meritorious Price of Our Redemption*—perfectly illustrates the seventeenth-century blurring of the languages of faith and commerce.

Despite their geographical, practical, and linguistic proximity, however, worship and trade have most often been cast as opposing forces in the culture of Puritan New England, where, it is typically assumed, piety and profit were incompatible. If modern scholars have failed to see the blending of economic and religious discourses in colonial America, it is because the literary historical narrative of New England has been utterly dependent on the opposition between commerce and community, between economic and spiritual gain. By repeating a narrative model of declension whose origins Mark Peterson locates in William Bradford and whose persistence he attributes to Perry Miller, studies of colonial and early national America have tended to either disregard or demonize economic concerns and contexts. By pitting the spiritual against—and then privileging it over—the material terms of early American identity, this declension paradigm not only subordinates economics but—by leaving it a relatively homogeneous and undifferentiated category—prevents more careful consideration of the varieties of class/status identity in early New England and of the tensions, conflicts, and alliances within and between them. In other words, by identifying New England's seventeenth-century settlers and their culture and literature predominantly in terms of reformed Protestantism, traditional scholarship has made it very difficult to talk about economics. And by ignoring the rich and complicated heterogeneity of economic identities and affiliations in early America, we have also missed a more rich and complicated understanding of dissent and its language in early America.

Recent historical studies by Mark Peterson, Stephen Innes, John Frederick Martin, and others have gone a long way toward correcting this picture of Puritan New England by insisting on the Puritans' integration of commerce with community, and by uncovering the economic inequality and profit-seeking that characterized significant portions of the region and period. Literary studies, however, have been slow to integrate such historical work into their analysis of colonial New England writing—although a handful of recent books indicate that this may no longer be so.[13] Ivy Schweitzer has recently called for literary scholars to position "New England Puritan culture firmly in specific social and especially economic contexts" ("Salutary" 589)—in part as an antidote to the decided neglect of material life in New England literary studies, and in part because these contexts are so crucial to understanding "[c]olonialism, imperialism, postcolonialism, and their cultural expressions" (589). Her call echoes a complaint lodged long ago by Philip Gura when he wondered why scholarship had refused to consider the "economic origins of the American self" ("John" 256). As others have suggested, this avoidance doubtless betrays an ideological investment in an American national narrative that wants to insist on the spiritual and communitarian rather than the material and commercial origins and character of the United States. *Folded Selves* grows out of an interest in seeing what colonial New England writing looks like once it is situated in the global context of a world economy rather than yoked to a nationalist trope of religious freedom, for without the relations of mercantile capitalism no Englishperson—Puritan or otherwise—might have even ventured across the Atlantic to America, much less have decided to write home about it.

Another explanation for the avoidance of economics in early American literary study might be that the final word would seem to have been said on such matters by Max Weber's powerful and controversial thesis about Protestantism's role in the development of the culture of capitalism. Puritanism encouraged the practices of asceticism, methodical account-keeping, the pursuit of an individual calling, and an ethic of labor that combined to foster "the development of a rational bourgeois economic life" (174) and promote "a duty of the individual toward the increase of his capital" (51). As a result of their religious ideology, Puritans were, for Weber, the cultural parents of capitalism. Whereas in the declension model inherited from Perry Miller capitalism destroys Puritanism, in Weber's narrative Puritanism capitalistically destroys itself. But despite its differences from the Millerian paradigm, the Weberian one is in many ways a nostalgic declension narrative all over again, telling the story of how pious Puritan profit-making destroys precapitalist pleasurable community, leaving its secular descendants to a life of competition and struggle. Weber's resembles Miller's account in other ways, too. Both position colonial identity and culture as anticipatory of U.S. nationalism, in a continuist narrative that makes Benjamin Franklin, for instance, the Revolutionary heir of the Puritans. Both also develop a relatively homogeneous model of Puritan theology and practice, presuming a religious and social consensus that has since been challenged on several fronts. And both—despite Weber's concern with capitalist ideology—remain inattentive to the material practices of economic activity in which Puritans and other colonial Americans were engaged.

Recent historical studies, however, have begun to make possible a more nuanced, post-Weberian discussion of economic culture in seventeenth-century America, and in doing so have begun to dismantle the narratives that have dominated early American studies more generally, and Puritan studies more particularly. Mark Peterson's account of the relative fates of Boston's prosperous Third Church and the impoverished church of Westfield over the course of the second half of the seventeenth century, for example, challenges the declension myth by exposing and exploring the fundamental integration of commercial and spiritual lives. Stephen Innes likewise provides a significant reassessment of Puritan economic identity by revising the terms of the Weberian paradigm. By recalculating Weber's understanding of the relationship between works and grace within Puritanism, Innes recognizes the far greater ambivalence within Puritan culture toward economic gain, and usefully casts New England Puritans as the unwitting and unwilling agents in creating a capitalist culture that they both "desired and abhorred" (*Creating* 37). John Frederick Martin takes even stronger issue with the declension consensus and its assumptions. His study illustrates just how central profit-making through corporate models of landownership was to prominent Puritan settlers and just how unevenly wealth and political power were distributed in towns as a result. The Puritans therefore "did not have to shed their religion before they could don their acquisitiveness. They could wear two hats simultaneously, and they did" (123). Christine Heyrman, too, rejects the declension narrative of change for one of continuity, where commercial commitments in Puritan culture coincided with and even helped to sustain communal ones (16–19). These scholars all replace the models of declension and opposition inherited from Miller and Weber with a more complicated, reciprocal, and mutually sustaining relationship between profit and piety in Puritanism. As Martin puts it, the "battle within New England culture was not principally chronological, but intellectual and psychological; nor was it waged so much between people of commerce and people of the cloth as between competing halves of the same New England mind" (128).

The World System and New England

In *Folded Selves* I turn to the world-systems theory of Immanuel Wallerstein and others in order to add to the local historical studies mentioned above a wider geographical framework in which to situate and interpret colonial American writing and economics.[14] For Wallerstein, early modern economics must be understood in the context not of the nation and its boundaries but of the "capitalist world system" that emerged in the wake of the European arrival in the Americas and consolidated during the seventeenth century. Capitalism is a world rather than a national system because its "economic factors operate within an arena larger than that which any political entity can totally control" (Wallerstein, *Modern* 1:348). This system is characterized by multiple cultures and political forms but by a single, geographical division of labor (Wallerstein, *Capitalist* 4–6). The system's overall stability is ensured by the fundamental inequality between different regions within the world economy, particularly between strong core-states and their underdeveloped peripheries (*Capitalist* 61; see also *Modern* 1:86).

In the early modern period, the emerging core state of England was among those nations that employed the ideology of mercantilism to govern its economic strategies and practices. As Wallerstein explains, seventeenth-century mercantilism "involved state policies of economic nationalism and revolved around a concern with the circulation of commodities, whether in terms of the movement of bullion or in the creation of balances of trade" (*Modern* 2:37). Within mercantilist ideology, nations competed with each other for the largest portion of the world's wealth, and overseas colonies became essential as external sources of bullion, raw materials, or markets that could enhance the economic, political, and military strength of the metropolitan center, which invariably sought to balance favorably its credit and debt.[15] Overseas colonial trade differed from local trade, not only by the immense spaces and times traversed, but by the possibilities of extraordinary profit (in many cases 200–300 percent) and the substantial amount of capital required in order to undertake these ventures (*Modern* 1:120, 121). The accumulated merchant capital in turn enriched core states, assisting in the seventeenth-century consolidation of the capitalist world-system.

As early modern nation-states entered into and shaped this developing world-system through voyages of conquest or exploration, they established a variety of models for the relationship between the American periphery and the European core. Historians and literary scholars alike have noted the differences, for instance, between Spain's pursuit of mineral wealth and its *encomienda* system; France's northern fur trade and its cooperative relations with Native Americans; the Portuguese trade in brazilwood and sugar; and the fur trade and land exchange relations of the Dutch.[16] Not all peripheries, of course, function precisely alike, and the region of New England fits only uneasily into the generic model supplied by Wallerstein. The colonies did supply some fish, fur, and timber to England, and the constant influx of new settlers especially during the first decades of colonization created a ready market for English goods. The mercantilist movement of coin back to England left the North American colonies beleaguered with a constant shortage of currency, and left those colonies underdeveloped in relation to the metropolitan core.

But the New England colonies were also, Wallerstein explains, more of a competitive liability than an economic asset for England for much of the seventeenth century (*Modern* 2:237). Moreover, the materials and markets they initially offered dwindled or dissolved by the 1640s. Many New England merchants responded to that crisis by investing instead in the triangular Atlantic trade, especially by supplying livestock and foodstuffs to the West Indies, where such materials supported the ongoing exploitation of slave labor.[17] New England thus became, Samir Amin argues, a kind of "annex" to southern plantation colonies that were themselves already "annexes" of merchant capital operating "in the service of nascent European capitalism" (*Unequal* 295, 296). Wallerstein classifies New England as a semiperiphery within the world economy (*Modern* 2:236) characterized by a mixture of both core and periphery activities—a kind of hybrid category others have defined as both underdeveloped in relation to the core and exploitative in relation to internal and external peripheries.[18]

Wallerstein's world-systems model has been criticized on several counts, including for positioning globalization far too soon in historical chronology and for displacing the nation as the central unit for understanding capitalist development.[19] But a world-systems model may precisely be of most value in disabling rather than reinforcing the nation as the central category of economic (or, indeed, literary) analysis. The virtue of such a geoeconomic model for American literary history is its incentive to trade in a national and temporal narrative for a more transnational and spatial one. While it is certainly the case that contemporary forms of globalization are of a different order than those that characterized the seventeenth century, a Wallersteinian framework encourages recognition of the global, transcontinental imagination illustrated so forcefully by Lewes Roberts' *Merchants Mappe*, and which informs the writing and reception of so many early modern texts. New England becomes, as a result, not the precursor to a nation or economic formation that would arrive only later, but instead a crisscrossed site engaged in uneven negotiations with European core-states and other peripheries, and marked also by its own unequally developed colonial centers and colonial peripheries. In this study I therefore follow Walter Mignolo—who adapts and renames Wallerstein's model the modern/colonial world-system, to better recognize the central role of colonialism in the emergence of modernity—in his call to move away from thinking of colonial American space as a nationalist site of "grounding" and toward imagining it instead as a site of "crossing" (69).

The charge that Wallerstein muddles the distinctions between mercantilism and capitalism by incorrectly associating capitalism with circulation rather than production is somewhat more vexing and deserves some consideration here.[20] The role of merchants and their money has bedeviled accounts of the seventeenth-century transition to capitalism at least since Karl Marx's famously unclear discussion of this phase as "mercantile capitalism." While some view merchants and international trade as a crucial determinant in the emergence of capitalism, others agree that merchant capital is incompatible with a capitalist mode of production and is instead a form of accumulation by trade that operates within, depends on, and supports feudalism.[21] As Fox-Genovese and Genovese argue, it is a mistake to identify "large-scale commerce" with capitalism. The capital accumulated by merchants as a result of such commerce not only "could not create capitalist social relations or a new system of production" but in fact "became an impediment to the emergence of the capitalist mode of production," reinforcing instead existing feudal social relations (6–8).[22] Merchant capital did fund (and reproduce itself through) the early European expansion into the Americas, but that exploration proceeded on behalf not of an incipient capitalist system but of a feudal system that was in crisis (12). Only in the seventeenth century was the "parasitic attachment" of merchant capital to feudalism severed, permitting this accumulated capital to come into the service of a new mode of production—capitalist agriculture and manufacture—in the core country of England.[23]

Class has been every bit as troubling a category in the seventeenth-century American context as capitalism has, and for similar reasons. Although there were plenty of traders and merchants who sought profit during this period, they were not capitalists. Nor did they constitute a class in the strictly Marxist sense, which traditionally reserves that category to describe groups differentially engaged in the property relations specific to capitalism as a mode of production.[24] Like merchant capital itself, seventeenth-century merchants operated within and on behalf of a feudal structure in crisis. In this study, I use such labels as "merchant" or "artisan" or "gentry" not to describe reified status categories with determinable boundaries, but to characterize early modern economic orientations that are unstable, that are very much in process, and that often overlap, perhaps particularly in the seventeenth-century colonial American periphery. I borrow from the work of James Holstun in using the more flexible formulation of "class/status" to describe socioeconomic formations in the seventeenth-century British Atlantic. As Holstun maintains, despite the fact that premodern status categories "do not refer exclusively to the mode of production," they "would collapse and become meaningless if they were not at least *partly* and even . . . *primarily* class relations" (99).[25]

The seventeenth century is thus typically seen as a final and critical period in England's transformation from a premodern feudal to a modern capitalist society, but many locate the emergence of a capitalist market economy in America only in the late eighteenth century at the earliest. Scholars continue to disagree over when and to what extent colonial American economies can be described as capitalist, and even whether there is such a thing as a colonial economy. As McCusker and Menard remark in the case of what would become the United States, "the concept of a colonial economy is anachronistic, the use of which goes unquestioned largely because of the postcolonial development of the United States" (8). Their comments suggest that narratives of American economic history have shared some of the same problems as narratives of American literary history, both of which have traditionally depended on teleological nationalist frameworks.[26]

Yet this is precisely where understanding the emergence of capitalism as a world rather than national system becomes useful. In doing so, however, it is critical to maintain the distinction between commerce and capitalism in discussions of particular regions like colonial New England within the world system. In response to charges that he mistakenly identifies the mercantilist early modern world as capitalist, for example, Wallerstein has carefully distinguished between a *world market* (which presumes the participation of all regions in a single capitalist market) and a *world system* (which recognizes that the capitalist market may not operate in many of the regions that nevertheless enable capitalism as a world system to function) ("Comments" 879).[27] This distinction allows us to see colonial America as a noncapitalist region that nevertheless supported a capitalist world-system through its participation in long-distance mercantile commerce. Aníbal Quijano and Wallerstein observe that the American colonies were critical to the modern world-system not because they were themselves capitalist but because they made the emergence of capitalism possible: "The Americas as a geosocial construct were born in the long sixteenth century. The creation of this geosocial entity, the Americas, was the constitutive act of the modern world-system. The Americas were not incorporated into an already existing capitalist world-economy. There could not have been a capitalist world-economy without the Americas" (549). Allan Kulikoff offers a somewhat analogous formulation when he observes that although the British North American colonies were "*noncapitalist*," they were also "born in a capitalist Atlantic economy" (*Agrarian* 7). Rather than try to assign a kind of economic ontology to colonial New England, therefore, it is more useful to define its role within this world economy.[28]

Andrew Delbanco may be right when he observes that the Puritans who migrated to New England "were in flight from what they themselves were becoming in England—a people fully involved in the pursuit of economic advantage, playing by the new capitalist rules, engaged in casuistical compromise over everything from church ceremonies to poor relief" (*Puritan* 12), but what looks like escape from a regionalist (and perhaps protonationalist) perspective looks more like implication from a world-systems perspective. The migration of Puritans and others to New England could be accomplished—and later their settlements could survive and thrive—only through a network of economic as well as religious supporters, through ties of investment and commercial exchange between the Old World and the New. Allan Kulikoff notes that "[b]efore a single ship could leave, merchants or the national government had to build and provision it, recruit immigrants, finance the voyage of those unable to pay, and provision the infant colony. Since the crown refused to finance emigration, colonization began only after English capitalists had accumulated sufficient surpluses to permit speculation in colonization" (*From* 40). Furthermore, as McCusker and Menard report, "[o]verseas commerce did not merely make colonial life comfortable; it made it possible" (71). If the Puritans fled from the troubling relations and practices of merchant capitalism, they also rushed right into them—and this tense cross-orientation is often embedded within their rhetoric and language, even when their ostensible subject has nothing to do with money matters. Of course, those New England inhabitants whose language seldom appears in the historical or financial record books—such as women, the poor, the enslaved, and the indigenous—were hardly primary or direct participants in the exchange and credit relations of transatlantic commerce. Yet their roles in regional, village, or domestic economies were often indirectly and secondarily linked to the mechanisms and relations of the world economy—for example, by providing labor whose invisibility permitted others to encourage overseas investment (in the case of the indentured servants and Native Americans at Thomas Morton's plantation, for instance); or through association with the local and long-distance exchange networks of their husbands, sons, and acquaintances (in the case of Anne Hutchinson); or by entering into debt with merchants and traders whose widespread credit transactions sustained transcontinental trade (in the case of the Native Americans who traded fur with Roger Williams and others, as well as many of the women and men involved with the witchcraft scandals at Salem).[29]

I offer the image of the fold as a way to conceptualize the colonies' instrumental annexation within the early modern development of a world economy. While the term *fold* might conjure images of an enclosed spiritual collective, especially in its use to describe Puritan-dominated New England, I mean it here instead to describe another kind of fold entirely: the bended site of colonial implication, a pleat that is both a part of and apart from the consolidating capitalist world-system. Perhaps one of the limitations of the center-periphery model is that its two-dimensionality insufficiently recognizes what might be called the curvature of circumatlantic space (and time) by the economic relations of investment and return.[30] In *Folded Selves* I argue that colonial American writing cannot be separated from transcontinental relations of credit, investment, and exchange—and that both literary and financial instruments contributed to the new curve and bend of transoceanic space, inaugurating a new geometry of selfhood and human relations that created, not only a kind of folded space and time, but also folded selves (an argument I develop in chapter 1). I read particular episodes of dissent in early New England as moments when that fold gets exposed, when seventeenth-century colonists confronted their unacknowledged implication in the new forms of language, money, and selfhood that developed along with an emergent capitalist world-system.

Subjectivity and Dissent

Janice Knight and Philip Gura are among those whose studies of Puritan dissent have challenged the consensus model of New England culture associated predominantly with Sacvan Bercovitch and, before him, Perry Miller. Gura suggests that radicalism from without the Puritan orthodoxy led to the strengthening and accommodationism of the center, that the New England Way became the New England Way only in response to the web of radical dissenting opinions that characterized early New England. Knight, on the other hand, suggests that the center neither was nor became as homogeneous as either Bercovitch or Gura suspect, but that it was from the beginning characterized by difference and disagreement. Both challenge Bercovitch's picture of New England as "a relatively homogeneous society" (*American* 20) that established a national pattern in which dissent is produced and appropriated by the very hegemonic authority it initially sought to challenge.

Represented for Bercovitch by the internally contradictory form of the jeremiad (which at once affirmed the Puritan sense of errand and castigated the Puritans for failing as yet to attain it), American middle-class ideology provides "a ritual of progress through consensus, a system of sacred-secular symbols for a laissez-faire creed, a 'civil religion' for a people chosen to spring fully formed into the modern world—America, the first-begotten daughter of democratic capitalism" (*American* 28). There is, as Michael Kaufmann perceptively notes, a certain performative power to Bercovitch's thesis, which itself ingests and absorbs any efforts to dissent from it (6). Kaufmann locates, however, a logical fallacy in Bercovitch's model of liberal capitalist selfhood, arguing that although he "offers an explanation of the *origins* of the American self . . . , his explanation actually presupposes the existence of such a self" (6). By seeking to understand instead "the historical development of individualism as it is reflected by particular moments of dissent" (6), Kaufmann joins such scholars as Theodore Dwight Bozeman and David Leverenz in challenging the presumed modernity of the Puritans, arguing that to the extent that there was a Puritan individualism, it was inseparable from affiliation with institutions, and suggesting that Puritans continued in many ways to strongly identify with premodern understandings of the self and society.

This book joins such scholarship in challenging Bercovitch's claims both of New England's homogeneity and of its essential modernity. But if these wider pictures of religious dissent are to alter Bercovitch's powerful arguments about capitalist ideology in America, they must also accommodate the socioeconomic dimensions of dissent that emerge from a more materialist reading of colonial writing. Perhaps because so many prominent colonial dissenters (including Thomas Morton, Anne Hutchinson, and Roger Williams) were exiled beyond the borders of the Massachusetts Bay Colony, it is tempting to imagine that what remained in the wake of such exiles was a coherent community that had successfully eliminated (while selectively ingesting) opposition to itself. But to imagine so is to forget that these exiled dissenters and their ideas were largely exaggerated versions of what remained behind and persisted within the so-called consensus of the New England Way. The difference represented by New England dissent might have been neither co-opted from nor exiled to the margins in order to strengthen the center, but might instead have inhabited a conflicted and self-resistant semiperiphery from the very beginning.

Folded Selves therefore asks how our perceptions of consensus and dissensus in America might change if we allow the promotional tract or bill of exchange to share ideological space with the jeremiad as the representative colonial genre; if the material economic practices of New Englanders are considered alongside, and in dialogue with, their devotional discourse; and if we position seventeenth-century New England as a semiperipheral fold within the early modern world-economy rather than at the origin of a national narrative. Colonial American studies have consistently identified dissent with particular individuals, and routinely defaulted to the term's more specific definition as theological disagreement. By situating colonial New England within the framework of the early modern world-economy, this book challenges these assumptions and complicates the conception of dissent that follows from them. The socioeconomic, political, and religious elements of dissent—understood in the term's more general meaning as disagreement, difference in thought or feeling—were folded together from the very beginning of the colonial project. Gura's own study intimates as much when he suggests that historians' underestimation of the economic roots and aims of New England radicalism has failed to produce the kind of analysis that Christopher Hill developed for seventeenth-century England (*Glimpse* 25).[31] Hill famously identifies in English radical writers and thinkers of the period a vision of the world "turned upside down." Parallel efforts by their contemporaries on the semiperiphery of New England may have been complicated by the practices of investment, commerce, and credit that enabled colonial emigration, settlement, and writing itself; they wrote from a world that had already been turned, if you will, sideways. I argue throughout this book that the eruption of dissent in New England repeatedly announces and grapples with the implication of colonial subjects and the colonial project within the folded terms of this consolidating capitalist world-system. Once New England is perceived as positioned within the fold of transatlantic space rather than protected within the seal of regional borders, dissent itself can be read as anxious resistance to the exposed terms of mercantile capitalism and its representational regime.

In the chapters that follow I show that the language of and about dissent in New England, even when it is about explicitly theological disagreements, reveals an extraordinary anxiety about commerce and hostility toward merchants and traders who are accused of misusing not just money but language—of lying, deceiving, and cheating. The heterodox and orthodox alike identified each other as mysterious, secretive, and deceptive—much as merchants and travelers engaged in trade were described by nonmerchants who were uneasy with the new instruments and relations of the expanding commercial world. The folded terms of long-distance mercantile relations generated the performance of a new kind of selfhood that became particularly identified with the slippery indeterminacy of merchants, and that appeared to have an inaccessible and troubling interiority. The often disproportionate anxiety and fear with which some New Englanders responded to the effects of this selfhood suggest its uncanny dimension, its simultaneous strangeness and familiarity. I suggest not that dissent erupted as a confrontation between mercantile and nonmercantile ideologies but rather that it registered the uneasy complicity of even the most anticommercial New Englanders in the capitalist world-system whose terms they otherwise feared and rejected. Indeed, it seems deeply significant that the most volatile eruptions of dissent occurred during periods of relative prosperity and prominence rather than during periods of relative poverty and ruin in seventeenth-century New England. In this way, writing from and about the ideological margins of the colonial world might be seen to expose the colonies' implication in—despite their marginal location within—a mercantile world-economy. If we refuse, for whatever reasons, to recognize these socioeconomic dimensions of early New England dissent (while recognizing, too, that these are never the only dimensions of dissent), American capitalist consensus is robbed of its own complicated ambivalence, leading us much too soon to overlook the discomfort and resistance that persists within capitalist culture and that continues to emerge at historical moments of crisis.

Keywords

Each chapter that follows is identified by a keyword that figures prominently in and among the texts I examine there and that, in many cases, resonates in the multiple registers of language, religion, and economics. Chapter 1, "Investment," examines the language of investment in early English travel writings about the New World, and the production in such writing of a folded subjectivity whose origins I locate in the rhetoric and practice of mercantile capitalism within the world system. Through a reading of early modern travel and economic writing, I argue that these genres share a paradoxical discourse of uncertain certainty. Both genres insist on an incontestable accuracy while simultaneously admitting that such certainty is never certain—a combined rhetorical strategy that constructed readers as investors who risked money as well as belief in the hope of always indeterminate future returns. The study of colonial American literature must begin with these writings, since such texts lay bare the transcontinental rhetorical and economic frameworks that equally determine the content and style of later "settlement" writings.

I position early New England writers and their texts within the rhetorical, aesthetic, and cultural traditions of these genres and discourses, and subsequent chapters consider particular New England writers and episodes of dissent in the context of this world system and its folds. It is precisely such a relationship with London investors, for example, that William Bradford catalogues in his history *Of Plymouth Plantation*. In chapter 2, "Merchants," I situate Bradford's text within the paired contexts of transcontinental colonialism and mercantile capitalism that characterized the world system in the seventeenth century. Once *Of Plymouth Plantation* is restored to these contexts, it emerges as a document registering considerable anxiety toward linguistic and economic change in the early modern Atlantic world, particularly among those subjects who most resisted their own implication in the commercial relations that characterized an emergent capitalist world-system. I survey Bradford's record of Plymouth's ambivalent relationship to merchants and argue that his use of plain style shares an ideology with his commitment to a production- rather than circulation-oriented economy—thus recognizing a materialist dimension to the early modern aesthetics of the plain style, and locating an element of economic protest that has gone largely unnoticed in Bradford's work.

Thomas Morton's confrontation with Plymouth and eventual exile from Massachusetts is often understood as the result of his own anti-Puritan idiosyncrasies, expressed in his only book, *New English Canaan*, which is typically read as a countertext to Bradford's *Of Plymouth Plantation*. This reading depends, however, on privileging the third and final section of Morton's volume, which presents a biting satire of the Plymouth Separatists. I argue in chapter 3, "Inflation," that *New English Canaan* in fact contributes to debates in the genre of contemporary travel writing about England's social and economic presence in North America. Read within the context of the world system, and in its three-book entirety, *New English Canaan* emerges as a text that constructs an aristocratic argument for English colonialism organized around what I call the mode of "trading-post pastoral" and its aesthetics of inflation. This chapter also identifies as central to Morton's vision and argument the suppression of the crucial role that Native Americans and their labor played in building and maintaining the colonial economy.

There is in Bradford's description of Morton an excessiveness both of style and anxiety that characterizes as well the response of John Winthrop and others to Anne Hutchinson and her role in the Antinomian Controversy. In chapter 4, "Vent," I read closely the language of Hutchinson and her opponents during the crisis for its revealing suggestions about the economic terms of antinomian dissent and the orthodox resistance to it. Hutchinson's critics frequently described her and other antinomians in language that not only associated them with mercantile commerce but that gendered the practices of circulation and exchange. In her trials, Hutchinson maintained a disparity between the inner and outer self—a subject position consistent not only with her theological beliefs but with her linguistic practice and her economic ideology. The fear and incomprehension generated by Hutchinson was ultimately a response to her performance of a protomodern subjectivity that terrified others, at least in part because it reflected the ways in which the orthodoxy were themselves implicated in a mercantile capitalism that they aligned with corporeal/colonial penetration and reproductive promiscuity.

Like Hutchinson, Roger Williams was punished for his unorthodox religious and political views by exile: he was sent across the border that represented both the geopolitical limits of the Massachusetts colony and the ideological limits of its dominant Puritan culture. I argue in chapter 5, "Equivalence," that Williams' dissenting opinions must be understood not only in terms of theology but in terms of his practice of other forms of border crossing—economic, linguistic, and ethnic. Williams established himself as a trader by actively and continually exchanging merchandise, as well as language, with the Narragansett Indians. Unlike his fellow trading-post manager Thomas Morton, Williams acknowledged the central role of Native American labor in the fur trade that sustained the colonial New England economy, and recognized, too, the natives' experiences of linguistic and financial uncertainty that resulted from their participation in the transcontinental credit system. Williams' trade practices not only distinguished him from other New England divines but contributed to his view of exchange—whether commercial, linguistic, or cultural—as fundamentally inequivalent. This view was furthermore consistent with his unique notions of religious typology, and with his insistence on paying the Indians for land occupied by English settlers. Williams' radical reformulation of the notion of equivalence—developed in part from his daily engagement in cultural, economic, and religious border crossing—helped determine his commitment to a practice of dissent and a dispossessive selfhood.

Cotton Mather's various accounts of the witchcraft affair are also concerned with violated borders, of both the flesh and the state. Chapter 6, "Debt," examines how Mather's concern with the penetrated boundary between the visible and invisible worlds, and the attendant debate over spectral evidence, raised troubling questions about the nature of representation that had earlier been raised in the very different but surprisingly analogous context of the production of paper money in Massachusetts, only two years before the witchcraft scare erupted at Salem. Much like the "shapes" of those accused of witchcraft, paper money provoked in New England a crisis of representation in which both the credit and the credibility of others became subject to radical doubt. As Mather's own language suggests, it was merchants and their credit culture that were perhaps most guilty of repeatedly opening and entering the borders of New England, much as the witches that Mather and others feared entered and exploited the gaps between their world and the visible one. Like the Antinomian Controversy earlier in the century, the witchcraft affair was a moment in which the bodies of women became potent sites, not only for the expression of the folded terms of an emerging modern subjectivity, but for the violent disciplining of that subjectivity.[32]

But unlike the case in Boston with Hutchinson, authorities in Salem were confronted by accusations that multiplied rather than consolidated, that dispersed among an ever widening series of bodies rather than taking shape in a single body. It is likely that because of the absence of a single central figure—or of an easily identifiable object of theological disagreement—the Salem witchcraft affair has more often been labeled a crisis or conflict rather than an instance of dissent in New England. The proliferating accusations and their use of antimercantile language indicate, however, a particularly wide and deep pulse of economic dissent within a semiperipheral colonial population unable fully to come to terms with its own participation within the spectral terms of an early modern/colonial world-system characterized by mercantile capitalism. My epilogue remarks that by recognizing the complex and foundational role of the Americas and of colonial writing within the dynamics of a global economy, we are better able not only to identify the economic and spatial terms of a folded modern/colonial subjectivity but to recognize the persistence of dissent within the capitalist world-system, even when that dissent is performed as the projection onto others of an anticapitalist discomfort experienced within.

Chapter One

INVESTMENT: UNCERTAIN CERTAINTY AND THE ECONOMIC SUBJECT

ONE OF THE MOST repeated anecdotes in early English travel writing is King Henry VII's response to Columbus' return from the New World. In his 1596 address to the "Favourers" who financially backed Sir Walter Ralegh's second voyage to Guiana, for example, Lawrence Kemys asks readers to imagine that moment of awful remorse when the English king heard "the strange report of a West *Indies*, or new world abounding with great treasure." Kemys recalls that, when first approached by Columbus with nothing more than a story and a request for money, King Henry refused to invest in his venture, finding the man "alien" and "subject to suspition" and his story beyond belief. Just like Henry, Kemys suggests, English people continue to "think it more credite to our common wisdome, to discredit most noble and profitable indevours with distrust." He reminds readers that "the penance of that incredulity lyeth even now heavie on our shoulders," and offers them his text as an opportunity for "repentance" (*Relation,* To Favourers, n.p.): readers are asked to put themselves in Henry's place and correct his costly skepticism. They can begin to undo the king's rhetorical and economic mistake by giving credit to both the Guiana venture and Kemys' account of it, which, he claims, has been written "without anie enlargement of made wordes" since "single speech best besemeth a simple truth" (*Relation,* Epistle, n.p.). A plain style and elaborate profits vie here as the ground and guarantee for truth and believability.

So, too, do they in John Smith's 1620 *New Englands Trials*, which invokes Kemys' same anecdote and same style to challenge English skepticism and tightfistedness.[1] Addressed to two merchant companies and several noblemen, Smith presents the narrative as the "observations and collections of a plaine Souldier" (394) written with "a souldiers plainnesse" (393). He expresses hope that, once these readers "make use of" (393) his text, it will "returne you such fruites from those labours" (394). But such returns depend on a risk or "adventure" of both belief and money that Smith's narrative must persuade them to take. He accordingly criticizes the "over-weening incredulity" (404) of the English, and suggests, like Kemys, that readers can remedy King Henry's past disbelief by imitating now the example of Queen Isabella, who "set [Columbus] forth with fifteene saile" (406). Smith admits that he "can promise no mines of golde," but he also asks readers "to consider and examine if worthy Collumbus could give the Spaniards any such certainties for his dessigne" (405–6). Having acknowledged this uncertainty, Smith goes on to assure a profitable traffic in fish, which "will afford as good golde as the mines of Guiana, or Tumbatu, with lesse hazard and charge, and more certaintie" (406).

This dual invocation of aesthetic plainness and economic profit characterizes nearly all promotional English travel writing of the seventeenth century. On the one hand, fish frequently stand in as a metaphoric substitute for gold in texts by Smith and others, but that metaphor itself depends on a material process of investment and exchange. Smith's mercantilist argument encourages readers to transform—by means of imagined commercial exchange—fish into gold, and to import the future profit back not only into England (where it might create a balance of trade) but into the textual present where, I suggest, it holds the place of truth. The "plain" style of seventeenth-century travel and economic writing worked much in the way that overseas mercantile practice did—within a suspended and recursive, or folded, temporality that renders these texts "true" only when their readers agree to become investors.

In order to understand the relationship between language and money elaborated in these texts, I bring the genres of early modern travel and economic writing together in this chapter. Just as promotional travel texts used mercantile language and techniques, mercantile texts incorporated travel imagery and information. Lewes Roberts, merchant and author of the remarkable 1638 guide to global exchange, *The Merchants Mappe of Commerce*, begins by insisting that all "*Merchants* or *Factors*, who are led thereto [to travel into foreign parts] by the *Motive profit*" (1) must learn geography, and he proceeds to offer instructions on how to read maps (4–10).[2] The merchant Thomas Mun likewise begins *England's Treasure by Forraign-Trade* (1664; written in 1622 or '23) with a long list of the kind of knowledge a merchant requires, including the ability to speak foreign languages since the merchant "is a Traveller, and sometimes abid[es] in forraign Countreys" (2). Mun and Roberts insist on the fundamental interdependence between early modern travelers and merchants, who often were, or became, each other. Just as travelers were generally funded by merchants, merchants relied on travelers to locate new markets, materials, and commodities. And just as many seventeenth-century economic texts include travel information and advice, seventeenth-century travel accounts are filled not just with descriptions of the journey, the landscape, and its commodities, but with advice on how best to initiate and sustain profitable trade with both Native America and Europe.

A close reading of mercantile and travel texts reveals that merchandising and traveling were often understood in terms of each other, and that they were both understood in terms of writing. Roberts later announces that his book is organized so that, among its four geographically defined sections, America is placed first—before Africa and Asia, and finally followed by Europe and London—in imitation of "the example of many *Merchants*" who, when attempting to sell a particular commodity, likewise "shew the *worst* first, and the *best* last." Roberts' language admits not just to the marketing of his book but to his book as itself a kind of textual marketplace within which words are goods offered for sale, much as he and other merchants marketed their wares within the network of trade routes, currencies, and exchange practices that characterized early modern long-distance trade—a network whose complexity necessitated and provided a market for guidebooks such as his. He hopes that his book will function as a "*Mapp*" by which the traveler-merchant can enhance "his owne profit and Commoditie." Roberts the writer, much like Roberts the merchant, is an adventurer whose text-voyage requires expense in order to yield profit.

Not only did the two genres borrow from each other, but they both developed in the context of mercantile capitalism—a term that I adopt to describe the investment and exchange relations that characterized colonial overseas trade in the early modern world-economy.[3] Although I focus here and throughout this book predominantly on the region of New England and writing from or about it, that region, its literature, and its political and social conflicts are, I maintain, incomprehensible outside their position within the transcontinental economic networks of the Atlantic world and the early modern capitalist world-system. The same is true of the aesthetics of plain style, which likewise belong not so much to the Puritans, the merchants, the travelers, or the scientists of the seventeenth century—all of whom were associated with various forms of plain prose—but to the world economy. "Plain" prose emerged as a means by which to manage the interdependent categories of truth and profit in the expanding spatiotemporal context of Atlantic trade. Early modern travel and mercantile writers resorted to plain style in order to persuade readers to invest in their linguistic and economic truth, but plain style itself must be understood in the context of the remarkable expansion in long-distance trade and the attendant development of mercantile relations that fueled these genres in the first place.

Repeatedly, it is the self-proclaimed simple style of early English travel narratives and economic tracts that brokers truth in the context of extraordinary risk. But as important studies by Robert Markley and others have demonstrated, there is really nothing "plain" about plain style, which is characterized less by its transparency or antifiguralism or neutrality than by the rather surprising force of its claims to be ideologically divested.[4] In their very efforts to market aesthetic guarantees for textual truth, early modern writings on travel and trade repeatedly betray their alleged "plainness." Lewes Roberts apologizes in the "Epistle" for his book's lack of stylistic sophistication by explaining that it issues from "the Pen of a *Merchant*" whose training has been distracted "from the study of *Arts* to the studie of *Marts*." Of course, the rhyme with which Roberts makes this claim not only betrays his own investment in the literary arts but lyrically aligns aesthetics with merchandising. And in his 1614 appeal for English investment in the shipbuilding and fishing industries, Tobias Gentleman apologizes that his experience as a fisherman has made him "more skilfull in Nets, Lines, and Hookes, then in Rethoricke, Logicke, or learned bookes" (3), a statement that not only rhymes but suggestively intimates that this otherwise humble "true relation" (4) written by "a Fishermans sonne" (3) has the power to seduce or entrap readers, as if they were fish netted and hooked by his lines of text. Robert Kayll's 1615 free trade treatise, *The Trades Increase*, makes explicit the rhetorical power of profit on which these texts depended, when he observes that "wherein if ever it were true, that a good cause maketh a good Orator, here is a subject to enable all meane Rhetoricians. Every man almost is taken with the attention to profite. Love doth much, but Mony doth all. Here is money, heere is profite in aboundance" (39). An early anecdote in the book tells the story of "an honest Romane Gentleman" who is tricked into purchasing a garden he is falsely led to believe contains a river filled with fish. This story is followed by an introductory note "To the Reader" that nevertheless invites one to read the book's appeal "frankely and plainely" (n.p.). Like their travel narrative counterparts, such economic texts seem surprisingly willing to admit, inadvertently or not, to the uncertainty of both their plainness and their profitability.

I argue that plain style depends on a linguistic economy of deferred reward that is inseparable from the investment relations of the consolidating capitalist world-system. While literary scholars are by now used to thinking of reading as a form of consumption, a careful reading of early English travel writing exposes the ways in which modern readers have perhaps always been imagined and produced as investors. The presumed or apparent truthfulness of plain style depends on its imported fantasy of a future profit that effaces and offsets present risk. In doing so, however, it positions truth within a complicated temporality because the certainty of present truth relies on a profit that exists only in an uncertain, and not-yet-arrived, future. Truth therefore depends on denying the time lag of exchange necessary to bring it into being.

The temporal dimensions of this long-distance investment matrix generate an emergent form of subjectivity characterized by an inaccessible interiority that both determines and destabilizes identity. These merchant selves appear as surprisingly modern selves, whose integrity and virtue ultimately rely—just as the texts by Kemys, Smith, and others do—on an investment rendered always uncertain by the spatiotemporal dimensions of the capitalist world-system. I argue that this effaced time-lag became identified as a kind of interiorized and inaccessible space folded within the merchant capitalist self, who appeared founded on an unstable, unfinished, and delayed ground. And in the early modern world-system, all selves—even those most opposed to the new relations of the capitalist world-economy—were in danger of discovering that their linguistic and economic exchanges resembled those of merchants.

Merchants and Colonial Credit

The predominant audience for promotional trade and travel accounts was merchants, a term whose definition is fraught with difficulty. I use that category here less to name those who had a particular occupation or rank than to describe those who participated in, depended on, and profited from an emerging long-distance, transnational commercial economy and its credit culture. Although merchants were of course already identified in the medieval era as "any man who earned his living by the buying and selling of merchandise" (Sacks 508), conceptions of this merchant class/status changed considerably as a result of English overseas expansion in the early modern era, when a significant split emerged between "a separate group of 'mere merchants,' limiting themselves to wholesale trade" (508), and those shopkeepers or businesspeople who sold locally and at retail the wares of such trade (572).[5] Much of what distinguished these "mere merchants" from others was their participation in what Sacks describes as "a new regime of private dealings . . . founded on credit" (513) that resulted from the extraordinary expansion and complication of long-distance foreign trade networks and that required "sophisticated financial and managerial techniques" (512). Sacks describes the marketplace in Bristol, for example, changing from an open space of public debate and predominantly local exchange to a largely private system of contractual relationships between known and trusted parties dominated by non-Bristolians who arrived at the market to deliver goods, place orders, and settle their accounts (513–28).

Of even greater interest for the New England focus of this study is that group Robert Brenner calls "new merchants" who began to invest in the American colonies beginning in the mid-1620s, when the larger London company merchants began to withdraw from colonial American ventures in the face of increasing losses and economic depression at home (*Merchants* 103). Brenner explains that these "new merchants" were often those barred from participation in the more secure and lucrative eastern and southern trades dominated by large companies of merchant adventurers. Whereas the Crown granted these large merchant companies trading monopolies in return for their risk, the "new merchants" were characterized by their willingness "to accept profit margins, take risks, and adopt methods of operation that neither the merchants nor the gentry would seriously consider" (Brenner 112). They were also drawn largely from social strata below that of the gentry or large-company merchants.

In the colonial periphery of New England, however, merchants would also have included "the younger sons of minor gentry or prosperous yeomen" as well as shopkeepers who engaged in trade in order to enhance their business (Brenner 114). What perhaps best distinguishes this complicated category of early modern merchants, therefore, is less a shared socioeconomic status than a shared attitude toward and participation in the credit practices and relations fundamental to the new overseas commercial networks. And on the North American periphery, nearly everyone was implicated in credit relations of one kind or another. As Walton and Shepherd note, a "complex credit structure" underpinned most market transactions in colonial America, where "[c]olonial merchants in the seaport cities usually purchased imported goods on one year's credit from British merchants or manufacturers. These goods would in turn be sold on credit to other merchants, often in small towns or the country, or to peddlers." Successful merchants with especially high balances due to them by customers could in turn use that credit as a form of money by transferring it to another (89). These customers could, of course, include women, who did not have any direct involvement in the relations of long-distance trade and investment, but whose role in the domestic and local economies nevertheless, if secondarily, entangled them in the financial mechanisms of the world economy.

Credit was absolutely crucial to enabling and sustaining the American colonies' role in the world economy, and it implicated in its complex and unpredictable structure a vast array of colonial subjects.

The mercantilism that determined English economic policy moreover gave to the colonies the role of helping create a balance of trade for England that would enhance its wealth and power. By supplying goods to England and providing a market for English goods, the colonies might help to reduce the outflow of bullion from England to other European kingdoms (Walton and Shepherd 36). As a result, bullion and coin were invariably scarce in the colonies, and various systems of credit and exchange were necessary in order to make commerce possible in the absence of coin. As McCusker observes, "little or no English coinage circulated in the colonial periphery—it was money of account only" (*Money* 121). In place of coins, trade relied on bills of exchange or forms of "bookkeeping barter" or "commodity money" (117) such as corn or meat or tobacco. Because exchanging such money forms into English coin always entailed some cost, colonial money of account was always of less value than its English equivalent; it "could [n]ever buy precisely the same sum in sterling" (121). The consequent fluctuations in and differences between currency values fostered new practices and professions that thrived on what came to be called "the art of exchange."

Overseas and transnational trade in particular depended on the bill of exchange, which, as Edward Misselden put it, allowed money to be moved long distances without having actually to be transported: "in a word, it's nothing else but a transmutation of money from place to place without transportation" (95). In his defense of the bill of exchange, Misselden argues that it protects from danger noblemen who might otherwise have to travel with large amounts of money, and it serves as credit for tradesmen who might possess a wealth that they do not currently hold (because that wealth may exist in debts owed them but not yet paid, or in goods possessed by them but not yet sold for money) (100). It also serves as a money-gaining device for young merchants with "little meanes, and lesse credit with the vserer," who can use it to acquire "great summes of mony" "vpon their own credits" (100). The bill of exchange was therefore fundamental to the transnational credit system that undergirded the capitalist world-economy, but it also created what seemed to many nonmerchants strange paradoxes: money that both moved and stayed in one place, wealth that was possessed but not held, the creation of vast sums of money out of nothing. All these paradoxes depended on the elision of the temporal delay of exchange, an elision performed also by plain style and by the selves of early modern merchants and investors who hoped to profit from such forms of exchange.

While McCusker and Menard have gone so far as to suggest that "[t]he fully self-sufficient yeoman farmer of colonial America is largely mythical: almost all colonists were tied to overseas trade" (10), Allan Kulikoff offers a rather more nuanced account of the relationship between farmers and markets in early America when he explains that "most colonial farmers participated in markets without being dominated by them" (*From* 206) and that the mixture of commerce and barter practices in New England "belies any notion of either full market embeddedness or self-sufficiency" (217). Even subsistence-oriented farmers, for example, sold surpluses in local and commercial markets, either on their own or through the agency of local shopkeepers who "linked farmers who rarely sold goods for export indirectly to commodity markets" (225). All this added up to a "complex network of merchants" who tied colonial urban and rural markets to each other and to overseas markets (207–8). It seems crucial therefore to recognize *both* the extraordinary range of colonists implicated in the seventeenth-century credit economy that helped the capitalist world-system to consolidate—including farmers, gentry, shopkeepers, company merchants, and new merchants—*and* the very different degrees of embeddedness experienced by these various groups and their members in that system and its credit culture. As Kulikoff observes, while the British North American colonies were, strictly speaking, noncapitalist, they were also "born in a capitalist Atlantic economy" (*Agrarian* 7). The same might be said about colonial American subjects, who were in without being of this capitalist world-economy in which they were compelled to produce, sell, and exchange (as well as to speak, read, and write).

The merchants and travelers who regularly operated and sometimes prospered within the risky terms of that world were often described as mysterious, secretive, and deceptive to those who shunned credit culture and its attendant risks. Subsequent chapters of this study examine seventeenth-century New England episodes of dissent as moments when more "embedded" merchant-traders reflect back to less "embedded" subjects images of their own commercial selves. This chapter establishes the terms on which such selves became founded. The case I wish to make here is that the new aesthetics of the English language that we find in travel and economic writing (among other places) is a mercantile investment aesthetics of uncertain certainty that emerges together with the economics of the capitalist world-system.

Anti-wonder and the Commodity List

In his influential book on Renaissance travel writing, Stephen Greenblatt argues that the "central figure" (14) in early European writing about the

New World is wonder, which registers a response to that which is "at once unbelievable and true" (21). From Mandeville and Columbus to Frobisher and Díaz, European travel accounts document the marvels of the New World, including the strangeness of new peoples and lands and the ease with which they are subdued and exploited. But Greenblatt's thesis, as well as it may describe late medieval and Renaissance travel texts, surprisingly fails to describe the decidedly anti-wondrous English travel accounts written much beyond the sixteenth century. One explanation of this shift is suggested by Mary Baine Campbell, who describes the transformation of wonder during the seventeenth century into a "suspect" and "inconvenient" (*Wonder* 4) sensation that would, in time, become aestheticized and associated with fiction. The early modern genre of travel writing plays a central role in the story Campbell tells, for it contains both the fantastic material of what would become prose fiction and the factual material of ethnology and other emergent sciences. But in order to understand the eclipse of wonder in seventeenth-century English travel writing, we must consider the investment relations that made possible the shift from gold or silver to fish or furs as the object of colonial travel.

Travel accounts were typically addressed both to present backers curious about the yield on their investment and to potential future backers. Increasingly these backers were not aristocrats or the monarch but merchants, including risk-taking "new merchants."[6] Writers like Lawrence Kemys and John Smith accordingly operate as merchants themselves, interested less in selling their book to consumers than in selling its story to investors. Of course, early colonial adventures like the Guiana and Roanoke projects were characterized by gigantic losses, and by the end of the 1620s every single English colonial company—including those responsible for the settlements in Virginia and New England—had failed both financially and organizationally (Brenner, *Merchants* 92). In the case of many such colonial projects, books became the only return on investments, and travel expeditions that resulted in losses were often reduced, literally, to words. Sir Walter Ralegh in 1596, for example, admits to his Guiana investors that he has thus far "only returned promises; and nowe for answere of both your adventures, I have sent you a bundle of papers" (iii). Likewise John Mason announces to the backer of his Newfoundland voyage that he can offer only a "bad markets returne, that is, papers for payment, for livers lines." Even the worst colonial losses were invariably answered with a literary plainness that took up the space left empty by monetary returns; as John Mason reports, the pages he returns in place of profits are "unpolished and rude, . . . , onely clothed with plainnesse and trueth." Even in the face of great skepticism brought on by complete financial failure, Mason's prose demands a rhetorical reinvestment that is never entirely divorced from economic promise. The new "plain" prose style of travel writing was in fact marked by what I will call "uncertain certainty," a condition that described, not only the relationship between the core of the world economy and its periphery, but the selves newly embedded in that circumatlantic economic space. If wonder (and its sensation of present excess) is the dominant aesthetic of gold and silver extraction, plainness (and its anticipation of future profit) is the dominant aesthetic of overseas mercantile capitalism.

Steven Shapin's influential argument in *A Social History of Truth* locates the seventeenth-century discourse of truth in "preexisting gentlemanly practices" (xxi) that were folded into the domains of natural philosophy and science. In a world where the profound distinction between the gentle and nongentle classes appeared to be dissolving, he argues, credibility came to be aligned with the social practices of the landed classes, whose leisure and freedom from labor and the market were believed to assure their virtue. This analysis locates emergent plain prose style in practices *apart from* and *opposed to* the traversed distances and fluctuating values of a capitalist world-economy. But Shapin's analysis underestimates, I believe, the ways in which plain style depended on and facilitated the very social changes it claimed to resist. Even (and perhaps especially) when it explicitly promises an aristocratic disengagement from the market, plain style is characterized by its implicit promise of profit from the market. Seventeenth-century plain style aesthetics made truth not an accumulated function of present assets but a suspended function of future profitability. In a sense, truth filled in for an imagined but delayed credit that would erase a current debit; truth *was* a bill of exchange. This formulation of truth was a necessary fiction required by an emergent capitalism, in which profit depends on what Immanuel Wallerstein calls "various deferrals of realized value" (*Modern* 1:46).

Julie Solomon's study of Francis Bacon and the origins of objectivity accounts for the commercial investments of seventeenth-century scientific discourse and its claims to truth in ways that Shapin and others have not. As Solomon notes, Bacon describes his method of scientific reasoning in terms of the ability to practice a "temporary cognitive self-distancing" (*Objectivity* 57) that was associated largely with travelers and merchants.[7] She also points to the writing and accounting practices of merchants—who kept a series of three books (journals, ledgers, and "waste books") that recorded their debits, credits, and transactions, as well as lists of current prices and exchange rates—as an important model for Bacon's three-tiered inductive method of scientific reasoning (129). Elsewhere, Solomon locates in Bacon the development of a scientific mode of reading that emerges in a dialectic between courtly and commercial models. Whereas courtly writers like Spenser and Sidney elicit readers' desire and encourage them to project themselves into and fashion themselves out of a text, Baconian reading and the merchant writings it drew from "virtually eradicate" readers' desire and assume that readers are "self-divested" ("'To Know'" 519). The rich and fantastic world of *The Faerie Queene* gives way, in commercial travel writing, to "nothing more than extensive lists of objects which the traveling observer is instructed to note" (521). The reader of such texts is as a result able, like merchants, "momentarily to suspend aspects of the self—its desires, values, habits, customs—to reap the material benefit that a thorough understanding of alien circumstances will provide" (521). Solomon describes a self-distancing and self-denial that promotes an objective clarity and in turn encourages more profitable business practice. Perhaps suspending the self encourages not objectivity, however, but an investment that only at a later moment in time will retroactively come to *look like* objectivity. After all, it is possible for lists to foster rather than eradicate readers' desire, but only if those readers become investors willing to defer their return of satisfaction to the future.

Wonder, on the other hand, generally offered all its returns in the reading present, and it accordingly discouraged investment. In contrast to the many earlier travel accounts characterized by the marvelous, seventeenth-century narratives of travel to New England seem virtually evacuated of wonder. What took its place was a rather mundane matter-of-factness, a spare and antifigural or "author-evacuated" (Campbell, *Wonder* 23) prose to which writers insistently brought attention in the letters and introductions that preceded their narratives. This stylistic attempt to represent truth was often described as "plain" or "simple" or "rough" or "rude," and it was those things, travel writers insisted, because it told the truth. The letter of dedication preceding Mourt's *Relation* (1622), for example, describes the text as "being writ by seuerall Actors themselues, after their plaine and rude manner; therefore doubt nothing of the truth thereof" (A3v). Likewise William Wood, in the note "To the Reader" that precedes his *New England's Prospect* (1634), insists that he offers "no such voluptuous discourse as many have made" but instead "presume[s] to present thee with the true and faithful relation of some few years travels and experience, wherein I would be loath to broach anything which may puzzle thy belief" (19). This linguistic distillation and its truth effect is perhaps represented best in the feature of the itemized commodity list. Consider the difference, for example, between Columbus' log-book sighting of "three mermaids who came quite high out of the water" (*Diario* 321) or his recorded account of "one-eyed men, and others, with snouts of dogs, who ate men" (133), and James Rosier's "briefe Note of what profits we saw the Countrey yeeld": "TREES. *Oke* of an excellent graine, strait and great timber. *Elme. Beech. Birch*, ... FOWLES. *Eagles. Hernshawes. Cranes. Ducks* great. *Geese. Swannes. Penguins*." Whatever marvelous qualities might have inhered in these objects and Rosier's encounter with them is almost deliberately drained out by their dry, antidescriptive, catalogued presentation; if anything, passages like these represent an antiwondrous discourse of investment potential that is closer to the modern genre of the company financial report or stock market prospectus.[8]

Of course, as Campbell and others remark, marvels can and do persist even in the list form designed to exorcise them. William Wood's descriptions of New England clearly contain and compress the marvelous attributes of number and size within entire paragraphs that are nothing more than a series of lists punctuated by brief commentary: "There is likewise growing all manner of herbs for meat and medicine, and that not only in planted gardens but in the woods, without either the art or the help of man, as sweet marjoram, purslane, sorrell, penerial, yarrow, myrtle, sarsaparilla, bays, etc. There is likewise strawberries in abundance, very large ones, some being two inches about; one may gather half a bushel in a forenoon. In other seasons there be gooseberries, bilberries, raspberries, treackleberries, hurtleberries, currants—which being dried in the sun are little inferior to those that our grocers sell in England" (36–37). What remains of the wondrous in such texts tends to persist in a muffled, ghostly, half-erased way, in part because when marvels are noted by seventeenth-century travel writers they tend to get deleted as soon as they are pronounced, a gesture that I like to think of as a kind of rhetorical backspace. Thus Christopher Levett remarks in his 1628 *Voyage into New England* that he could have told us about "strange Fish . . . with wings flying above the water, others with manes, eares and heads, and chasing one another with open mouths" but has instead left such details out of his account. Wonder—which had become associated with exaggeration, overpromise, and falsehood—might have sold books, but it would not promote investment in a book's story, because its promise of future profit was not balanced with an acknowledgment of present risk. Plain style manufactured that balance. Levett, for instance, deliberately positions his account against earlier excesses:

> And to say something of the Countrey: I will not doe therein as some have done, to my knowledge speake more then is true: I will not tell you that you may smell the corne fields before you see the Land, neither must men thinke that corne doth growe naturally (or on trees,) nore will the *Deare* come when they are called, or stand still and looke one a man, untill he shute him, not knowing a man from a beast, nore the fish leape into the kettle, nor on

> the drie Land, neither are they so plentifull, that you may dipp them up in baskets, nor take *Codd* in netts to make a voyage, which is no truer: then that the fowles will present themselves to you with spitts through them. (22)

Levett's clever parody both includes and eliminates the extravagant promise of the marvelous, before replacing it with a deliberate linguistic modesty: instead there is, he soberly notes, "fowle, *Deare*, and Fish enough for the taking if men be diligent" (22). Levett's restrained and sparse description offers an uncertain certainty that replaces the fullness of wonder with a stricter temporal accounting of credits and debits. It is as if the linguistic excess that might best represent enormous profit is reserved for a future that the reader-investor is encouraged privately to calculate in the present.

At the same time that Levett manufactures certainty as a way to motivate tentative investors, he takes great pains, as many other contemporary travel and promotional writers did, to insist on the fundamental uncertainty of investment in overseas ventures. The discourse of wonder as both unbelievable and true gives way to the discourse of investment as both certain and uncertain. John Mason likewise asserts and erases exaggerated promise when he criticizes earlier accounts of Newfoundland and its commodities for "too much extolling it, . . . , preferring the temperature of the aire thereof before ours, the hopes of commodities there without paines and mineralles, as if they were apparent (which as I deny to bee a veritie, yet I affirme not to be impossible)." Mason argues that those "narrations dissenting from the trueth, . . . although done out of good affection, yet had they better beene undone." As a remedy, Mason offers his own *Briefe Discourse of the New-found-land*, "set downe in few and plaine tearmes out of that experience I have gained in three yeares and sevventh monthese residence there, the trueth, as thou shalt find by proofe thereof." Mason's claims to certainty paradoxically depend for their credibility on his admission of uncertainty.

John Smith was perhaps the master of such uncertain certainty. In *A Description of New England* (1616) he both assures and denies assurance to readers about the existence of mines in New England when he notes that he "could say much if relations were good assurances." His own discoveries "perswade mee I need not despaire, but there are metalls in the Countrey: but," he goes on to say, "I am no Alchymist, nor will promise more then I know" (336). Here Smith is actually a kind of reverse alchemist: by asserting and then deleting the very same claim, he promises nothing out of something. In a sense, his travel narrative functions as a bill of exchange, as paper that stands in the present place of future coin, and which he invites his readers to trust as if it were legitimate currency. He constructs his readers as merchant-investors by offering them the uncertain certainty that is the central condition of mercantile capitalist investment.

Bookkeeping and Truth

It seems to me characteristic of seventeenth-century English writing on New England to move in these two paradoxical ways at once: to overtly insist on the uncertain profitability of this and other overseas ventures, and to proclaim to be quite certain of the profitability of this and other overseas ventures. This paradox of uncertain certainty marks the aesthetics of both travel writing and mercantile account-keeping in the capitalist world-system. In her fine study *The History of the Modern Fact*, Mary Poovey locates a "self-actualizing fiction" in seventeenth-century accounting practices that is parallel to what I am calling "uncertain certainty." Her analysis of double-entry bookkeeping observes that the numerical balance that appeared at the bottom of each page of the ledger, and which brought the columns of debits and credits into numerical agreement, produced an

> effect of accuracy [that] was just that: an effect, not a verifiable reflection of the fit between words or numbers and measurements or counts. In part . . . a degree of *in*accuracy was necessary to the system: because all early modern merchants depended for their profits on some long-distance trade or credit transactions, the ledgers could never be temporarily aligned with the company's actual money; some of the debts owing to the merchant would only eventually be paid, for example (and some would never be), even though the books recorded these debts as if repayment could be taken for granted. By the same token, the rhetorical function of the ledger—to display the merchant's honesty and thus his creditworthiness—always tended to surpass the ledger's referential function. It was necessary, in other words, for the merchant to represent himself as solvent even if he was not *in order* to establish the credit necessary to make himself so. (63–64)

The merchant's ledger might therefore tell a lie in order to make that lie become true. Both truth and creditworthiness become established within a suspended and recursive temporality in which it is made to appear, through writing, that "the future has already arrived" (62). Many travel narratives themselves include not only itemized lists of commodities but detailed and exhaustive financial columns listing and calculating initial costs, against which is balanced the total income that, in a second detailed column of figures, could be made from trade in a commodity such as fish over the course of subsequent years. Christopher Levett concludes his *Voyage into New England* with what is essentially a narrative version of such an account book, when he compares the expected profits of outfitting a fishing ship to the expected profits of establishing a plantation devoted to fishing. While the plantation may exact a larger initial expense from merchants, Levett illustrates through a precise tally its greater net gain, and asks, "Now tell me seriously, which is the more profitable course?" (35). In *England's Treasure by Forraign-Trade*, the merchant Thomas Mun argues that English wealth depends on reinvesting in foreign trade rather than hoarding its profits, but he repeatedly does so by similarly inviting his readers to calculate an uncertain future as if it were certain. At one point, he asks readers to

> suppose Pepper to be worth here two Shillings the pound constantly, if then it be brought from the *Dutch* at *Amsterdam*, the Merchant may give there twenty pence the pound, and gain well by the bargain; but if he fetch this Pepper from the *East-indies*, he must not give above three pence the pound at the most, which is a mighty advantage, not only in that part which serveth for our own use, but also for that great quantity which (from hence) we transport yearly unto divers other Nations to be sold at a higher price: *whereby it is plain* [my emphasis] that we make a far greater stock by gain upon these *Indian* Commodities, than those Nations doe where they grow. (10)

Repeatedly in Mun's text, the word "plain" appears to mean something like "obvious," "clear," or "true," but it very often arises in the context of a numerical calculation.[9] For Levett and Mun both, their texts became most "plain" or "true" when readers calculated the future return on a present outlay and ended up with a positive number.

In *New Englands Trials* (1620), John Smith uses both enumeration and lists to argue for English investment in a New England fishing industry. He begins with the example of Holland, where "they have neither matter to build shippes, nor merchandize to set them foorth, yet they asmuch encrease as other Nations decay." Smith moves from what he calls "these uncertainties" to information of which "I am certain," all of which is supplied in the form of lists. The first includes the varieties of fish consumed by Europe and available in the waters of New England: "Herring. Salt-fish. Poore John. Sturgion. Mullit. Tunny . . ." (397). He then notes other resources available on land ("wood, water, fruites, fowles, corne"), markets for fish ("Terceras, Mederas, Canaries, Spaine, Portugall, Provance, Savoy, Sicilia, and all Italy"), and merchandise for which fish might be exchanged ("wines, oyles, sugars, silkes, and such merchandizes as the Straites affoord"), before concluding that "our profites [those of the English] might equalize theirs [those of the Dutch]" (398). In a text that resembles a narrative version of double-entry bookkeeping, Smith makes the periphery of the world system central to the wealth of core states, and to the anticipated wealth of his reader-investors. The credibility of his text depends on its readers' willingness to become merchant capitalists, by balancing the lists and numbers Smith provides and allowing that future gain to stand in as present truth. Any visions of excess must be exiled from plain style, because such gain belongs to a future that is both imagined in and deferred from the present. That excess of future profit takes up its residence instead within the merchant-investor self, where it unsettles, often in ways difficult or impossible to detail concretely, the honesty or virtuous integrity of that self.

Prompting merchants and others to invest in such trade therefore required yoking the expectation of future profit to the admission of present risk. Seventeenth-century English travel writing obviously remains as frankly promotional as earlier travel accounts, but it replaces wonder with a particular formulation of "truth" that borrows from the rhetorical accounting strategies of mercantile writing. In this context, uncertain certainty represents a new discursive formula for the production of truth and value consistent with a shift from mines to merchants, from extraction to exchange, from the Spanish example to the Dutch one, from gold to fish. The discourse of wonder has given way to the discourse of adventure, understood in its double early modern sense as the risk of monetary investment and the heroic and hazardous risk of self.

The Mystery of the Profitable Self

Many critics have remarked on the linguistic dimensions of Europe's contact with the New World, including the performative elements of possession-taking, and language's exploitative and colonizing power.[10] Others have noted that Europe's encounter with the Americas resulted in the modification of existing words and the emergence of completely new ones, generating what William Spengemann calls "a new world of words." But this encounter, fostered and sustained by the intertwined developments of mercantile capitalism and transcontinental colonialism, also helped to initiate a far more radical shift in the relation of words to things.[11] Michel Foucault describes this transition as one from a Renaissance episteme of resemblance to a Classical one of representation. The dominant sixteenth-century assumption that signs were organically bound to their signifieds by a fundamental similitude gave way in the seventeenth century to an arbitrary and fabricated relation between sign and signified that interposed a gap between words and things (63, 43). As a result, the ability of words to tell the truth came under increasing suspicion.

Foucault points to an analogous shift in the realm of economy: the similitude that formerly bound together "the weights of coins and their nominal values" (169) is replaced by the representational function of money; henceforth "the value of things will no longer proceed from the metal itself" but will rather "take on value . . . in relation to each other" in the process of circulation and exchange. The metal of coins does not constitute their value as it once did; instead "the metal merely enables this value to be represented, as a name represents an image or an idea, yet does not constitute it" (176). The mercantile writers Edward Misselden and Thomas Mun explain this representational model in their replies to the pamphlets of Gerald de Malynes, who argued that England's trade problems could be solved by fixing the rate of foreign exchange. Misselden savagely attacks Malynes' confusion of value determined by "the *Intrinsique* or inward finenes" (97) of a coin with value determined by its "*extrinsique* or outward valuation" (98). Whereas Malynes assumes that the two values—a coin's weight and its denomination—organically cohere, Misselden insists that it is precisely the discrepancy between them that is necessary for long-distance trade to flourish, since without that discrepancy "there would be no aduantage left neither to him that deliuereth, nor him that taketh, when mony must be answered with mony in the same *Intrinsique* value" (97). Just as the extrinsic or representational value of coin is, Misselden argues, "vncertaine, because it is greater or lesse, according to the circumstances of *time*, and *place*, and *persons*" (98), so is there "no certainty of gaine or losse to the parties taking or deliuering of mony, vntill the time be run out, and the returne come backe, from those parts and places, whether the mony was first deliuered by *Exchange*: during which time, the manifold occurrents which are contingent to trade, may vary the gaine or losse to either party" (99).[12] Monetary value is rendered uncertain by the temporal and spatial distances involved in long-distance exchange. Expanding commercial networks thus helped instigate dramatic transformations in once-dominant conceptions of both money and language. And it was travelers and merchants—those intimately involved with financing colonial ventures, exchanging goods and money in complex and perplexing new ways, manipulating and profiting from new markets and trade routes—who were repeatedly aligned with this new and troubling representational mobility. Thus whereas Misselden defends value's fundamental uncertainty—arguing that it enables trade and ultimately increases the wealth of the kingdom along with the power of the king—Malynes and many others see such uncertainty as evidence of "some great mystery in this kinde of *Exchange*" (Misselden 99).

Lewes Roberts explains and defends against similar charges the bill of exchange, which allowed money to be converted into paper, transported across long distances, and reconverted back into money—a process that required between two and four people in at least two places (usually, a remitter and drawer in one place, and a receiver and payer in another) and that strangely seemed to generate extra money. As the practice developed, Roberts explains, the deliverer came to receive a fee (in return for his risk and for the remitter's loss of time until repayment), which led "the second payment . . . to be somewhat greater than the former." This payment led some to begin exchanging money not out of necessity but merely in order to make a profit, thus transforming such exchanges "into an *art* or *mysterie*" (*Merchants* 14). Roberts' phrase "art or mystery" was a conventional formula used during the seventeenth century to describe the indenture experience of an apprentice who was learning the skills associated with a particular trade. This sense of mystery as a trade or art overlapped during this period, however, with its sense as enigmatic or indecipherable. While the word "mystery" was used to describe a specific secret or riddle as early as the Middle Ages, its use to describe a generalized sense of the unknown emerged only in the seventeenth century ("Mystery"). Roberts' account thus indicates both that money exchange became its own highly specialized skill that required training to master it, and that it became an arena characterized by an inability to determine truth. Roberts recognizes that some perceive bills of exchange to be "a certaine kind of *permitted Usury*," but insists that the "gaine and profit" enabled by "this *art* and *mysterie*" fosters trade in general and benefits the kingdom (15).

There may be no other word used as often as *mysterious* to describe trade in the new transcontinental markets that increasingly relied on credit relations and their tools such as the bill of exchange. In fact, long-distance commercial exchange is continually described as unstable, confusing, impenetrable, and unreadable—incomprehensible to all but merchants, whose ability to exploit the spatial, temporal, and representational gaps allowed them, almost magically it seemed, to become rich.[13] Merchants themselves, like travelers, were often suspected of deceit and fraud in their linguistic as much as in their financial transactions, not necessarily because they lied but because it was never quite possible to tell whether they were lying or not. While merchants might have been described as liars or cheats for centuries, there is a new seventeenth-century sense in which these terms describe an almost terrifying instability that cannot be pinned down or understood, and that inhabits the underside of a surface plainness. As Mary Fuller remarks, the merchant's "complexity consisted partly in the maintenance of a space of privacy, of hidden knowledge" (8–9), which appeared as a private interior that "transcended any particular referent" (15). It was as if merchants were themselves an account book or ledger that was always open, representing a series of outstanding debits and credits that could be balanced but never really closed. Gerald de Malynes ascribes this quality of unfathomability to merchants, depicting them as conjurers or magicians able to make wealth appear out of nothing. It is therefore no surprise that merchants spend so much time defending their profession and character, even in texts devoted to issues of national economic policy.[14] Thomas Mun, for example, challenges Malynes' representation of "the admirable Feats (as he termeth them) which are to be done by Bankers and Exchangers, with the Use and Power of the Exchange," claiming that "how these Wonders may be effected, he [Malynes] altogether omitteth, leaving the Reader in a strange Opinion of these dark Mysteries" (52). Mun insists that "we Merchants deal not with such Spirits, we delight not to be thought the Workers of Lying Wonders, and therefore I endeavour here to shew the Plainness of our Dealing" (53).

In their effort to make plain what appeared to be the suspicious mystery of mercantile exchange, seventeenth-century economic texts like Mun's laid claim to the same style that characterized travel texts. In his instruction in *The Merchant's Magazine; or, Trades-Man's Treasury* for writing a bill of exchange, Edward Hatton describes that style as writing "only what is absolutely necessary, avoiding all Complements and superfluous Expressions" (206). Whether it took the form of words or numbers, mercantile writing asserted its own transparent accuracy. Roberts notes, for example, that a merchant's account books should include "all circumstances of time, price, and other conditions, in every bargaine, contract, adventure, receipt of goods, sales, &c. in which though there should afterward appeare an errour . . . yet it will easily at a second view be both corrected and amended" (36). Like the catalogued lists in travel texts, mercantile account books produced the appearance of absolute certainty. But here, too, as with travel prose, this apparent accuracy belied an undergirding uncertainty. Everyone knew, merchants better than most, that the apparent certainty of numbers and accounts was not certain at all; why else would Lewes Roberts' third rule for account keeping instruct the merchant to "keepe *them*, *just*, *true*, and perfect, and not to falsify any parcell, matter, or thing, nor yet interline or shuffle one matter with another, but to set every thing . . . plainly, directly, and orderly downe" (*Merchants* 36).

Yet, however hard the writers of plain-style texts worked to dispel the "mystery" (in the sense of skill) of exchange, they never seemed able entirely to disassociate "mystery" (in the sense of indecipherability) from the self of the merchant. Christopher Levett explains that "I have studied no other Art a longe time but the Mysteries of *New Englands* Trade, and I hope at last: I have attained to the understanding of the secrets of it. . . . But it shall be no longer concealed, for that I thinke every good subject is bound to preferre the publicke, beforre his owne private good" (31). The trade "secrets" that Levett so plainly divulges, however, include pretending to Native traders that he does not want or need all the goods they offer him (so that they will lower their asking prices), and initially offering Native traders more in exchange than they expect (so that they will continue to choose him over others as a trading partner and thus ensure his continued profit) (10). Such advice is analogous to the accounting records of cost and profit presented at the end of Levett's narrative: by sacrificing more in the certain present, the merchant-trader will gain more in the uncertain future. In contrast to this kind of mercantile investment, Levett presents the experience of an apparently well-to-do fellow named Chapman who arrived in Plymouth with over "80 pound worth of provision" to support only himself and two servants (27). He quickly sold those provisions "at a low rate" in order to support his enormous expenses for "wine, Tobacco, and whores." These expensive habits of consumption eventually lead to Chapman's economic fall, and in the end he is "glad to become servant to one of his servants" (28). On the colonial periphery, servants can become the masters of once-rich noblemen merely by investing rather than spending, deferring rather than indulging desires.

In many ways, the bill of exchange itself modeled the ideal restraint of plain style. John Marius' incredibly popular *Advice concerning Bills of Exchange* (1651) begins by explaining that "[e]xchange is by some held to be the most mysterious part of the Art of *Merchandizing* and *Traffick*" although it is accomplished "only by two or three Lines written on a small piece of Paper, termed, *A Bill of Exchange*" (3).[15] A page later, Marius abruptly stops himself from discoursing about how such bills function by remarking that "I love not to spend more words then need, or tell a large Story to little or no purpose" (4). The bill of exchange joined mercantile writing, double-entry bookkeeping, and travel writing in recursively suspending the spatial gap and temporal lag of long-distance trade. But though the lag became effaced, it was not—as Poovey suggests—erased. That fundamentally horizontal lag-time became instead verticalized and imported within the merchant-traveler, who—despite (or perhaps as a result of) the truth claims of plain style—came to be perceived as possessing a troubling depthlessness or mysterious interiority that we now associate with a modern subjectivity, and that might be said to describe a self who always awaits a certain return from an uncertain future that it pretends has already arrived. Future promises are acted on in the present as if they have already been met and fulfilled. Merchant selves came as a result to resemble bills of exchange: pieces of paper whose surface plainness in fact managed a mysteriously complex network of agents, factors, goods, and prices. What finally most aligned overseas travelers and merchants was that each undertook, in the expectation of gain, the hazardous risk of money or of self (or, in the words of these early modern texts, the risk either of "purses" or of "persons") in the passage back and forth across the vast spatial gap between England and America and the correspondent temporal gap between investment and return.[16] Merchants and travelers alike were aligned with that temporal suspension and spatial traversal, with the unending movement of circumatlantic travel and trade, and with the perpetual deferral represented by the complicated system of debits and credits in mercantile account books. The financial credit and social credit (or reputation) of merchants and travelers was as a consequence put into a kind of suspense of its own. There was a sense that their very selves were incalculable, indeterminable, and slippery.

It was this divide or gap that made truth so suspect and trust so necessary, but that also made profit possible. Language was in the difficult position of having at once to risk suspicion in its always uncertain promise of future profit, and to ensure trust through its professedly certain strategies of truth telling. Travelers and merchants were, in essence, in the business of selling their words as a way of selling their wares; both were trafficking in language, and both did so through the uncertain certainty that characterized the discourse of adventure. What was therefore fundamentally a horizontal gap (understood spatially) or lag (understood temporally) was more often perceived—particularly by those less embedded in the commercial and credit relations of long-distance trade—as a vertical depthlessness or, to use the language of the Antinomian Controversy that would rock Massachusetts Bay in the mid-1630s, a "bottomlessness." Imagine the early modern transatlantic world inscribed, like a map, on a sheet of paper. Now imagine folding this sheet of paper loosely over upon itself, creating an empty space between its two edges. I am suggesting that the selves who regularly negotiated this transcontinental zone of commerce were perceived as enclosing within themselves a version of the empty space created by and hidden within that fold. That continual deferral that merchants knew and manipulated so well became, as it were, imported within the merchant self to suggest a kind of inaccessible and hidden interiority that we now associate with a modern subjectivity. As the next chapter will show, even those early modern colonists most opposed to merchant capitalism often found images of themselves reflected back in the uncertain and deceptive selves of merchants, and when they did, they sought to exile and to name as dissent their own alliance with a growing transcontinental culture of commerce and credit.

Chapter Two

MERCHANTS: WILLIAM BRADFORD AND PLAIN STYLE

WILLIAM BRADFORD IS KNOWN as the writer of *Of Plymouth Plantation*, an account of the settlement at Plymouth that he began writing in 1630, the year when John Winthrop and others arrived to settle in and around Boston. At that time, Bradford had been in New England for ten years already, and his first known piece of writing about the New World is the contribution he made to the collaboratively written tract originally titled *Relation or Iournall of the Beginning and Proceedings of the English Plantation setled at Plimoth in New England, by certaine English Aduenterers both Merchants and others*. The *Relation*, usually attributed to a G. Mourt and often referred to as Mourt's *Relation*, was published in 1622 and consists of narratives of the planters' arrival in New England, their explorations once they arrived, and what they found there. It is an example of the kind of colonial travel writing examined in the previous chapter and bears many of the conventions of contemporary promotional tracts. It begins by apologizing, for example, for its style, which is written "after their [the planters'] plaine and rude manner," but assures readers that this style should lead them to "doubt nothing of the truth thereof" (A3v). It also makes recourse to the commodity list, such as when its writers announce that they discover the area where they have landed "all wooded with Okes, Pines, Sassafras, Juniper, Birch, Vines, some Ash, Walnut" (3). And it suggests cautious promise about the prospects for profit from fishing and trading ventures in New England.

One letter near the end of the book, which claims to offer "*a briefe and true Declaration* of the worth of that Plantation" (60), makes it clear that the manuscript of the *Relation* went back to England on a ship along with representative New World goods or materials, and that its audience included the London merchants who funded the voyage. This letter attempts to set the terms of the relationship between the colonial planters and the metropolitan investors, asserting that the planters are ready to embark on

> the fishing business, and other trading, I doubt not but by the blessing of God, the gayne will giue content to all; in the meane time, that we haue gotten we haue sent by this ship, and though it be not much, yet it will witnesse for vs, that we haue not beene idle, considering the smallnesse of our number all this Summer. We hope the Marchants will accept of it, and be incouraged to furnish vs with things needfull for further imployment, which will also incourage vs to put forth our selues to the vttermost. (63)

Following this letter is the final narrative contained in the *Relation*, which is devoted to justifying the lawfulness of the English settlement but which reveals a great deal along the way about the economic motives and anxieties that attended the Plymouth project. Reflecting on what they left behind in England, its writer recalls a place of competition and inequality, where "each man is faine to plucke his meanes as it were out of his neighbours throat, there is such pressing and oppressing in towne and countrie, about Farmes, trades, traffique, &c. so as a man can hardly any where set vp a trade but he shall pull downe two of his neighbours" (70), and a place where "[t]he rent taker liues on sweet morsels, but the rent payer eats a drie crust often with watery eies: and it is nothing to say what some one of a hundreth hath, but what the bulke, body and cominalty hath, which I warrant you is short enough" (72). These two concluding pieces reveal the Pilgrims' rejection of changing trade and property relations in England, and their hesitancy in being allied with profit-seeking English merchants.

Although he began writing in the transcontinental rhetorical tradition of the promotional travel narrative, Bradford is remembered as the writer of a history about a settlement that has been imagined as largely isolated and communal. A close reading of the entire text of *Of Plymouth Plantation* indicates, however, that it is written in the same context of commercial anxiety that produced the 1622 *Relation*. On the first page of *Of Plymouth Plantation*, Bradford declares that the small Scrooby congregation determined to separate from the Church of England "whatsoever it should cost them." The defiance of this vow quickly gives way to embittered sadness when he announces, "And that it cost them something this ensuing history will declare."[1] Here already is the pattern of declension that many Bradford scholars see as characteristic of the entire history, which slides from the optimistic promise of book 1 to the increasingly mournful sense of failure in book 2.[2] These readings assume that Bradford hopes from the beginning to narrate an important and exceptional story about Plymouth's place within the broader religious and political framework supplied by the Protestant Reformation and by English overseas expansion but that, over the years, this story becomes increasingly impossible for him to tell. Even if Bradford had precisely such ambitions in mind when he began *Of Plymouth Plantation*, any reader of his entire text knows that his most overt and anxious concern is not Plymouth's place within the grand sweep of history but the far more mundane problem of finances. In fact, Bradford's use of the verb "cost" in the opening sentences better anticipates the remainder of his book than his references to separatism and the Reformation. More than anything else, *Of Plymouth Plantation* tells a detailed and complicated story of economic mismanagement and loss. So consumed is this narrative by matters of money that it might best be described as a history of the plantation's financial accounts.[3]

Although economic matters dominate Bradford's text, the sections concerning finances are routinely excluded from American literature anthologies. Aside from a few notable exceptions, critics typically dismiss the text's economic content as insignificant or tedious when they do not ignore it entirely, or they cite its irrelevance as evidence of a narrative disarray paralleling Plymouth's own eventual fragmentation.[4] Kenneth Alan Hovey has accurately observed that "[m]ore of Bradford's work is devoted to the Pilgrims' financial and legal difficulties than to any other topic"; but in his subsequent acknowledgment that most readers find the "financial and legal history . . . tiresome," he identifies without comment a profound discrepancy between the concerns of the seventeenth-century Englishman William Bradford and those of his twentieth-century American critics (49). By suppressing or ignoring the economic elements of the text, critics have effectively alienated it from its immediate sociohistorical environment, and have missed Bradford's often bitter resentment of the developing mercantile capitalist economy in which he reluctantly took part. As a result, Plymouth has been allowed to appear as an isolated and exceptional religious community predictive of American independence, rather than as an economic project fully dependent on English mercantile backing and fraught with the tensions produced by transatlantic colonialism and commerce. To this extent, literary studies of Bradford (and of the Puritans more generally) have shared the "asocial bias" that Russell Reising and other recent critics attribute to the dominant liberal tradition of American literary criticism.[5]

Bradford and American Literary History

It is easy to see why this selective reading of *Of Plymouth Plantation* has prevailed. The once-conventional placement of Bradford's text at the beginning of American literature anthologies gave it the burden of inaugurating American literary history, and Bradford's expressions of community and religious freedom provided far more attractive themes for such a national narrative than did his financial worries. As a result, two of the contracts described in the early pages of *Of Plymouth Plantation* have been invested with extraordinary symbolic status; both the religious covenant that bound together the members of the Scrooby/Leyden congregation and the political compact signed aboard the *Mayflower* have been positioned as anticipatory precursors to an American national community and its Declaration of Independence.[6] But Bradford himself devotes the vast majority of his text to explaining, discussing, and analyzing a third contract: the business agreement between the Plymouth planters who settled the colony and the London merchants who provided the capital for their venture.[7] Once this mercantile relationship is recognized and restored, the text's direct engagement with the transcontinental social world in which it was written cannot be overlooked. Moreover, reframing *Of Plymouth Plantation* within these economic terms provides an overlooked materialist dimension to Bradford's Puritan aesthetics. For Andrew Delbanco, the Puritans' language was one "under terrible stress," forced to accommodate its words and meanings to a new world and therefore "to devise a new language even as they clung to the old" (*Puritan* 15). But Delbanco imports the declension model (and the familiar oppositions that form its basis) into the realm of language, noting that "[t]he language of family was sent into combat against the language of commerce" (22). Far from being in "combat," I suggest that these languages were in fact both conceptually and materially dependent on each other.

One of the most cited passages in Bradford's text is his opening promise to write his history "in a plain style, with singular regard unto the simple truth in all things" (*OPP* 1). Here the history might be seen to repeat the apology for stylistic simplicity—and the attendant assurance of truth—that begin the earlier *Relation*. A rather limited understanding of Bradford's "plain style" has predominated, however—the outcome, in part, of dismissing the text's financial dimensions as tedious or tangential, and of divorcing settlement from discovery literature. Certainly plain style was consistent with Puritan theology's desire to eliminate necessarily flawed human invention by returning to the simplicity and purity represented by scripture.[8] But Bradford's dedication to plain style also shares with his commitment to a production economy an ideology evident in his record of the Plymouth planters' relations with a series of merchant adventurers who backed, challenged, and cheated them. Thus two early and seemingly disparate seventeenth-century developments reveal in Bradford's text their fundamental intersection: the emergence of a new "plain style" in English prose writing and the massive expansion of mercantile commerce as a result of colonial overseas expansion. Once *Of Plymouth Plantation* is restored to these contexts, it emerges as a document registering considerable anxiety toward linguistic and economic change in the early modern Atlantic world, particularly among those subjects who most resisted their own implication in the commercial relations that characterized an emergent capitalist world-system.[9]

William Spengemann has argued that new attention to the linguistic can disengage colonial American literature from its construction around nationalist terms. The European encounter with the New World posed profound challenges to language, since the task of describing the "new things" encountered in the Americas required that "every Old World language involved in the discovery would have to change" (*New* 44). One of the measurements of such change, Spengemann notes, is the number of newly coined words and familiar words with shifting definitions. But as chapter 1 argued, the intertwined developments of mercantile capitalism and transcontinental colonialism also resulted in a new relation of words to things. What was once perceived as an organic and inseparable unity between words and the things to which they referred came instead to be regarded as an arbitrary and fabricated relation. As Foucault describes, for the seventeenth century "[t]he relation of the sign to the signified . . . resided in a space in which there [was] no longer any intermediary figure to connect them" (63) and, as a result, "[t]hings and words were to be separated from each other" (43). This shift is evident as well in the realm of economy, where the similitude that bound together "the weights of coins and their nominal values" (169) was replaced by the representational function of money; thus "the value of things" came not from "the metal itself" but rather through a process of circulation and exchange. "[T]he metal merely enable[d] . . . value to be represented, as a name represents an image or an idea, yet does not constitute it" (176). Since their value was so unstable and shifting, words and coins both acquired a potentially untrustworthy dimension, a correspondence that suggests why it was merchants—those intimately involved with financing colonial ventures, importing strange new goods and exporting familiar ones, manipulating and profiting from new markets and trade routes—whose linguistic practice was so often accused of evincing this troubling instability.

Foucault attributes this transformation in the realm of economy to "the long mercantilist process" (180) that occurred over the course of the seventeenth century. While his archeological method results in a description more than an explanation of this epistemic shift, Foucault's occasional references to trade routes to and from the Americas nevertheless suggest the crucial and perhaps constitutive role European colonial expansion played in this transition. Joyce Appleby's study of economic writing and thought in seventeenth-century England illustrates how this remarkable commercial and colonial expansion rendered a once "visible and tangible economy" increasingly "incomprehensible" to anyone except merchants, who came to be seen as the only experts on its new complexity (26).[10] Merchants alone seemed to possess the experience and specialized knowledge that enabled them to take advantage of the gap between an object and its shifting value, between New World products and Old World markets, between the price of investment and the profit of return. Plain style emerged—as Bradford's text, among others, suggests—as a stylistic attempt to close the corollary gap between words and things. But as its association with merchant speech and writing suggests, plain style in fact participated in the very dangers it sought to combat, serving in the end to fold over rather than to close the gap associated with a representational economy.

Plain Economics

After his invocation of "a plain style" at the very opening of his history, Bradford's next use of the adjective "plain" occurs in a different but quite illuminating context, for he uses it to describe not his prose style but his economic identity and practice. Bradford's record of the Scrooby group's emigration from England to Holland in 1608 describes an anxiety of displacement founded on economic difference, for he explains that the Pilgrims "were not acquainted with trades nor traffic (by which that country [Holland] doth subsist) but had only been used to a *plain* country life and the innocent trade of husbandry" (*OPP* 11, emphasis added). Here Bradford's use of the term "plain" invokes several seventeenth-century meanings at once, including its association with simple, honest, and direct forms of behavior or presentation, and its description of a social status that is ordinary, common, or lowly ("Plain"). In fact, Bradford's sentence explicitly associates the qualities of simplicity and honesty with the Pilgrims' agricultural identity. And if for Bradford the "innocent" culture of "husbandry" accommodates directness and honesty, then the "trades" and "traffic" of Holland's largely mercantile economy and culture implicitly convey the threat of confusion and deceit.

Although Bradford identifies the Pilgrims here with husbandry, most members of the group were, as Ruth McIntyre notes, artisans of one sort or another.[11] Among those who eventually left Holland to settle in Plymouth were cloth workers, wool combers, tailors, watchmakers, cabinetmakers, carpenters, tobacco-pipe makers, and printers. Artisans shared with farmers, however, a production-oriented economic practice and ideology that was substantially at odds with the circulation-oriented economy of merchants. Even though many among the Pilgrims would have sold in public markets the goods they produced, remarkably few of them "had either the experience or capital to be a merchant" (McIntyre 11). Unlike artisan-traders, merchants earned profits by buying and selling goods that they themselves did not produce, and as trade routes lengthened and became increasingly complex, those merchants who best understood and manipulated the new credit relations and instruments profited most.

The Pilgrims' lack of mercantile experience did not serve them well in Holland, a country alternately envied and decried in England precisely for its merchant-oriented economy and the materialism associated with it. Seventeenth-century Holland was the site of a burgeoning and international class of wealthy merchants who capitalized on the transcontinental trade routes that were in turn enabled and sustained by various colonialist ventures. Merchants made profits by serving as middlemen in networks of exchange; they bought and sold goods imported from and produced elsewhere, and they often ventured money on colonial projects that would facilitate further trade and gain.[12] In port cities like Antwerp and Amsterdam, where the Scrooby group first arrived, products such as precious metals from the New World and spices from the East were routinely imported, exchanged for goods or credit, and dispersed throughout the continent. As a result, Amsterdam became a place known for its "chronically high cost of living," "where the rich were richer than anywhere else, and the poor as numerous and perhaps even worse-off" (Braudel, *Perspective* 185). Bradford echoes this characterization when he describes Holland as a country with "fair and beautiful cities, flowing with abundance of all sorts of wealth and riches," but where the Pilgrims themselves encountered "the grim and grisly face of poverty coming upon them like an armed man" (*OPP* 16). Their removal within a year of their arrival from Amsterdam to Leyden only worsened the Pilgrims' "outward estates" (17), perhaps a result of their settlement in a city characterized by profound inequities between poor textile laborers and their wealthy employers (see Schama 340).

But the group's poverty was only one symptom of the alienation and disorientation prompted by their move from the English agricultural countryside to the Dutch commercial city, where they encountered a mercantile capitalist culture that would increasingly characterize the Atlantic world in an era of imperialist expansion. Holland was a place where strange new economic institutions and their seemingly incomprehensible practices flourished, including banks, stock exchanges, systems of credit, and networks of merchant middlemen. For the artisans and yeoman farmers whom Bradford describes as coming from "plain country villages (wherein they were bred and had so long lived)" (*OPP* 16), this mercantile culture and economy was anything but plain. Bradford's brief account of the Pilgrims' twelve years in the Netherlands represents only the first entry, so to speak, in a long register of their encounters with transatlantic commerce and the mysterious, deceptive, and dangerous men who profited from it. *Of Plymouth Plantation* relentlessly records the economic, cultural, and linguistic anxieties that arose when the Pilgrims' largely premodern worldview confronted the early modern ethos of mercantile culture. This fundamental conflict—which pits production against commerce, the notion of just and fair prices against constantly changing market values, and the preservation of the common good against the advancement of individual profit—undergirds not only the content but the very style of Bradford's history. Early on, Bradford joins the two problems of language and money in his remark that the group, upon arriving in Holland, "must learn a new language and get their livings they knew not how, it being a dear [expensive] place" (*OPP* 11). By the time he is settled in Plymouth and begins to write *Of Plymouth Plantation*, however, these two problems of language and money are, for Bradford, much more inevitably and disturbingly interlaced.

The Puritans have long been associated with modernity and characterized as future-oriented, "errand"-bound millennialists. For Sacvan Bercovitch, the Puritans represent "the movement toward modernity" (*Rites* 6), and their New England Way provided "a distinctive rhetoric for the major free-enterprise culture of the modern world" (7). Once the New England Puritans are situated within more transcontinental and horizontal spatial and temporal frameworks, however, such claims to their modernity are less easily upheld. Stephen Foster's study of transatlantic Puritanism, for example, recasts New England as neither exceptional nor particularly modern but as a continuation of the tensions that marked earlier, Elizabethan Puritanism. Theodore Dwight Bozeman has likewise argued that Puritans were not the "millennial futurists" that Bercovitch and others describe but rather "primitivists" oriented toward a primordial and "ancient" past. In their exclusive focus on the religious dimensions of Puritan culture, both Foster and Bozeman identify an antimodern orientation that pulls against and resists the dominant paradigm of Puritan modernity. Such resistance and reluctance also characterize the Puritan response to the emergent world-economy in which they nevertheless found themselves participants.

The Plymouth venture embodied such ambivalence from the outset. On the one hand, it offered the Separatists an opportunity to escape from new and old dangers associated with Holland: the political threat of a renewed war with Spain, the ongoing social perils posed to their children by the "manifold temptations" (*OPP* 25) of a diverse and wealthy Dutch society, and the poverty and alienation they experienced within the Dutch mercantile world. But on the other hand, while the Pilgrims may have imagined that their New World colony would offer, among other things, an escape from the "trades" and "traffic" of Holland, their departure was made possible only through an alliance in a joint-stock company with merchants who expected returns on their investment. Bradford's *Of Plymouth Plantation* must be read not only as a record of the tensions between these two groups but as an attempt at the very level of style to avert the economic, social, and linguistic dangers associated with merchant capitalism. In his book, merchants invariably appear secretive and deceptive; in their unreadability they display a surprisingly modern selfhood that disturbed and haunted Bradford and the Pilgrim group, perhaps most of all because they recognized their own implication within it.

Plain Style

Studies of seventeenth-century plain style have understood its emergence and dominance in relation to various contemporaneous religious, aesthetic, and historical developments. Bradford's use and advocacy of plain style in *Of Plymouth Plantation,* for example, have been viewed most often as typically Puritan, much as the book's pattern and philosophy of history have been aligned with Puritan theology. As many critics have noted, the demand for an "unadorned, simple, and direct" (Westbrook 187) language is consistent with Puritanism's iconoclastic opposition to the embellishments associated with the services and sermons of the established Anglican church.[13] Perry Miller further argues that the brevity and simplicity of the Puritan sermon was borrowed from the logic and rhetoric of Petrus Ramus, which provided "a method for discovering or unveiling arguments concealed in matter and not a way of devising them by mere human wit" ("Plain" 160). Anne Kibbey, however, situates Puritan theories of language more broadly within a particular anxiety about the relationship between words and things; she explains that, for the Puritans, "A manner of speech that calls attention to itself alone is a 'vain' use of the material shapes of words, because it forcibly divides the manner and matter of speech, violating the holistic character of the sign as figure" (Kibbey 20). A good many other seventeenth-century prose style developments shared precisely this attitude toward language, suggesting that while plain style is certainly consistent with Puritan theology, theology alone cannot fully account for it.

Francis Bacon, for example, has variously been aligned with two other seventeenth-century styles that privileged plainness over ornamentation:

anti-Ciceronianism and the scientific method. Morris Croll locates Bacon within the anti-Ciceronian movement that developed in the seventeenth century in reaction to the elaborate conceits of Anglican preachers like John Donne. Against such rhetorical excess, Bacon and others urged a plainness that Croll calls "Attic" (or later "baroque") prose, which aimed "for a bare and level prose style adapted merely to the exact portrayal of things as they are" (67). Accounts of the new scientific discourse likewise locate its origins in Bacon (as well as Descartes) and its culmination in Thomas Sprat's call for members of the Royal Society of London to adopt a style of economy, brevity, and simplicity. Such prose was identified as neutral, accurate, and transparent, qualities that served to establish and transmit scientific truth.[14]

Furthermore, writings by members of the Royal Society often compare linguistic excess, ornateness, and obtuseness not just to deception but to aristocratic luxury, just as Ciceronianism, Anglicanism, and the Renaissance metaphysical style were also linked with wealth and the nobility.[15] Thus the antiornamental prose styles that emerged in the seventeenth century were rooted in a shared attitude toward language and its potential dangers, and they were conventionally allied with an antiaristocratic social and economic status, as the etymology of the word "plain" might suggest. Similar class/status-based claims have been made for William Bradford's own fondness for "homely, sometimes earthy words and phrases," which several critics ascribe to his country origins (Westbrook 127).[16] Only by situating these intersecting accounts of plain style within the historical contexts of transcontinental colonialism and mercantile capitalism, however, might we understand why, at this particular historical juncture, plainness became the privileged linguistic vehicle for truth: it was precisely within these crucial contemporary developments that language's capacity to tell the truth took on a new value as that capacity became increasingly suspect.

Plain style registers a reaction to linguistic diversity, complexity, and confusion, as do other seventeenth-century linguistic developments, such as the interest in reforming orthography to attain "an exact relation between letters and sounds" (Cornelius 126) and the pursuit of a universal language whose words would perfectly describe the things they signify, thus eliminating incomprehension as well as religious and political disagreements (36–37). One of the poems in the prefatory materials to Cave Beck's *Universal Character: By Which All the Nations in the World May Understand One Another's Conceptions* (1657) suggests what Beck's proposal for a universal language might make possible: "*Babel* revers'd; The traveller's Relief; / Ferry of Nations Commerce" (Beck A6; qtd. in Murray Cohen 2). By reversing the confusion of tongues brought about by the Tower of Babel, a universal language would eliminate the difficulties of travel and commerce caused by linguistic variety. In turn, by opening up and making more accessible routes of trade and travel, a universal language would further advance the nation's glory and wealth.

Travel narratives reported the existence of new and strange languages, including those that seemed to promise a return to the linguistic purity and universality forever lost with Babel.[17] Whether based on real or imagined findings—such as Chinese characters, the presumed Hebraic origins of Native American words, or the hieroglyphics of Thomas More's Utopians—these travel narratives evoke the possibility of recovering a prefallen language like that spoken in the Garden of Eden, where words and things were in precise correspondence. In fact, Bacon's own interest in making language once more about things rather than words was probably influenced by accounts of the Chinese use of characters, "which express neither letters nor words in gross, but things and notions" (*Advancement* 137). Even those seventeenth-century linguists who rejected the belief that a primitive language could or would be recovered often set out, like Athanasius Kircher, to invent "an artificial universal language" that would replace words with numbers (Cornelius 21–22).

Travel narratives not only contained reports of newly discovered languages but were themselves typically written in plain style. Writers about and promoters of English travel such as Richard Hakluyt and John Smith gained credibility for their tales of adventures and encounters in the New World by narrating them as plainly as possible, encouraging readers to associate plainness with veracity.[18] Like scientific prose, the prose of travel narratives aimed to make "distant readers who had not directly witnessed the phenomena—and probably never would"—into "*virtual witnesses*" (Shapin, *Scientific* 108). Thus one critic argues that Hakluyt's *Principal Navigations,* for example, which imitates the speech of "plaine folk," presents voyages "as if they were historical experiments of a sort, attempts to combine adventurous curiosity, personal gain, and increased wealth and prestige for England" (Montgomery 75). Travel narratives that appeared accurate and honest were of course also likely to stimulate mercantile investment and colonial settlement. This conjunction of credibility with credit demands that we acknowledge, however, the economic interests plain style served, no matter how insistently and convincingly it asserted its own neutrality or disinterest.

Consider, for example, Francis Bacon's assault on words in *Novum Organum,* published in 1620, the year the Pilgrims departed for the New World. Bacon describes the defeat of truth by a language that is insufficiently precise, that does not accurately define the words it uses. And yet, he quickly notes, "definitions cannot cure this evil. . . . For definitions themselves consist of words, and words beget words, so that we have to go back to particular instances" (*Novum* 64) or, as he notes elsewhere in the text, to "things themselves" (13). This distance between words and the notions or "things" they represent causes an "underlying deception" that Bacon famously and suggestively terms the "idols of the marketplace" (20). It is in the marketplace, Bacon claims, in "the commerce and meeting of men," that "words plainly do violence to the understanding and throw everything into confusion, and lead men into innumerable empty controversies and fictions" (55). Indeed, Bacon specifically associates one category of lying—that of lying "for advantage"—with merchants ("Of Truth" 1). Language is for Bacon "a medium of exchange" (Montgomery 74) that, like money itself, must be used carefully to avoid corruption and deception. As Douglas Anderson notes, William Bradford's friend and partner William Brewster owned a copy of Bacon's *Advancement of Learning* (15).

Plain style and its seventeenth-century practitioners like Bacon are often called modern since they seem to predict an individualism as well as an emphasis on reason that would later characterize the Enlightenment. But plain style must be seen as a linguistic development that is as antimodern as it is modern, that looks "backward as well as forward in time" (Cornelius 23), since it marks a resistance to, even as it unwittingly participates in, those elements of an emerging modernity that appeared most alienating and destabilizing. Merchants and travelers may have employed plain prose in order to facilitate economic profits and to keep track of commercial exchanges, but for William Bradford, as for a great many other seventeenth-century writers, plain style appeared to offer a kind of antidote to the linguistic and economic confusion associated with merchants and their profits. Like the Puritans themselves, plain style had one foot in and another out of an emergent modernity and its developing world-economy.

Merchants and Credit

The commercial world of Holland alienated Bradford and the other Pilgrims, but in order to escape it they became rather unwilling and uncomfortable participants in the joint-stock company that was formed to fund their New World project. Plymouth Plantation depended on two groups: the merchant adventurers, led by Thomas Weston, who remained in London but invested money in the colony in hopes of reaping future profits, and the planters who provided their labor to settle the plantation and make it profitable. Weston insisted on a last-minute alteration to the original terms of this contract by requiring each planter to work exclusively for the common store rather than private gain for the first seven years of the venture. After those seven years, the merchants and settlers would divide equally the company's profits and assets. By agreeing to this change, the

Pilgrims' agent, Robert Cushman, much to Bradford's dismay, increased the merchants' potential for gain by reducing that of the planters.

In 1622, after two years of constant tension in his dealings with both the Plymouth and the London groups, and with little profit on his investment, Weston sold his shares and arranged to establish his own plantation at nearby Wessagusset, becoming thereby another source of trouble and competition to Plymouth. The following year, a third group arrived in Plymouth: men called "particulars" who did not belong to the joint-stock company, who paid for their own voyage to Plymouth, and who worked for their own profit.[19] In the same year the particulars arrived, the Plymouth planters ceased their "common course" by assigning private plots of land to individuals, allowing them to "set corn every man for his own particular" (*OPP* 132). Despite Weston's departure, the London adventurers, now led by James Sherley, continued to support Plymouth until a 1626 agreement entirely liquidated the joint-stock company. At that time, a group of eight undertakers from Plymouth, led by Bradford, took over the remaining debt and became responsible for managing the plantation and its trade. While serving as their London agent, Isaac Allerton entered into a series of private agreements that advanced his own personal finances while plunging Plymouth into further debt.

This compressed history of Plymouth's economic formation and development highlights some of the fundamental tensions and complex interdependencies that characterized the colony. Each of the major episodes in that history—the Weston affair, the disputes with the particulars John Lyford and John Oldham, and the Allerton crisis—is represented by Bradford as a conflict between those who worked for the so-called "General Body" (*OPP* 140) and those particulars who were interested in their own individual profit rather than the common good. It is precisely one such early conflict that Robert Cushman addresses in a 1621 lay sermon delivered in Plymouth on the text "Let no man seek his own, but every man another's wealth" (1 Corinthians 10.24). Cushman puts the Plymouth group's religious and national covenant into economic terms when he tells them, "It is now therefore no time for men to look to get riches . . . but rather to open the doors, the chests, and vessels, and say, Brother, neighbour, friend, what want ye? any thing that I have? Make bold with it; it is yours" (265). This representation of a selflessness mindful of maintaining the common good acquires more force when Cushman contrasts it with the quest for individual gain: "[W]ho, I pray thee, brought this particularizing first into the world? Did not Satan?" (266).

Published in London in 1622, Cushman's sermon addresses at once the Plymouth planters, discontented with their economic exploitation by the London adventurers, and the London merchants, discontented with

Plymouth's lack of profits. In the sermon's dedication, Cushman assures the adventurers, whose aim "has been, first to settle religion here, before either profit or popularity" (261) that "no labor is lost nor money spent, which is bestowed for God" (262). Cushman insists, and implicitly urges his London audience to agree, that the Plymouth project is guided by a purely providential economy in which the planters' profits and losses are ascribed to God and in which all economic successes come by plain dealing. The merchants' interest in "particularizing" represents, by contrast, a worldly and individualized self-interest that Cushman, by aligning such behavior with Satan, portrays as frankly evil.

Cushman evidently shared with Bradford not only an economic but a stylistic ideology, for he claims that "to paint out the Gospel in plain and flat English, amongst a company of plain Englishmen, (as we are,) is the best and most profitable teaching; and we will study plainness, not curiosity, neither in things human nor heavenly" (260–61). Cushman's opposition of "plainness" to "curiosity" seems itself more curious than plain, but curiosity's association with inquiry into that which is hidden, secret, and inaccessible nicely evokes a sense of an interiority that is at odds with the self-evident truth of surfaces associated with plainness. If the real antagonists in *Of Plymouth Plantation*, as Alan Howard has suggested, are the uncertainty and confusion that result from not seeing fully or clearly (Howard 252), it was merchants who repeatedly embodied those threats. For both Cushman and Bradford, merchant capitalists represented an excess and deceit that challenged the integrity of the covenant community. *Of Plymouth Plantation* is a record of such challenges to the Pilgrims by a series of merchant middlemen. In the course of pursuing the profits that might follow the adventure or risk of their money, figures like Weston, Lyford, Oldham, and Allerton appear as subjects whose unreadability threatens the present and future coherence of the Plymouth project. As Bradford warns, in a modification of Psalm 145, quoted while recounting the planters' relations with Thomas Weston, "'Put not your trust in princes,' (much less in merchants)" (*OPP* 112).

In Europe merchants had long been associated with deception and concealment. Fernand Braudel explains that the face-to-face trading practices of the public market, where peasants arrived from the country to exchange goods for money with which they in turn purchased other goods, were gradually eclipsed by the more private and concealed exchanges of merchants who traveled between town and country buying and reselling goods in order to increase their store of money. Likewise, artisan shopkeepers who sold the goods they produced were increasingly replaced by middlemen who bought and sold goods produced by others (Braudel, *Wheels* 42, 62–64). Seventeenth-century court cases reveal that these new merchants were "detested, hated for [their] cunning, intransigence and hard-heartedness" (47). But the characterization of merchants as employing secret and deceptive modes of speech has an even longer history. As early as the fourteenth century, protests were recorded against mercantile exchanges that were conducted "by whispering in each other's ear, by speaking low or by signs, and in strange or hidden words" (qtd. in Braudel, *Wheels* 49). Florentine merchants of the fourteenth and fifteenth centuries were likewise described as not only misrepresenting themselves in order to "conserve and increase their riches" but circulating stories about "the cheating and lies of others, when, in the secrecy of their consciences—unless they wanted to deceive themselves—they feel themselves just as impure" (Salutati 40; qtd. in Jed 77). Stephanie Jed identifies in such writings about merchants the repeated "designation of a secret space within the mercantile conscience" (78) that echoes efforts by merchants to "protect the secrecy of their writing." And merchant books and diaries commonly used linguistic codes and formulas that likewise encouraged the emergence of a sense of privacy and of a private self (83).

Such observations provide very early evidence of a self that could be imagined as consisting of an exterior and interior that were not necessarily bound to or consistent with each other. It is in many ways not surprising that merchants were among the first social group to be identified with this new model of the self and its dangers. As noted earlier, the epistemic shift Foucault locates in the seventeenth century exposed a new gap in the realm of economics between inherent value and market value, as well as a commensurate gap in the realm of language between things and words. Even in the small community of Plymouth on the periphery of an emerging capitalist world-system, the simple act of receiving goods on credit from a merchant implied a series of complicated and long-distance exchanges. That Plymouth merchant, as Rutman notes, would have obtained those goods on credit from a Boston merchant who in turn got those same goods on credit from an English merchant, often in exchange for sugar or wine from the Caribbean or Madeira—which had been traded and shipped to New England for agricultural products shipped to the West Indies or elsewhere (*Husbandmen* 20–21). Significant profits could often be made simply by selling in Plymouth a manufactured item purchased in Boston, much less by engaging in longer-distance Atlantic trade (21). Merchants therefore lived in and represented the world of credit, an ephemeral world in which profits resulted from a series of deferred and distant exchanges. While such merchants might have appeared to balance their account books by writing in the expectation of future revenue or payment, in fact those balances were perpetually outstanding. In the unstable and expectant space of those time lags emerged the excess of mercantile profit, the linguistic danger of deception, and the devious and impenetrable selves of merchants—performances that often got marked and disciplined in colonial New England as dissent.

Fictional Selves

The repeated descriptions in *Of Plymouth Plantation* of merchants as self-interested profiteers and deceivers whose words cannot be trusted reflect Bradford's discomfort with this world. In his review of a series of letters written by Weston and others among the adventurers, for example, Bradford exposes a suspicious "unconstancy and shuffling" that suggests a concealed "mystery" (*OPP* 113) that he is unable to access or decode. Weston, whom Bradford early suspects of "run[ning] in a *particular* way" (*OPP* 113, emphasis added), is later accused of "pretending" only in order to create "profit to himself" (*OPP* 116). Repeatedly, Thomas Weston's economic self-interest and his linguistic dishonesty are directly linked. Just as the planters soon learn that Weston "pursued his own ends" rather than those of the general good, they discover that his early "promised help turned into an empty advice" (*OPP* 118). Not only are the words and actions of Weston unreadable, but he and his allies appear as shifting and unstable men who cannot be pinned down and perceived clearly. Once Weston deserts the Plymouth and London groups to establish his own "particular plantation" at nearby Wessagusset, Robert Cushman warns Bradford in a letter not to trust the members of the new settlement: "[I]f they offer to buy anything of you, let it be such as you can spare, and let them give the worth of it. If they borrow anything of you, let them leave a good pawn" (*OPP* 119). Soon after, Weston himself arrives "under another name, and the disguise of a blacksmith" (*OPP* 131)—acts of deliberate misrepresentation that are for Bradford at once perfectly consistent with Weston's use of fiction to gain wealth and perfectly illustrative of the kinds of dangers posed by merchants to men like Bradford committed to the common good.

Although Bradford portrays Weston throughout as a difficult and base man, this hostility cannot be read simply as the result of a personality conflict or an isolated assault on Plymouth's well-being by a singularly selfish individual. The Weston affair tells a larger story about a profound clash between the still largely feudalist ethos subscribed to by the farmers and artisans of Plymouth and the mercantile capitalist orientation of Weston.[20] At the same time, the excessiveness of the case Bradford makes against Weston suggests an almost worried determination to differentiate the individualist merchant from the farming collective at Plymouth that has only recently abandoned its collective structure so that each member could "set corn every man for his own particular" (*OPP* 132). Perhaps because of such periodic blurring within Bradford's carefully maintained opposition, he insistently projects self-interested trickery onto merchant others external to the plantation who seemed to threaten the stability not only of Plymouth but of language itself.

Nowhere are such threats more clear than in Bradford's account of the John Lyford and John Oldham conspiracy, in which the strategies of plain style are called upon to distinguish the "poor Plantation" from these "sly merchant[s]." Bradford likens John Lyford to "that dissembling Ishmael" who graciously greeted the worshipers whom he meant to kill (*OPP* 164). Lyford and Oldham create, through secret means, a faction among the particulars and the London adventurers who supported them. Bradford explains—echoing earlier European accounts of merchants—that there were "private meetings and whispering amongst them" even though "outwardly they still set a fair face of things" (*OPP* 165). But if Lyford tells secrets, his more devastating deception occurs through writing. Bradford and others intercept a bundle of Lyford's letters bound for London and find them "full of slanders and false accusations" (*OPP* 166). In fact, they find that Lyford has opened the letters of some planters, copied them, and included them with commentary in his own letters. In his account of this episode, Bradford describes Lyford, who was sent by the adventurers to serve as a minister to the Plymouth group, as "this sly merchant" who "takes these copies and seals them up again; and not only sends the copies of them thus to his friend and their adversary, but adds thereto in the margin many scurrilous and flouting annotations" (*OPP* 166).

In the trial that follows the discovery of these letters, Lyford and Oldham are accused of organizing a "conspiracy and plots" against "this poor Colony" (*OPP* 169). Bradford reports that Oldham's response to these charges was to "ramp more like a furious beast than a man, and called them all traitors and rebels and other such foul language as I am ashamed to remember" (*OPP* 167). He later "began to rage furiously because they had intercepted and opened his letters, threatening them in very high language" (*OPP* 168). In his response to the charges that Lyford outlined in his letters, Bradford repeats the familiar terms of a conflict between two fundamentally opposed economic ideologies. To Lyford's claim that the Plymouth church rejected all outsiders, Bradford claims that "they were willing and desirous that any honest men may live with them, that will carry themselves peaceably and seek the common good" (*OPP* 169–70). To Lyford's claim that the planters belonging to "the General" "sought the ruin of the Particulars" by refusing to trade with them, Bradford replies that the "Particulars" came by their goods falsely, through illegal purchase and theft.[21]

Weston, Lyford, and Oldham were, of course, all outsiders. They were neither members of the group of original planters nor of the Separatist church, and thus the troubles they caused and dangers they posed were easily represented as external ones solvable by exiling all three of them from New England. The later problems with Isaac Allerton, however, could not be explained or resolved so easily, and they suggested the disturbing possibility that the troubles and dangers associated with merchants had penetrated to the very core of Plymouth itself. Allerton was one of the "Pilgrim Fathers" who had arrived on the *Mayflower*, a member of the original Leyden congregation, the first assistant to Governor Bradford, and the son-in-law of the revered Elder Brewster. When the Plymouth undertakers "ran a great adventure" (*OPP* 207) by buying out the London adventurers, accepting the remaining £1,800 debt, and claiming a trade monopoly in an effort to repay that debt, Allerton was chosen as the middleman to negotiate between Plymouth and England, where they hoped to find "some of their special friends to join with them in this trade" (*OPP* 218). But almost immediately, Allerton acted less as an agent for the Plymouth collective than as an individual with secret and self-interested motives: he brought over a minister unsolicited by the church who proved to be "crazed in his brain" and transported "some small quantity of goods upon his own particular, and sold them for his own private benefit" (*OPP* 233). Later transatlantic voyages by Allerton yielded even worse results: he carried Thomas Morton back to New England after Plymouth authorities had earlier exiled him, and he brought yet more "retail goods, selling what he could by the way on his own account" (*OPP* 240).

Allerton begins to resemble those deceitful and selfish merchants who had plagued Plymouth earlier. He is accused of using "crafty wits" to cheat the planters and pursue his own "private gain" (*OPP* 242, 241), and like Weston, Lyford, and Oldham before him, he combines lying with profiteering. The other undertakers "saw plainly that Mr. Allerton played his own game and ran a course not only to the great wrong and detriment of the Plantation who employed and trusted him, but abused them in England also in possessing them with prejudice against the Plantation" (*OPP* 259). But as a Plymouth insider, Allerton's participation in these practices represents the penetration of the emergent world of transcontinental mercantile commerce—a world whose dangers the Pilgrim planters so feared—into the very center of Plymouth itself, where even those whom Bradford might have thought he knew best suddenly appear unknowable. Allerton the man comes to resemble his account books, which Bradford describes as so complex as to be indecipherable to the colonists. In the end, Bradford encloses his account of both "this tedious and uncomfortable subject" of Allerton and "that long and tedious business between the partners here and them in England" (*OPP* 358) within the apparent clarity and simplicity offered by plain style. Bradford minimizes his own words and commentary as he inserts the letters written by others, hoping thereby to "deliver the truth in all, and as near as I can in their own words and passages. And so, leave it to the impartial judgment of any that shall come to read or view these things" (*OPP* 285). Bradford marshals his spare linguistic economy against an excessive economics of self-interest.

Douglas Anderson argues that Bradford's book is committed to the "disinterested goal of . . . the pursuit of simple truth as he unfolds the tale of Plymouth Plantation" (43) and that Bradford achieves this goal through a surprisingly modern, Baconian use of protoscientific language, which positions its readers as unbiased and passionless observers (28). The many letters Bradford incorporates into his history, often deliberately without comment, serve in this reading as evidence on which readers can formulate their objective positions. Yet it is also possible to see the letters as entries documenting the monetary (as well as moral) credits and discredits accumulated by the plantation over the course of the years—a kind of epistolary account book that places various credible and suspicious persons and their writing against each other.

His style and structure might seem in this regard to be among the tools of an emergent modernity and the mercantile capitalist world-system, but Bradford uses these tools to challenge the institutions and relations that come with that system. While his history duly records the passage of time, as any good account book also would, one also senses that Bradford is waiting throughout his journal for colonial time (and colonial consensus) to really begin. There is a sense of urgent desire in *Of Plymouth Plantation* to close these open accounts, to put outstanding debts to rest, to rejoin words with things, to disengage the plantation from the folds of transoceanic time and space and the troubling dissenters who appear themselves incomprehensibly folded. It is, I suggest, this unmet desire that helps to produce the "pattern of incomplete completion" (147) that Anderson identifies in the narrative at large. The plainness of Bradford's presentation is an effort to hasten and promote that closure, to disengage the colony from the folds of transoceanic time and space, although his plain style also signifies Plymouth's own folded position within the webs of commercial and mercantile relations. In the end, the perpetual delays and deferrals mandated by transcontinental credit relations turn out to be the very condition of colonial existence.

The Failure of Language

When the settlement and expansion of the Massachusetts Bay Colony in the 1630s opened up a vast new market for Plymouth goods and merchants, the economic opportunities and competition prompted many of Plymouth's inhabitants to move and establish churches elsewhere. Bradford acknowledges these changes as causes of the gradual dissolution of the Plymouth church and community, signaling as well the failure of the Separatists' special covenant with God. With this coincident covenantal failure and financial success, Bradford's book stumbles into the silence of its notoriously empty last page, which contains only the heading that identifies the years: "Anno 1647. And Anno 1648."

It has become a critical commonplace to read the sudden silence with which the book ends as a despairing sign not only of the final collapse of the Separatist settlers' initial hopes but also of Plymouth's final eclipse by John Winthrop's "Citty upon a Hill." But this reading does not take into account Bradford's obsession with money; it fails to appreciate the many pages in *Of Plymouth Plantation* dedicated to financial discussions and the degree to which Bradford's vision centers on merchants and their practice of deceit. Considering that Plymouth's outstanding debt to the London adventurers is finally paid a mere two dozen pages before the history ends—thereby concluding once and for all the complicated business arrangements that both enabled and crippled the colony—it would appear that Bradford's writing as well as its plainness is sustained against such mercantile forces. The book ends, in a sense, once the central financial tangle that sustains it is finally over. The account book becomes unnecessary once all outstanding debts have been paid and payments received. At that point, however, it is perhaps more clear than ever that the "particularizing" ways of those merchants have penetrated Plymouth itself. Just as Plymouth has won its lengthy battle to escape the control of transnational merchants, it becomes despairingly evident that the bigger war against the deceitful and disunifying forces of mercantile capitalism has been lost.

Bradford wrote little else than *Of Plymouth Plantation,* but the few later texts that remain offer interesting extensions of his celebrated history and its concerns with linguistic uncertainty and mercantile deceit. These writings include, for instance, dialogues between "young men" who are curious about the origins of Plymouth and the Separatist movement and "ancient men" who provide information and clarification in response to the youngsters' questions. The 1648 dialogue is less a nostalgic return to the past than a determined effort to set straight the apparently inaccurate historical and cultural record. Repeatedly the "ancient men" respond to the youths' questions and assumptions by correcting the misrepresentations handed down to them and by offering evidence in the form of oral, eyewitness accounts that counter and correct the errors and misinformation the young men have acquired from written sources.[22] That Bradford presents these concerns and corrections in the form of a conversation furthermore suggests his ongoing effort to find ways in which language can best convey truth—even if, in the end, he records this suspicion of writing in a dialogue that is itself written.

Although Bradford makes little or no mention of Weston, Lyford, Oldham, or Allerton in this 1648 dialogue, the verses he wrote in 1654 return to the problem of mercantile commerce, and he explicitly identifies it as a central cause of Plymouth's troubles. In these verses, he notes that as Boston grew, it quickly dominated "Not only . . . the Massachusetts Bay, / But all trade and commerce [that] fell in her way" (469). The prosperity that followed, however, also resulted in poverty for some:

> For merchants keep the price of cloth so high,
> As many are not able the same to buy.
> And happy would it be for the people here,
> If they could raise cloth for themselves to wear;
> And if they do themselves hereto apply,
> They would not be so low, nor some so high. (470)

The verse makes it clear that Plymouth has developed unevenly in relation to the new colonial center of Massachusetts, which is itself on the semiperiphery of the capitalist world-system. Bradford's description of the difficulties faced by the Plymouth planters in New England in 1654 curiously parallels his description of the difficulties confronted by the small group of farmers and artisans who had arrived in Holland nearly half a century before. It also repeats the complaint about commercial competition and inequality in England that concludes the 1622 *Relation*. He finds himself, decades later, once again poor in a country filled with wealthy merchants, yearning for a return to a production-oriented economy in which people might make their own goods instead of having to buy them from merchant middlemen who profit, in ways that continue to appear mysterious, from the complex new markets created by European colonial and commercial expansion.

One of the few details we have of Bradford's later life, after he put away his history of Plymouth, is his decision to study Hebrew. Historians from Cotton Mather to Perry Miller have registered this biographical detail as evidence of William Bradford's admirable devotion to learning, a devotion they see as all the more admirable since it seems such a departure from his agrarian and artisan background. Douglas Anderson considers it evidence instead of Bradford's continued intellectual vitality and cosmopolitanism (20). But the choice of Hebrew suggests an attachment to a pre-representational world, since it was Hebrew that, in the aftermath of the destruction of the Tower of Babel and the subsequent linguistic fragmentation and confusion, acquired a privileged relation not only to God but to truth and linguistic clarity.[23] Those seventeenth-century linguists, philosophers, and scientists who were committed to the possibilities of a universal language saw themselves as recovering or at least reinventing Hebrew. William Bradford's own late turn to Hebrew and his gradual abandonment of writing suggest the possibility that, despite his commitment to plain style and its purported ability to represent "the simple truth in all things," the English language, plain or not, finally failed him in America.

Chapter Three

INFLATION: THOMAS MORTON AND TRADING-POST PASTORAL

WHILE FEW OF THE EPISODES detailing Plymouth's financial relationships with Weston, Lyford, Oldham, Sherley, and Allerton ever appear in standard anthology excerpts from *Of Plymouth Plantation*, the episode chronicling the 1628 conflict between Plymouth and Thomas Morton invariably appears in every anthology, where it is typically paired with those selections from Morton's own book *New English Canaan* that offer a dissenting account of those same events. Most analyses of this confrontation have repeated what Matt Cohen identifies as "Hawthornian comedy-versus-prudery readings" (2). In his recent study of Bradford, however, Douglas Anderson offers a very different understanding of this conflict by perceptively identifying in Bradford's version of Ma-re Mount a compressed mirroring of Plymouth's own history.[1] Bradford explains that the plantation at Mount Wollaston fell into Morton's hands only after its original leaders, finding that it did not meet "their expectations nor profit," left to sell their servants on the Virginia market. After their departure, Morton, one of only two freemen left at the site (Salisbury 157) and who apparently "had some small adventure of his own or other men's amongst them," overthrew the lieutenant in whose command the post had been left and asked the remaining servants to become his "partners and consociates; so may you be free from service, and we will converse, plant, trade, and live together as equals and support and protect one another."[2]

Yet the communalist dimensions so prominent in Bradford's description are strikingly absent from Morton's own book: in spite of attributing the utopian dimensions of "Platoes commonwealth" to the Native Americans, Morton never details the terms of his own relationship to the indentured servants among him. And rather than conform to the indigenous people's way of life, I argue in this chapter, he insists that they conform to his. But Ma-re Mount's egalitarian origins do recall Plymouth's own utopian beginnings, which Bradford compared to Plato's ideal before it succumbed to the temptations of individualism, materialism, and luxury. What Bradford sees in Morton and his men is not only an inflated and monstrous pursuit of personal gain, therefore, but a distorted reflection of Plymouth's own pursuit of gain.[3] If merchants like Weston and Allerton reminded the Pilgrims of their resistant implication in the mercantile capitalist relations beginning to define the Atlantic world, Morton's performance may have reminded them of the more communalist, premodern identity they seemed to have left behind in a rapidly receding past.

Why then does Bradford's own language become itself so relatively inflated when he writes about Thomas Morton, as if the Plymouth governor has momentarily and unwittingly "gone merry" himself even in the very process of condemning the mirth taking place at the nearby plantation that Morton named Ma-re Mount? Douglas Anderson reads Bradford's stylistic shift not as a desperate or angry attempt to get language to describe accurately his disorderly subject but rather as a deliberate and self-conscious mockery of Morton's own unruliness. I would like to press further Anderson's observation about Ma-re Mount's mirroring of Plymouth to suggest that when William Bradford resorts to a suddenly allusive, erudite, and emotive style when he writes about Ma-re Mount, he may be, consciously or not, demonstrating his own access to the literary and cultural traditions associated with a socioeconomic identity that Morton denies him. Bradford may, in other words, be mimicking Morton's own linguistic performance of a gentlemanly class/status, with the effect either of claiming membership in the learned elite that Morton refuses him and his fellow Separatists or of exposing any such claims—Morton's and his own—as a kind of theatrical class/status effect that is produced not by nature or breeding but by language. Both the "comedy-versus-prudery" readings and Anderson's account miss the economic dimensions of Thomas Morton's stylistic as well as social dissent.

In 1633, while Thomas Morton was back in England simultaneously writing *New English Canaan* (published in 1637) and preparing a legal case challenging Plymouth's land patent, King James' *Book of Sports* was reissued by Charles I. As David Underdown notes, this republication encouraged countryside celebrations to reemerge during the 1630s from their repression at the hands of English Puritans who objected to the ceremonial indulgence of drink, dance, and song associated with them (67).[4] The political, religious, and social divisions that marked these disagreements also took the form, however, of aesthetic debates, for the Puritans who opposed the indulgent excesses associated with such celebrations offered the alternatives of "godliness, plain speech, and plain manners" (Zwicker 36). These competing aesthetics clearly separate the linguistic plainness, self-effacement, and stylistic restraint of Bradford's *Of Plymouth Plantation* from the linguistic obscurity, self-promotion, and stylistic excess of Morton's *New English Canaan*.[5] But as this chapter argues, the aesthetics of Thomas Morton's dissenting actions at Ma-re Mount and expressions in *New English Canaan* are tied also to a particular socioeconomic ideology, much as the defense of "public mirth" was in England.[6] *New English Canaan*'s satirical critique of the Separatist Puritans' incapacity for enjoyment—a relatively brief portion of the book that has been the nearly exclusive focus of literary criticism on it—is in fact interwoven with the book's sustained theory of English colonial economics. The book condemns the New England Puritans as financial and cultural illiterates whose ungoverned access to colonial trade destroys at once the order of a traditional social hierarchy and the natural productivity and wealth of New England. Drawing on the literary forms of the masque and pastoral, Morton presents the Separatists as inept performers of an illegitimate class/status identity, and he urges an aristocratic reordering of the colonial society and economy that, he insists, is already modeled in the landscape itself.

Oddly enough, it is when William Bradford comes to his account of Thomas Morton in *Of Plymouth Plantation* that his prose begins aesthetically to resemble his neighbor and enemy's. In remembering Ma-re Mount, Bradford's language becomes uncharacteristically effusive, as its barely controlled rage erupts into what looks like literary playfulness. He complains that Morton and his fellow traders erected an "idle or idol maypole" and invited Indian women to join them in drinking and dancing together "like so many fairies, or furies, rather. . . . As if they had anew revived and celebrated the feasts of the Roman goddess Flora, or the beastly practices of the mad Bacchanalians" (*OPP* 227). He dubs Morton the "Lord of Misrule" and proclaims him guilty of "maintain[ing] (as it were) a School of Atheism" at the Mount Wollaston plantation that Morton renamed "Merry-mount, as if this jollity would have lasted ever" (*OPP* 228). Morton's own version of these events explains that the celebration, complete "with Revels, and merriment after the old English custom," aimed simply to commemorate the change in name of their plantation from its "ancient Salvage name [Passonagessit] to Ma-re Mount" (134). They brewed beer, prepared a song, and erected a maypole, to which was nailed "a pair of buck's horns" (134), which "stood as a fair sea-mark for directions, how to find out the way to Mine Host of Ma-Re Mount" (135). Morton remarks that because the maypole offended the "precise Separatists that lived at New Plimoth," who "termed it an Idol," these neighbors threatened to make the place "a woeful mount and not a merry mount" (136).

The festivities staged by the Anglican Morton at Ma-re Mount certainly offended both the religious and the aesthetic sensibilities of his Puritan neighbors. But Bradford actually reserves his greatest outrage for Morton's practice of selling firearms and ammunition to the Indians, who have as a result become "ordinarily better fitted and furnished than the English themselves" (*OPP* 229). With sudden and surprising passion, Bradford exclaims, "O, the horribleness of this villainy!" and anxiously worries that

> many both Dutch and English have been lately slain by those Indians thus furnished [with guns by Morton], and no remedy provided; nay, the evil more increased, and the blood of their brethren sold for gain (as is to be feared). . . . O that princes and parliaments would take some timely order to prevent this mischief and at length to suppress it by some exemplary punishment upon some of these gain-thirsty murderers, for they deserve no better title, before their colonies in these parts be overthrown by these barbarous savages thus armed with their own weapons, by these evil instruments and traitors to their neighbours and country! (*OPP* 229–30)

Bradford concludes this explosive aside by confessing, "I have forgot myself and have been too long in this digression," and promises "now to return" (*OPP* 230) to his chronicle. But while his language resumes at this point the more dispassionate tone and restrained style that typify the rest of his history, Bradford is unable yet to leave the subject of Morton and his dissent behind.

The riotous excess of Ma-re Mount's merrymaking is in fact linked for Bradford, figuratively as well as literally, with the profitable excess of their trade in guns and furs. Morton, drawing on his own West Country experience, instructed the Indians in the hunting practices of English country gentlemen. This instruction simultaneously increased the Indians' acquisition of valuable animal skins for trade and drove their desire for firearms and ammunition, making those commodities increasingly scarce and expensive. The gun and fur trade established by Morton was clearly quite profitable, since Bradford remarks that those at the Ma-re Mount trading post were able to drink as much as "£10 worth in a morning" (*OPP* 227). Bradford laments the growing cost and unavailability of lead, "which is dear enough, yet hath it been bought up and sent to other places and sold to such as trade it with the Indians at 12*d* the pound. And it is like they give 3*s* or 4*s* the pound" (*OPP* 229). By purchasing lead not for local and English use but in order to resell it in another market at a higher price, Morton and his colleagues have "sold for gain" the lives and safety of fellow English settlers. As Bradford tells it, Morton and his eclectic group of Ma-re Mount traders are guilty of creating and then profiting from numerous forms of economic and social inflation; their actions have led to the inflation of prices, the inflation of consumption and spending practices, the inflation of the social position of servants and Native Americans, and the self-inflation of Morton himself, whom Bradford calls a mere "pettifogger" (*OPP* 226) who now thinks himself "high" (*OPP* 231).

Bradford's disgust with Morton's profiteering—and its impoverishing effect on Plymouth colonists—would seem to align Morton in many ways with Lyford, Oldham, Allerton, and other merchants and "particular" investors who appear in the pages of *Of Plymouth Plantation* seeking private gain. But Morton is in more important ways unlike these other men, all of whom appeared, at least initially and however wishfully, to be committed to the community's success. Moreover, as the previous chapter argues, these other figures trouble Bradford not just because they emerge as deceptive but because they approach inscrutability; they repeatedly appear as someone other than who they seemed to Bradford to be, and this very slipperiness leaves them impossible to read clearly. Morton, on the other hand, is from the beginning a defiant outsider and competitor, openly hostile to both Plymouth and Puritanism and, for Bradford, all too easily read as a figure of simple excess. If the merchants and their mysterious accumulations cannot, for Bradford, be linguistically *located*, Morton and his inflationary performances cannot be linguistically *contained*.

While Morton and the London-tied merchants both remind Plymouth of the returns the Pilgrims struggled to produce for their demanding English backers, Ma-re Mount represents a very different kind of challenge to Plymouth's socioeconomic identity and ideology than that posed by men like Allerton, Lyford, or Oldham. Whereas the latter deceptively hoarded and concealed their profits, Morton's prompt spending and ostentatious consumption of his profits figure forth an altogether different economic subjectivity, one that summons the bountiful self of the aristocratic country landlord out of England's recent feudal past. Morton—probably a recently risen member of the "middling gentry"—might be seen himself to performatively claim this identity even as he accuses the Puritans of illegitimately performing their class/status. In the North American colonial periphery of an emergent world-system increasingly organized in terms of mercantile capitalist relations, Morton and Bradford alike cling to pre-modern economic identities as they project onto each other their own symptoms of commercial implication.

It bears remembering that at the time of the Plymouth–Ma-re Mount conflict there was literally no working model of a profitable plantation in New England (although there were some profitable individuals). The economic drama of *New English Canaan* is therefore staged against a backdrop of landownership disputes, trading rights and pricing conflicts, and colonial financial failure on the plantation level. Morton attributes New England's financial disaster to the paired economic and cultural illiteracy of Plymouth's common farmers and artisans. Designed for an audience of English aristocrats, Morton's economic dissent is expressed in both the content and the style of his book, which apparently annoyed Bradford nearly as much as his gun trading and maypoling did. Morton is guilty not only of inflating prices but of an inflated linguistic style that parallels what Bradford terms his "riotous prodigality and profuse excess" (*OPP* 228). Bradford identifies Morton's inflationary aesthetics in the inexplicable "rhymes and verses" (*OPP* 227) he nailed to the maypole, in his use of "scurrilous terms full of disdain" (*OPP* 231) in his reply to letters from Bradford and others, and in his insolent rejection of the authority not only of Governor Bradford but of the former King James himself.

Morton's trading success coincided with Plymouth's economic reorganization, an arrangement that freed the colony from control by the London merchants but that also made a group of eight Plymouth "undertakers" (including Bradford) responsible for both its large debt and its trade potential. Plymouth therefore found itself hopeful of entering into the lucrative New England fur trade in order to begin to repay this debt, at a moment when its Ma-re Mount neighbors were already profitably engaged in that trade. A good many critics have located in this competition the repressed center of Bradford's heightened animosity toward Morton.[7] But although Ma-re Mount and Plymouth found themselves competing in the same fur trade, Morton suggests that each plantation was engaged in that trade as a means to advance very different colonial economic visions: for Plymouth, trade was a form of labor engaged in by a largely agrarian community, while for Ma-re Mount trade was a laborless means to support a leisured class of manor lords in the image of the old English countryside.[8] Both groups looked backward, in different ways, to economic formations that predated the capitalist world-system, although both participated in mercantile capitalist arrangements central to that world system in their efforts to arrive there. Although scholars are correct to pinpoint the fur trade as a pressure point in the Bradford-Morton conflict, therefore, we might locate within that competition an even more profound disagreement about plantation economics and a colonial class/status system. What Bradford saw as Morton's dangerous social and economic forms of inflation, Morton represented as the natural and pleasurable reproductivity of the New World. Whereas Bradford saw in Ma-re Mount opportunistic waste, Morton saw in Plymouth wasted opportunity. The linguistic economy of each man's text offers an index to their competing colonial visions, and only by reading these two texts together, and in their entirety, might we begin to expose not only the mercantile capitalist investment sensibility that supports Bradford's plain style but the obscured labor relations that underlie Morton's aristocratic pastoral ideology. The two plantations, leaders, and texts might exist in a different kind of dialectical relation with each other than scholars have supposed, each exposing the other's participation in a consolidating capitalist world-system that they both proclaim, in very different ways, to resist.

Literary Form and Land Rights

As long as critics have written about it, Thomas Morton's *New English Canaan* has been positioned as a counterhistory to the canonical *Of Plymouth Plantation*, but Morton's volume is read and taught in small and selective excerpts even more often than Bradford's. As the previous chapter notes, Bradford's journal has often been positioned by American literary histories and anthologies at the beginning of a national narrative whose story celebrates a liberal individualist pursuit of religious and political freedom. Morton's book—which by challenging Plymouth's self-definition also challenges its contribution to this narrative—has typically either been dismissed as a flawed anomaly or celebrated as a more laudable expression of individualism and freedom than that represented by the Pilgrims. Both responses keep intact the central terms of this American nationalist narrative.

Charles Francis Adams, in his 1883 edition of *New English Canaan*, introduces it as "a singular book" (v) whose deliberately "inflated, metaphorical, [and] enigmatic" (103) style caused it to go unread. Such criticisms have persisted well into the twentieth century. Donald Connors, otherwise among the most careful and sympathetic readers of Morton's text, describes the book as filled with utterly baffling passages as well as with "tonal and stylistic discrepancies" (81). Connors' comment that the book lacks "any underlying unifying principles by means of which to bring the entire book into focus" (81) is echoed by Robert Arner, who calls it a "troublesome book" (217) that is not quite history and not quite literature, and that is furthermore undercut by its own cross-purposes and by conflicts in both "tone and imagery" (217). Daniel Shea, in a comment that might well sum up this line of modern criticism on Morton, has called the book "greatly flawed" (52), "an apparently failed attempt to rewrite the rewriters" (56).

This critical reception, because it repeats and affirms Bradford's own befuddled and anxious response to Morton's linguistic and cultural aesthetics, continues, of course, to privilege the historical content of Bradford's over Morton's narrative.[9] A smaller but equally impassioned vein of literary criticism has in turn elevated Morton over Bradford's Pilgrims on the basis of his communal egalitarianism, protoenvironmentalism, or multiculturalism *avant la lettre*.[10] By emphasizing instead Morton's commitment to colonial trade, others critics such as Karen Kupperman and Edith Murphy have usefully complicated these bifurcated representations of Morton.[11] Here I wish to combine this emphasis on trade with the efforts of more recent critics (such as Philip Round, and Peter Linebaugh and Marcus Rediker) to situate Morton and Ma-re Mount within a transatlantic literary and cultural arena. Moreover, the very stylistic and structural difficulties associated with Morton's volume might be made more legible by reading all three of the books that make up *New English Canaan* in the context of Morton's already intersecting regional and transatlantic economic relationships.

Critics who have sought a central agenda for *New English Canaan* have been stumped by the generic and stylistic discrepancies between the book's three sections. The first book offers a protoethnographic description of the native Algonquins, and it differs from similar manners-and-customs portraits found in contemporary New World travel narratives only in its overtly sympathetic portrayal of the natives. The second book—a promotional tract that describes in detail the New England landscape and its commodities—is also a common element of contemporary travel literature. The third book's critical history of the region's present English inhabitants has, of course, dominated critical responses to Morton's volume.[12] Rather than treat the first two books as appendages to the politicized history of the last one, however, I instead reconsider all three in terms of the travel narrative genre to which the first two so clearly belong. Of the three books, the middle one's extensive description of the landscape has been the most routinely neglected in both criticism and literary anthologies, though I would argue that its pastoral concern with the use and exchange of the land's "Catalogue of commodities" supports the entire volume.

One of the effects of privileging Morton's third book is that it tends to prevent critics from seeing *New English Canaan* within cultural and literary contexts other than New England regional politics and Bradford's then-unpublished history.[13] The literary influences on *New English Canaan* certainly do include biblical, classical, and Renaissance literature,[14] but Morton engages those sources, I suggest, largely in the context of contemporary travel writing. The texts that formed the most powerful and immediate print context for this 1637 volume were contemporary promotional and descriptive travel accounts of New England such as John Smith's *Description of New England* (1616) and *Advertisements for the Unexperienced Planters of New England* (1631), Mourt's *Relation* (1622), Edward Winslow's *Good Newes from New England* (1624), John White's *Planter's Plea* (1630), and William Wood's *New England's Prospect* (a book published in 1634, and to which Morton refers repeatedly and critically in his own volume). Unlike any of these texts, however, Morton's is not addressed to present or would-be investors, because the very premise of his book is that New England yields rather than needs wealth. In doing so, Morton was likely echoing and building on the most well-known travel collection of the time, Samuel Purchas' *Hakluytus Posthumous; or, Purchas His Pilgrimes* (1625), which, like *New English Canaan* (but unlike the travel narratives mentioned above), targets a gentry more than a merchant audience. In Morton's view New England requires not merchant investors but gentry landholders, and his book is designed to appeal rhetorically to those he believes would govern the land best: elite English gentlemen with the means to settle and ability to rule a manor-style colonial plantation supported by a kind of trade tenancy. To advance this economic vision, Morton pastoralizes promotional travel writing. *New English Canaan* blends and cross-fertilizes such "high" or "court" literary forms as the masque and pastoral with such "low" or "commercial" literary forms as the colonial brochure or promotional tract.[15]

Included in Purchas' collection are writings by several of the explorers and agents associated with Sir Ferdinando Gorges, president of the Council of New England (which held a royal patent to northern New England) and for whom Morton worked as a lawyer. It is believed that Gorges first used Morton's name on a grant for New England land as part of an effort to convince Virginia Company critics that the Council's patent did not constitute a monopoly.[16] After his 1628 exile from Massachusetts and return to England, Morton worked as a land patent lawyer, defending Gorges' New England land grants and challenging the Plymouth patent while also writing *New English Canaan*.[17] Among the competing promotional travel narratives he read must certainly have been Gorges' own 1622 tract, *A Briefe Relation of the Discovery and Plantation of New England*, written primarily to encourage further settlement in New England in the face of growing skepticism about its safety and profitability. In it, Gorges presents a plan for recreating in New England the economic and social relations of the old English countryside.

Gorges proposes to divide the land "into Counties, Baronries, Hundreds, and the like" (*Briefe Relation* Ev), and "these Lords of Counties may of themselues subdiuide their said County into Mannors and Lordships, as to them shall seeme best." He furthermore determines that these lords will govern the manor through keeping local courts, "as is heere vsed in *England*, for the determining of petty matters, arising betweene the Lords, and the Tenants, or any other" (Ev–E2r). While the countryside will be inhabited by these manor lords, the cities or towns will be home to merchants who, Gorges claims, will "gouerne their affaires and people as it shall be found most behouefull for the publique good of the same" (E2r).[18] Gorges' colonial vision places country gentlemen and city merchants in geographically and politically separate worlds. Morton's interest in *New English Canaan* is clearly in the former, and his book largely endorses his colleague Gorges' vision of a New England countryside governed by a colonial aristocracy of landholders. Land is absolutely integral to Morton's *New English Canaan*, which develops an aesthetics of colonial pastoral that finally locates within the landscape itself the right of English gentlemen to possess New England's land and wealth.[19]

In the first book of *Hakluytus Posthumous*, Samuel Purchas presents King Solomon's discovery of gold at Ophir as an exemplary voyage that inaugurates the empire building continued by Columbus, Cabot, and countless others. Morton, too, mentions early in his book King Solomon's act of sending "ships to fetch of the gold of Ophir" (17) shortly after introducing Sir Ferdinando Gorges as "our Solomon" who has directed "the English Nation" to its own "golden mean" (11).[20] Whereas Solomon discovered the precious metal of gold, Gorges has found a land whose "gold" is its geographical location. Daniel Shea has argued that Morton, who was well acquainted with Jonsonian masque from his days at Clifford's Inn, presents *New English Canaan* as a masque designed to produce a "metamorphosis" that would install Morton in New England while excluding the disorder of the Separatists' antimasque (58). Indeed, *New English Canaan* might be seen as a colonial masque that performs its pastoral excess not for the court and the king but for the Council of New England and its leader, Gorges. Just as Ben Jonson's court masques celebrated the authority of and encouraged loyalty to James I, Thomas Morton's *New English Canaan* affirms his loyalty to Gorges and the Council. And as the playwright Jonson often became associated with the king in his masque productions, so does Morton also cross-identify with his own Gorges-Solomon figure. Just as Gorges' wisdom led him to discover New England (13), Morton's wisdom and knowledge qualify him to write this account exposing "the real worth of that eminent Country," a worth that other, previous reporters have "concealed from publike knowledge" (3). *New English Canaan* presents New England as a pastoral utopia of potentially unlimited pleasure and profits, but only if it is organized around a hierarchical socioeconomic order supported by colonial trade rather than King Solomon's gold or Plymouth's labor. Morton's book, which culminates with a traditional masque revels, invites its aristocratic readers to join with and reproduce the colonial economy summoned by the book's masque, and to restore to Morton the land and trading privileges denied him by the disordered antimasque of the Puritans.

Pastoral and Masque

In his recent study *What Is Pastoral?* Paul Alpers suggests that literary form needs not only a diachronic but what he calls a *diachoric* dimension that would account for aesthetic differences across space as much as those across time (x). I adopt Alpers' proposal here to suggest that Thomas Morton's book develops a colonially specific instance of English pastoral that incorporates elements of seventeenth-century court and country-house pastoral, but transforms them into what I call "trading-post pastoral."[21] Morton's trading-post pastoral in *New English Canaan* mocks Plymouth's class/status alliance with agricultural and artisanal labor, challenging what Timothy Sweet identifies as Bradford's georgic vision. *New English Canaan* might be seen to transcontinentalize the political and socioeconomic effects of seventeenth-century English pastoral. It appropriates colonial land for a specifically aristocratic English imperialism, but it also imports the pastoral aesthetics of the English court and countryside into the landscape of New England and into the genre of colonial American travel writing. Morton's trading-post pastoral imagines a colonial world of gentlemanly leisure and luxury made possible by profiting from the naturalized labor of Native Americans and the unacknowledged labor of indentured servants.[22]

The final three words of *New English Canaan*—"*Cynthius aurem vellet*" (199)—come from Virgil's *Eclogues*, and align Morton as "Mine Host" with the Roman poet whose pastoral verses appeared in a new English translation in 1628, under the reign of Charles I and just as Plymouth was in the process of exiling Morton from New England.[23] Raymond Williams explains that traditional Virgilian pastoral depends on a contrast "between the pleasures of rural settlement and the threat of loss and eviction" (17). If the pastoral mode serves the land patent lawyer Morton well, it is because when he writes *New English Canaan* he has been evicted from land and trading privileges to which he believes he was entitled through Gorges and the Council. Morton's inflated celebration of the New England landscape registers precisely the discrepancy between his present loss and his former pleasure. *New English Canaan* represents, as Alpers suggests all pastoral does, a "convening"—a gathering for dialogue and song—in order to acknowledge (and aestheticize) this loss.[24] But Morton—who by losing the land has also lost the trading rights and profits that accompany that possession—develops a pastoral not of the shepherd dispossessed of pasture but of the landowner dispossessed of his trading post. Morton's is a pastoral in which colonial gentlemanly leisure can be supported by the "natural" profits received from a trade practiced largely by the labor of others.

New English Canaan makes in this way a very different kind of appeal to a very different class of readers than the plain style of so much contemporary promotional travel writing. It transforms the loss of colonial profits and land suffered by Morton into present aesthetic abundance, rather than mortgaging that loss toward a certain-uncertain future in a rhetorical-accounting ploy that, as chapter 1 argued, is calculated into the aesthetic restraint of plain style. Pastoral's inflationary aesthetics offer a linguistic measure of the discrepancy between former possession and present loss, much as the economic inflation that Bradford blames on Morton (as well as other Gorges associates) reflects the discrepancy between a commodity's fair value (or "just price") and its market price.[25] Bradford's account highlights the latter market gap, and the excessive profits and dangerous consumption that result from Ma-re Mount's exploitation of it. Morton, on the other hand, emphasizes not the market and its prices but the land and its possession. Unlike *Of Plymouth Plantation*, which frequently takes numerical note of prices paid or debts owed, *New English Canaan* rarely includes a monetary notation. Morton records his dispossession instead through a pastoral language whose very richness measures the loss sustained by himself, the Council, and the English empire. The density and obscurity of Morton's rich language deliberately work, as Philip Round perceptively notes, to exclude a certain class of nonaristocratic readers from the text's "truth." But Morton's book simultaneously excludes these readers and fellow traders from New England's economic bounty, for he depicts his Puritan neighbors as laboring farmers and artisans turned would-be merchants who are no better able to read the trade economy than they are able to decipher his poems. Far from a Leveller-like figure, as some have suggested, Morton presents New England as a place where country gentlemen like himself are illegitimately evicted from their estates by Puritan farmers who incompetently "play" at gentlemanly status; for him, New England requires not leveling but reordering.

For Raymond Williams, seventeenth-century English pastoral operates in the interests of "a developing agrarian capitalism" (22), and he situates the development of the pastoral form within the rapidly changing economy of a period marked by the interrelated emergence of land enclosures, vagrancy, and capitalist relations. Annabel Patterson similarly tracks the early modern fate of pastoral and its class allegiances when, following Anthony Low, she aligns pastoral with the aestheticized and intellectualized realm of "an aristocratic and later royalist elite," and the alternative form of the georgic with the "radical scientific thought or . . . social protest" of "those involved in 'work,' whether commercial or agricultural" (138).[26] The world of agrarian labor and rural poverty became, as Williams argues, screened out within early modern pastoral, which erases the tensions that characterized classical pastoral to leave its figures suspended "not in a living but in an enamelled world" (18). And by idealizing the social and economic relations of English country life, the pastoral of the country-house poem screens out, not only the labor of the rural poor, but also the country landowner's increasing participation in the "forces of pride, greed and calculation" that characterize the new capitalist age (28).

Countryside pastoral and the country-house poem share with city and court forms of pastoral this ambivalent disavowal by the aristocracy and the court of their participation in an emerging capitalist economy. Pastoral became a form through which both the country gentleman and the court identified themselves with older social and economic arrangements, as if to mask their increasing participation in newer forms of mercantile and colonial commerce. As Leah Marcus explains, the Stuart monarchs sought to erase the "emerging commercialization of court and countryside by urging a return to older forms of aristocratic life," including the celebration of traditional forms of hospitality and revelry (19). We might see Morton's *New English Canaan* performing for its gentlemanly audience, who were members and supporters of the Council, this same aristocratic disavowal, much as pastoral masques did for the monarch or country-house poems did for the gentry. It offers a vision of New England that resembles the old English countryside, where landowners and laborers gather together in scenes of traditional hospitality and revelry that elide this vision's very dependence on complex regional and transcontinental commercial arrangements. Morton's use of pastoral and masque traditions negotiates his own disavowed participation in these commercial relations just as much as Bradford's plain style does, but it does so by separating from the present an idealized and abundant past, rather than importing into the present a certain-uncertain future.

If Morton ends his book by invoking Virgil, he begins it with the conventional pastoral tropes of a temporal golden age and a spatial golden mean. As his book's title already explains, New England is an earthly paradise, an Eden, a "second Canaan" (93). In fact, New England even exceeds Canaan in the "delicacy" and "conveniency" of waters, and offers in the place of milk and honey an extraordinary "plenty of birds, beasts and fish, whereof Canaan could not boast herself" (91). He explains that the present planters of New England have as yet penetrated "very little way into the iland. The riches of which Country I have set forth in this abstract," which reveals the country as "nothing inferior to Canaan of Israel, but a kind of parallel to it, in all points" (13), "a country whose endowments are by learned men allowed to stand in a parallel with the Israelites' Canaan" (54), a "land that for her excellent endowments of nature may pass for a plain parallel to Canaan of Israel" (91). Morton's descriptions unabashedly recall the earlier prose of Columbus or Ralegh, whose accounts of the indescribable beauty and abundance of the New World became increasingly associated over the course of the seventeenth century with unbelievability. But rather than follow contemporary travel writers' recourse to a more "factual" plain style, Morton accuses the plain language of recent travel accounts of concealing behind its apparent "truth" the riches of a country that its writers seek to keep for themselves.

The idyllic site of New England is characterized by both a geographic and an economic "golden mean." Morton reminds readers that the ideal sites for colonization are those situated within "the temperate Zones" between the extremes of "hot and cold." New England is precisely located "within the Compass of that golden mean" (8), and "Massachusetts" is furthermore situated in "the middle part" (12) of New England, an observation made earlier in Gorges' *Briefe Relation*, when he placed New England "not onely . . . in the temperate Zone, but as it were in the Center, or middle part thereof," where it shared the same climate as "*Constantinople*, and *Rome*, the Ladies of the World," and "*Italy*, and *France*, the Gardens of Europe" (Dv). By going on to call for "industrious people, to reape the commodities that are there to be had" and join the present colonists in their "health and plenty" (D3v), Gorges introduced the need for human industry that was a traditional element of colonial promotional writing. Since at least the earliest tracts by Richard Hakluyt, English writings justifying North American colonialism argued that their goals of spreading Christianity and gaining economic profits could be reached only through the hard work of training, planning, and planting.[27]

By eliminating this rather conventional call for industrious colonists, Morton deviates from the appeal of Gorges and others, and he moreover does so without returning to the earlier colonial economic model of gold or silver discovery that underpins the writing of Columbus or Ralegh. Morton is able to erase altogether the need for English labor, for Morton's colonists will not work but rule over a land that already works for them. He argues that man is justified, by virtue of his "wisdom," to rule over all the creatures that fall within "the Compass of that golden meane," but that this dominion must be regulated by the characteristics of "moderation, and discretion" (8). The possibilities of exploiting this geographic golden mean, or "*Zona temperata*," are thus dependent on dedication to an economic golden mean, expressed in the aphorism "The wise man says, give me neither riches nor poverty." The golden age might be realized by avoiding the pride that results from excessive "riches" and the "despair" that results from poverty (8). This paradise emerges, however, only by the same "magical extraction of the curse of labour" that Raymond Williams discovers at work in the pastoral country-house poems of Jonson and Carew (32). For Morton, the paradise of New England is a laborless world because the very climate that makes it a geographic golden mean also makes it an economic golden mean. As he notes, the winds not only bring the rain but "do blow Trade" (10) in the same direction. And as this sentence suggests, the work of trade in this second and superior Canaan is associated less with human beings than with the natural world itself.

For instance, one of Morton's most delightful descriptions of an Edenic golden age in the golden mean of Massachusetts exposes also, on closer inspection, a revealing account of the kind of labor and economic relations that enable such bountiful beauty to bring pleasure to the leisured owner-observer. In the pastoral paradise of New England, Morton finds

> so many goodly groves of trees, dainty fine round rising hillucks, delicate fair large plains; sweet crystal fountains and clear-running streams that twine in fine meanders through the meads, making so sweet a murmuring noise to hear as would even lull the senses with delight asleep, so pleasantly do they glide upon the pebble stones, jetting most jocundly where they do meet; and hand in hand run down to Neptune's Court, *to pay the yearly tribute which they owe to him as sovereign Lord of all the springs*. (53–54; emphasis mine)

The landscape here is a place of supreme leisure (it "lull[s] the senses with delight asleep"), extraordinary bounty (there are "so many" trees and hillocks, "large" plains), and playful happiness (the streams "pleasantly . . . glide," "jet most jocundly," and run to the court of Neptune "hand in hand"). Yet what is a pleasurable performance of nature from the position of the recumbent "Lord" (whether the resting Morton or Neptune himself) is also, from the perspective of the running streams, an act of labor and financial payment. The "tenant" waters are meanwhile working continuously, if with great apparent happiness, to pay their rent to the "landlord" (or waterlord, perhaps, in this case) of the sea. The natural world itself models a socioeconomic arrangement that is repeated among its inhabitants, since the relationship here between Neptune, the lord of the sea, and the laboring streams, is precisely that between Morton, trading-post owner, and the Indians, who have a "coveteous desire . . . to commerce with our nation, and wee with them" (17).

Morton's pleasurable description of the pastoral landscape follows immediately after his initial announcement that he arrived in New England "with 30 servants, and provision of all sorts fit for a plantation" (53). He undertook the "survey of the country" that resulted in the above description, he claims, "while our houses were building" (53), a phrase whose passive tense elides the human labor of the servants engaged in house construction.[28] Just as often, however, Morton's descriptions of the country's natural inflationary excess exclude the presence of human beings altogether. In Book II in particular, sentence after sentence struggles to make language rich enough to describe the wealth of the country:

> Contained within the volume of the land, fowls in abundance, fish in multitude, and discovered besides, millions of turtledoves on the green boughs; which sat pecking of the full ripe pleasant grapes that were supported by the lusty trees; whose fruitful load did cause the arms to bend. With which here and there dispersed you might see lilies, and of the Daphnean tree; which made the land to me seem paradise. For in mine eye, 'twas Nature's Masterpiece: Her chiefest Magazine of all, where lives Her store. If this land be not rich, then is the whole world poor. (54)

This is a landscape so wealthy that it literally bends over to offer itself to its reclining inhabitants. Morton has likewise seen so many bass "stopped into the river close adjoining to my house . . . as will load a ship of 100 tons" (84), and "[o]f Smelts there is such abundance that the Salvages do take them up in the rivers with baskets, like seives [*sic*]" (86). Morton's would seem to be precisely the kind of narrative that Christopher Levett and others mocked for its absurdly unbelievable descriptions of fish and fowl that literally deliver themselves to arriving colonists. Some fish are so big and numerous, claims Morton, that "fishermen only eat the heads and fins, and throw away the bodies," whereas others "do almost come ashore, so that one may step but half a foot deep and prick them up on the sands" (87).

Morton deliberately contrasts both the content and the style of his description with those of William Wood's *New England's Prospect*, published in 1634 while Morton was writing *New English Canaan*, and which Morton repeatedly refers to as "a woodden prospect" (57). Wood, whose book adopts plain style, insists on the necessity of both colonial investment and labor. A rich man, Wood emphasizes, coming to New England "must first scatter before he gather," or become momentarily poor through expenditure before "his increase comes in double" later (68). Future prosperity can arrive only if human labor is expended in the present, for "whereas it is generally reported that servants and poor men grow rich, and the masters and gentry poor, I must needs confess that the diligent hand makes rich and that laboring men having good store of employment, and as good pay, live well and contentedly" (73). Morton characterizes this expenditure of labor as, at best, unnecessary and unintelligent waste, and at worst, a deliberate misrepresentation designed to dissuade competing claimants to the country. Why work, Morton asks, when trees bend over to deliver their fruit, and fish wash ashore at one's feet? Morton's New England, in contrast to Wood's, is a land not of labor but of leisure, because the land itself yields all the commodities any inhabitant might need.

Book III, which might appear to abandon the promotional pastoral of the previous book for its satirical history of the Plymouth Separatists, actually relies on Morton's earlier description of the land's abundance to support his critique of the Puritans' economic mismanagement of New England. After narrating his return to Massachusetts with Isaac Allerton in 1629, Morton describes an attempt by "Captain Littleworth" (Captain John Endicott) to organize the beaver trade within the region granted them by the "Patent of the Massachusetts" (164). Captain Littleworth, whose very name announces his financial valuelessness, required the planters to sign "Articles" promising to *"follow the rule of God's Word"* (165) if they wished to reside within the compass of the patent, and required them to contribute funds to the "general stock" if they wished to participate in the beaver trade within that patent. But after only six months, the participating partners called for an accounting and discovered that "instead of increasing the profit, they had decreased it; for the principal stock . . . was freetted [fretted, wasted or worn away] so, that there was a great hole to be seen in the very middle of it which cost the partners afterwards one hundred marks to stop" (166). Morton, on the other hand, as the only planter who had refused to sign the Articles and to enter into the trade agreement, "did not only save his stock from such a Cancar [canker or open wound], but gained six and seven for one" (167). As if their regional financial arrangements mimic transatlantic ones, the Separatist planters make a poor investment that yields only loss. Morton represents another economic possibility altogether, in which, without any apparent risk, his possessions multiply six- or sevenfold. The Puritans' economic ineptitude is repeatedly aligned by Morton not only with their religious, but with their socioeconomic, identity.

When Littleworth/Endicott responds to the failure of his trade arrangements, for example, by organizing a raid on Morton's home, his actions betray not only his financial ignorance but also his ignorance of the traditional hospitality and feasting customs of the English countryside. Littleworth reportedly entered Morton's house under the pretense of recovering corn and other goods belonging to the Separatists, although Morton maintains that Littleworth's loss was his own fault, the result of having "improvidently trucked his store for the present gain in beaver" (167). Littleworth's greed caused him to sacrifice his colony's common store of food for the promise of failed future returns (167). While Morton was securing his ammunition in the woods, the "Commissioners entered the house; and wilfully bent against Mine honest Host, that loved good hospitality. After they had feasted their bodies with what they found there, they carried all his corn away, with some other of his goods, contrary to the laws of hospitality." Morton charges the men with violating old English countryside traditions of good hospitality, but such violations are themselves the result of the Puritans' blindness to the pastoral excess that surrounds them. After they left, for instance, Morton simply killed some "fowl, and venison" with his gun, taking advantage of "the plenty of the country, and the commodiousness of the place affording means by the blessing of God. And he [Morton] did but deride Captain Littleworth, that made his servants snap short in a country so much abounding with plenty of food" (168). Endicott and his men experience poverty and hunger, and must resort to theft, because they lack the knowledge and ability to reap the landscape's natural abundance that country gentlemen like Morton possess.

Indeed, the hierarchy of class/status groups that brought order to the traditional English world so often invoked by Morton, has clearly collapsed in New England. One chapter in Book III, titled "Of the Degrading and Creating of Gentry in New Canaan," tells the story of how one English gentleman newly arrived in New England was arbitrarily "degraded" in rank by "Joshua Temperwell" (John Winthrop) simply because the man "incurred the displeasure of great Joshua" (174). Meanwhile, a pious Separatist who had become wealthy through the beaver trade was, upon renouncing such commerce for religious reasons, "made a Gentleman of the first head" in the place of the authentic English gentleman whose "title, prerogative and preheminence" had been taken away (175). Morton suggests that the newly promoted Puritan, who had when younger been "apprenticed to a tomb-maker" (173), was able in New England to buy his way into the "title of a Gentleman" merely through "the help of beaver and the command of a servant or two" (174). In Puritan New England, the hierarchy that organizes the traditional social order has collapsed, and class/status distinctions can be arbitrarily made and unmade simply through the strategic performance of wealth.

The Separatist Church is likewise characterized by this collapse of the traditional socioeconomic order, for any of those who govern the church, "though he be but a Cowkeeper," might become a public preacher (181). The danger of this social mobility, Morton observes, might be seen in the example of King Louis XI, who "advanced his Barber to place of Honor, and graced him with eminent titles," permitting him even to address political matters with "foreign princes" (183). The French monarch soon learned, however, that the man "behaved himself so unworthily (yet as well as his breeding would give him leave)" that he had to be exiled from the kingdom. For Morton, the Separatists are precisely such a group of commoners who have duped themselves into believing they can become gentlemen. Book III is in large part an effort by Morton to expose the Puritans' "ass's ears [that] will peep through the lion's hide"; he intends to expose the socioeconomic identity of "these illiterate people" (184), who, as common laborers, lack (from Morton's point of view) the ability and legitimacy to govern and manage the paradise that is New England.

Morton turns to the genre of the masque in Book III to depict to the Council and Gorges in theatrical terms the conflict between the Puritans and himself, employing the songs, dances, mythological figures, and revels that characterized the Stuart court masque. Like Ma-re Mount's revels were perceived by Bradford, Stuart court masques were perceived by many to be a wasteful and excessive display, particularly at a time when England was in an economic depression. In his critical 1625 essay on masques, for example, Francis Bacon calls them expensive "Toyes" and sharply takes them to task for their costly extravagance. In Patricia Fumerton's brilliant analysis, the Jacobean court masque emerges as a performance of the Crown's ambivalent relationship to colonial commerce. The masque form answered what for Fumerton was the "question for the private aristocratic self: how to dress up in ornaments the foreign trade and bourgeois barbarousness in which it was involved so as to sustain at least the fiction of the gift culture while allowing business to continue as usual?" (173). Fumerton reads Jonson's 1624 masque *Neptune's Triumph* as an effort to celebrate a traditional economy against the world of the market that was contained and demonized within the embedded antimasque. The performative work of the masque was therefore to "mask the fact that the 'private' sel[ves]" of the aristocrats enjoying the production were "the very embodiment of such greedy consumption" (173). *New English Canaan* offered the same satisfying identity to its English aristocratic audience, although its distinction between the world of the masque and the antimasque is the presence not of trade but of labor. The intrusion of the disorder of the antimasque—represented by the ignorant, blind, and incompetent Separatists—represents the entrance of commoners, exposed by their labor, into the realm of gentlemen landlords.

Moles, Insects, and Labor

If Book II presents a landscape of natural abundance that reproduces itself without the need of human labor, Book III presents its Puritan inhabitants as a kind of plague whose misguided labor brings morbidity and infertility to Canaan's paradise. Morton frequently describes the Plymouth Separatists as moles, first calling them by this name when he records their unacknowledged inability to interpret the poem he nailed to the maypole in celebration of the renaming of his plantation. He mocks their "most pitifull" inability "to expound" the poem (135) and scorns their misreading of his maypole, concluding that they "despise" learning and "vilify . . . the two universities . . . not considering that learning does enable men's minds to converse with climents of a higher nature then is to be found within the habitation of the Mole" (141). Morton proceeds to offer his own analysis of "the Poem according to the true intent of the authors of these Revels, so much distasted by those Moles," and his literary explication is designed "to convince them of blindness as well in this [literary interpretation] as in other matters of more consequence" (139). As moles who live in the darkness, aligned here with both a common social ranking and the soil itself, the Separatists have no access to elite knowledge, but also no access to the climate of New England's temperate zone, and its abundant productivity.

The "habitation of the Mole" is of course more specifically the tilled soil where crops are planted, an association that Edward Johnson makes explicit in his *Wonder-Working Providence* when he identifies moles with what Timothy Sweet calls "too much intensive concentration on farming" (57; see 29 in Johnson). This agrarian exclusivity has for Johnson the effect of blinding these farmer-moles toward other economic possibilities, including most particularly that of trade. But in Morton's representation, the Puritans cannot profitably manage trade even when they try, for the economic blindness associated with their social ranking renders them unable to even see New England's natural abundance. *New English Canaan* brings to light the abundant value of New England, which has been hidden by the Separatist moles (and their writers like William Wood); as Morton's poetic prologue declares, "Admired things producing which there die, / And lie fast bound in dark obscurity— / The worth of which in each particular, / Who list to know, this abstract will declare" (7).[29] The Puritans' class/status might prepare them to be able laborers of the soil but not competent traders of commodities.

Consider the example of "Master Bubble," the unidentified character whose exploits Morton describes in the chapters leading up to his account of the Ma-re Mount revels. Bubble is described as one who spends countless hours uselessly recording the language of the natives, since he is unable to understand what he has recorded, making his efforts a complete "loss of labor." He also is described as being so dull an orator that he "lulled his auditory as fast asleep as Mercury's pipes did Argus' eyes" (123), rendering his own listeners at least temporarily blind. When he comes to visit Morton, the grace he delivers—with closed eyes—at the dinner table is so long that Morton decides to help himself to the food during "this blind oratory . . . and had half-done before this man Bubble would open his eyes, to see what stood afore him" (124). And Bubble's idiocy and blindness extend to his trading ability as well, for Morton explains that he would "buy anything that was to be sold" regardless of its price, and solely on the basis of how much time he was allowed for payment (123). Later, while trying to take advantage of the inland beaver trade, Bubble convinces himself of some illusory Indian conspiracy, and runs away without his shoes and with "his breeches . . . on his head" (128), a blindly inverted trader running away from profit. He recovers all the goods and equipment he brought with him only because the Indians are honest enough to bring them back. Morton later observes, in his list of the Separatists' tenets, that they pray with their eyes closed "because they think themselves so perfect in the high way to Heaven that they can find it blindfold. So do not I" (188). And Morton observes that after burning his house down upon finding him guilty in court of several charges, "they had found their error (which was so apparent that Luceus' eyes would have served to have found it out in less time)" (190–91).

In the poem praising Morton that opens *New English Canaan*, one "R. O. Gen." defends Morton's publication of the book on the basis of "His love unto his Country," and asks, " . . . is the sun to be disliked and blamed / Because the mole is of his face ashamed? / The fault is in the beast, not in the sun . . ." (7). If the Separatists are blind moles, then Morton and his book are the sun, shaming the Puritans in the act of exposing their greedy incompetence. Morton occasionally accuses the Plymouth group of deliberately concealing from their merchant-investors and others abroad the abundance and potential for profitability in New England. The extraordinary and labor-free bounty of New England has been hidden, according to Morton, by those whose self-interest has led them "to keep both the practice of the people there, and the real worth of that eminent Country, concealed from publike knowledge." It is Morton's task to "lay open" that "real worth" in his book (3). In fact, plain style itself is, according to Morton, simply a literary mechanism for a kind of rhetorical hoarding, by concealing the wealth and excess that he claims to lay bare in his book. Wood's failure to mention minerals, for example, leads Morton "to suspect his aim; that it was for himself, and therefore will I not discover it" (80). Wood's misrepresentation of the region in *New England's Prospect* is not only delivered in "wooden" prose whose poverty and barrenness Morton deplores, but is the result of what Morton repeatedly identifies as its misdirected vantage point, for he accuses Wood of incorrectly describing the New England coast as "high land" (23). Wood cannot see clearly, because his "prospect" or perspective is literally distorted. Good trees, for instance, cannot be seen or found on "the upland ground" where Wood's "woodden prospect" (57) is perched, but "in the lower grounds" (45) or "bottom grounds" (57). He accuses Wood of either stupidly or deliberately describing the coast as "highland" rather than "lowland," suggesting that "he is of weak capacity that conceiveth otherwise of it" (93). Like his fellow Puritans, Wood is rendering himself blind by illegitimately advancing himself to a higher geographical-socioeconomic level.

Book III repeatedly characterizes the Separatists as laborers whose unnecessary work produces nothing of value. Book I's protoethnographic account of the Indians is, on the other hand, an inadvertent record of the necessary human labor that quietly sustains Morton's aristocratic pastoral vision. In their study of the Revolutionary Atlantic world, Peter Linebaugh and Marcus Rediker identify "new forms of self-organization" among workers that appeared in response to the "processes of expropriation, exploitation, and colonization" that characterized the early seventeenth-century Atlantic world. These new forms were often characterized by members of the ruling class as "monstrous," and Linebaugh and Rediker identify the image of the seven-headed hydra as one of the most common formulations of this monstrosity (40). Thomas Morton uses precisely this image to describe the Puritans' perception of his small group, and Linebaugh and Rediker accordingly nominate Morton's Ma-re Mount as one of many alternative communities within early modern capitalism, describing Morton as one who "advocated acquiring the land through cooperative trade with the Native Americans," who "praised their midwives, medicine men, and uses of the land," and whose "followers, servants and fugitives of several languages and colors, hoisted the maypole and joined the round dance, earning the wrath of the Puritans" (62). But it is perhaps less easy to celebrate Morton's collective as this description suggests, for when Linebaugh and Rediker describe the ruling class's erasure of workers' labor from landscape descriptions, they could very well be describing Morton's own text: "the field is *there* before the plowing starts; the city is *there* before the laborer begins the working day. Likewise for long-distance trade: the port is *there* before the ship sets sail from it; the plantation is *there* before the slave cultivates its land" (42). The abundant landscape of New England is likewise for Morton *there*, before the indentured servants and Native Americans work and hunt and build it. Morton's pastoral vision—much as the wealth that will effortlessly arrive for the gentlemen landlords whom he invites to New England—depends on the toil of others, on the occluded labor of the Native Americans and indentured servants who also inhabit New England. For the fur trader Roger Williams, the voices and bodies of Native Americans would be central in his guide to New England commerce and culture; for Morton, however, they are silent and largely invisible.

If the Puritans are moles, then the Indians are ants and bees. The two animals who prosper best in the "*Zona Temperata*" are, Morton notes, "the Ant and Bee" (10)—both of which are identified with industriousness and with hoarding. Morton's interest in ants and bees is evident in several other references, which link the productive qualities of these insects with the imperialist figure of King Solomon. In Book II, for instance, Morton describes the incredible abundance of the country, which is "so infinitely blest with foode, and fire, to roast or boyle our Flesh and Fish" and so temperate that no man should have cause for complaint "unless he be one of those that Solomon bids go to the Ant and the Bee" (89). In this passage, Morton quotes, if somewhat inaccurately, from Proverbs—a book traditionally attributed to Solomon—where it suggests that the "lazybones" should "Go to the ant" and learn from the insect's diligence and hard work how to avoid poverty and want (Proverbs 6.6–11).

It is, however, neither the colonial organizer Gorges nor the landholder Morton who is aligned with these industrious insects, but the Native Americans who inhabit New England. In fact, Morton's reference is particularly revealing when we remember that in his description of the Indians' method of storing corn underground during the winter months, he compares their practice "to the Ant and the Bee" (36). Morton's portrayal of the Indians as generous, tractable, and even "ingenious" (37) does of course offer a sympathetic portrait of them, as it also convinces would-be planters that they need not fear Indian violence in New England. But he is more subtly here castigating those reports and individuals that have characterized New England as intemperate, or unproductive, or barren—and suggesting, Solomon-like, that these "lazybones" should "go to the Indians." But Morton is suggesting, not that settlers and planters need themselves learn how to become hardworking ants and bees like the Indians, but only that they need to trade with them in order to take advantage of the productivity and abundance that already, by virtue of the natives' entirely naturalized labor, flourishes in New England. Like aristocratic landowners in England, the colonial landowner can live in pastoral leisure, free from labor, collecting profits from trade in the place of rents. If Ma-re Mount operated as other colonial New England trading posts or "truck houses" did, for example, Morton would have first extended credit—in the form, for example, of guns, food, clothing, or tobacco—to Native Americans, who would have been expected to repay their debt by returning with marketable animal furs and hides. Those furs would then have been sent to Europe, where there was increasing demand for beaver pelts and other "luxury furs" (DePaoli 177).

While it is unclear just what comprised Morton's own activities at the trading post, he significantly never represents himself as engaged in any activity other than the country gentleman's sport of hunting. Even when labor is clearly required in order to make game into a marketable commodity, this labor is either left undescribed or ascribed to the Indians. He remarks, for example, on the "great abundance" of geese, which have often appeared as "1000 before the mouth of my gun. I never saw any in England for my part so fat as I have killed there in those parts. The feathers of them make a bed softer then any down bed that I have lain on; and is there a very good commodity. The feathers of the Geese that I have killed in a short time have paid for all the powder and shot I have spent in a year, and I have fed my dogs with as fat Geese there as I have ever fed upon myself in England" (62–63). The economic usefulness of the geese he shoots appears almost a by-product of the sport of hunting, and Morton never describes himself preparing or exchanging any of the game he kills (i.e., plucking and selling its feathers). He does, however, frequently describe the work of the Indians in building homes, catching fish and game, and preparing goods, such as when he notes in his report on elk that "[t]heir hides are by the Salvages converted into very good leather," and "[o]f this leather, the Salvages make the best shoes, and use to barter away the skins" (70).

If an English landowner like Morton need not work, it is because the land and its inhabitants will work for him. While Morton himself engages in the English gentleman's leisure activity of fowl hunting, the Indians are often described in terms that, at least inadvertently, reveal their physical labor. They build houses by "gather[ing] poles in the woods" and "placing them in form of a circle or circumference; and bending the tops of them in form of an Arch, they bind them together with the bark of Walnut trees, which is wondrous tuffe." These poles the Indians then "cover with mats, some made of reeds and some of long flags, or sedge finely sowed together with needles made of the splinter bones of a Crane's leg, and with threads made of their Indian hemp, which their groweth naturally." They construct beds of "planks commonly about a foot or 18 inches above the ground, raised upon rails that are borne up upon forks" and use as blankets "coats of deerskin, otters, beavers, raccoons and of bears' hides, all which they have dressed and converted into good leather with the hair on for their coverings" (21). While accounts such as these do contain a wealth of fascinating ethnographic detail, in their very detail they also seem to dwell on the amount of labor expended by the Indians to transform the landscape's raw materials into useful products.

Moreover, in the best English countryside traditions, the natives who work to construct such homes offer guests leisured hospitality, and "will spread a mat for him, of their own accord, and lay a roll of skins for a bolster, and let him lie," only waking him in order to feed him meat they have prepared (22). The description of Indian labor here resembles Morton's account elsewhere of the beaver, who "cuts the bodies of trees down with his foreteeth. . . . And with the help of other beavers . . . they draw the log to the habitation appointed, placing the logs in a square; and so by piling one upon another, they build up a house, which with boughs is covered very strongly, and placed in some pond to which they made a dam of brushwood like a hedge" (72–73).[30] In fact, Morton sustains throughout his book such parallels between the Indians, the animals, and the landscape of New England, representing all three as "naturally" productive and fruitful. Morton's pastoral effectively blurs the dependence of his own leisure on the laboring bodies of Native American men and women who hunt, build, prepare exchangeable animal skins, and produce children.

The skins prepared by the Indians are, of course, the most valuable of their productions for the trading-post owner Morton, and he observes that the Indians have sometimes had so many moose hides that "they have bestowed six or seven at a time upon one Englishman whom they have borne affection to" (70). Likewise one deerskin acquired through this kind of gift economy can be exchanged for "2, 3, or 4 beaver skins, which will yield pounds apiece in the country," and Morton notes that "I have made good merchandise of these" (71). Beaver skins "are the best marchantable commodity that can be found to cause ready money to be brought into the land, now that they are raised to 10 shillings a pound" (73), and he reports that even English fishhooks can be traded to the Indians in exchange for a valuable beaver skin, which in turn can be traded for even greater profit.

Morton extends this naturalized and aestheticized productivity to Indian women as well, and marvels that even when Indian women are "as great as they can be" with child, "yet in that case they forbear neither labor nor travel. I have seen them in that plight with burthens at their backs enough to load a horse, yet do they not miscarry, but have a fair delivery, and a quick. Their women are very good midwives, and the women very lusty after delivery, and in a day or two will travel or trudge about" (26–27). In Book II, Morton reminds us, he demonstrated "how apt [the country] is likewise for the increase of Minerals, Vegetables, and sensible Creatures" (120). Not only are commodities abundant and the soil fertile, but "in New Canaan the deer are accustomed to bring forth 2 and 3 fawns at a time" (92)—evidence of a remarkable natural fertility. Likewise, he insists, "the increase of . . . Children" (120) proceeds effortlessly in New England; despite the fact that far fewer women live there than in Virginia, more children have been born in seven years in New England than were born in twenty-seven years in Virginia. In his tale of the "Barren Doe of Virginia, Grown Fruitful in New Canaan," Morton yokes wealth and eros together, Solomon-like, by insisting that profit and pleasure are simultaneous in a land as fertile as New England.

In the poetic prologue that presents New England as a "fair virgin, longing to . . . / meet her lover in a Nuptial bed," Morton claims that the country, like the virgin, is "most fortunate / When most enjoyed"—and he insists throughout his book that it is, indeed, necessary to enjoy New England, to take pleasure in it, in order to make it prosper, to make it "fortunate." Morton offers his own pastoral colonial economy as a (re)productive alternative to the Puritans' fruitless labor, arguing that, at present, Canaan's "fruitful womb, / Not being enjoyed, is like a glorious tomb" (7). The erection of the phallic maypole, and the invitation in "The Song" to "Lasses in beaver coats" (138) to come and join them—an expression of hope that "wives [might be] brought over to them" (139)—represent Morton's identification of Ma-re Mount with masculine sensuality but also with reproduction and trade (since the women will arrive, apparently, wearing exchangeable commodities). Edith Murphy's analysis of the "Rise Oedipus" poem as the depiction of a contest between a "virile lover" and a "new husband" over possession of a widow—in which the manly Morton and the feminized Pilgrims compete for the hand of the land itself—further suggests the ways in which Morton contrasts his erotic economy of abundance to the Puritans' wasteful and empty infertility. For Morton and his fellow traders, profits are generated by pleasure and consumption, rather than by labor and hoarding.

Morton cites the words of Solomon again, this time from Ecclesiastes, when he describes in Book I the risky and pointless travels of explorers like "Captain Davis" (actually Hudson, according to Adams 118), who ventured into the *Frigida Zona* of Greenland and the Arctic, scoffing that such hazardous and difficult pursuits are performed in order "to get and hoard up like the Ant and the Bee, and yet as Solomon saith, he cannot tell whether a fool or a wise man shall enjoy it" (10–11). Why should Englishmen labor to accumulate goods, when the *Zona Temperata* of New England allows them to immediately enjoy its products and profits without any work? While Morton emphasizes the "getting and hoarding" capacities of ants and bees, it is crucial to note that what makes New England so attractive is that it does not require English gentlemen to labor like such insects, since the industriousness and productivity of the ant and the bee do not represent qualities demanded of those settlers who would hope to inhabit and plant New England so much as they represent qualities already possessed by a landscape and inhabitants that Morton portrays as naturally productive.

Morton deliberately bars from his dense and difficult text those moles doubly associated with cultural illiteracy and agrarian labor. The meaning of Morton's text cannot be accessed by such common readers, no matter how hard they might try, just as the abundance of New England cannot be enjoyed by labor. *New English Canaan* therefore depends on a courtly reading model that, as Julie Solomon describes it, elicits readers' desire and encourages them to project themselves into and fashion themselves out of a text, much as aristocrats would have read Spenser and Sidney. As we have seen, Solomon locates in Bacon and merchant writings the development of a new, scientific mode of reading that, by contrast, "virtually eradicate[s]" readers' desire ("To Know" 519). Thus over the course of the seventeenth century, the rich and fantastic world of *The Faerie Queene* gives way to commercial travel writing and its "extensive lists of objects which the traveling observer is instructed to note" (521). Part of what makes Morton's text so unintelligible (and also so interesting) is that he mobilizes this earlier courtly reading model in the service of what is largely (though not exclusively) this newer commercial content. By including the texts and explications of his several poems, he asks his readers to locate their desire and to fashion themselves as colonial aristocratic lords precisely in response to his merchantable "Catalogue of commodities." Morton's inflationary language is itself a kind of site of fertility, reproducing readers as leisurely country gentlemen who watch as the "natural" processes of commodity trade reproduce New England in the image of the English countryside.

New English Canaan offers its readers a kind of aristocratic colonial fantasy; it promises would-be planter-gentlemen the pastoral possibilities of unlimited pleasure and leisure rather than the burden of hard labor and the necessity of sacrifice. But what is also clear is that English readers, gentlemen or not, were buying neither Morton's book nor, it seems, the colonial economic theory it proposed. Although the details of the publication of *New English Canaan* remain murky and speculative, they do suggest that the English print market in the 1630s was receptive to neither Morton's vision nor his language. Of course, by the time Morton's book was published in Amsterdam in 1637, English readers interested in colonial New England affairs already had available a more immediately intriguing subject in the emerging Antinomian Controversy and the figure of Anne Hutchinson. Far from the object of celebration that it was in *New English Canaan*, female reproductivity became, in the language of Hutchinson's orthodox opponents, a figure for the dangers of mercantile commerce and a figure against which the fantasy of an American exceptionalism took shape. That exceptionalism also helped to determine the predominantly theological and regional terms in which colonial American dissent has for so long been understood—obscuring not only such dissenting figures as Thomas Morton but also, as the next chapter shows, the world economic dimensions of Hutchinsonian dissent.

Chapter Four

VENT: ANNE HUTCHINSON AND ANTINOMIAN SELFHOOD

COLONIAL AMERICAN STUDIES has been transformed by a series of challenges to the continuist, exceptionalist, regionally narrow, and prevailingly religious terms that have dominated its traditional enframement. Among other things, critics have challenged the cultural and geographic privilege of the Puritans and New England, often explaining such privilege as one effect of a retrodetermined paradigm that imposes on colonial American literature the role of anticipating later events, such as the American Revolution, American Romanticism, or U.S. nationalism.[1] Others have argued that these nationalist literary narratives deliberately suppress the mercantilist ideology and imagination so evident in John Smith and the southern Virginia planters (T. H. Breen, "Right" 50; Gura, "John" 265). But such efforts to set John Smith against John Winthrop, and the region of Virginia against that of New England, run the risk of overlooking the transoceanic mercantilist context that informs all colonial American writing, including that of the Puritans and New England. The dominant narrative whose terms these critics seek to revise has historically tended to suppress attention not just to John Smith and the southern colonies but to the pressures of economic conflict, class/status tensions, and colonial exploitation within early American literature generally, including those Puritan New England texts that have otherwise seemed to represent America's origins in a coherent community dedicated to religious and civil liberty. Among those studies which have suggested alternative models for American literary history, Houston Baker's *Blues, Ideology, and Afro-American Literature*—which expresses a desire to abandon accumulative literary histories structured around a religious "errand into the wilderness" and to replace them with an emphasis on the economics of exploitation and "commercial deportation" (24)—is particularly suggestive for colonial America. While Baker's reformulation successfully foregrounds minority and subaltern texts and peoples, it should also prompt a reconsideration of the transcontinental economic terms that help shape dominant literary texts and figures.

New England's Antinomian Controversy, the earliest large-scale social, political, and theological crisis in the Massachusetts Bay Colony, generated a significant number and variety of documents noteworthy for their anxious insistence on the stability of the colonial community in Massachusetts and the coherence of its religious mission. Indeed, American exceptionalism might be said to emerge in the aftermath of the Antinomian crisis, when figures such as John Winthrop, John Cotton, Thomas Weld, Thomas Shepard, and Edward Johnson struggled—in print, in public testimony, and under the discerning gaze of England—to define New England by opposing and exiling what New England was not. As Amy Schrager Lang notes, their writings worked to produce the long-dominant cultural consensus that "declared Americans a peculiar people inhabiting a wilderness theirs by promise" (*Prophetic* 16). To read the political gesture of exile as well as the language of the controversy in economic terms is to confront a culture that was fraught with much more than just a glitch in its religious errand. For what the orthodoxy sought to exile in their efforts to define New England was the effects of a mercantile capitalist world-system that had helped to fashion New England and its subjects.

At the center of the Antinomian Controversy was, I argue in this chapter, a tense and fractious contest over the economic terms of selfhood in early modern New England. The contest was largely played out through attempts to define the highly overdetermined figure of Anne Hutchinson who, both as a body and as a subject, represented the dangers of a mercantile sensibility. It was a contest in which colony leaders struggled to deny and reject their own folded implication in the mercantile capitalist relations that sustained colonial existence within the world system. At the same time, this debate generated two radically different conceptions of the colony as a body, and of colonial subjectivity: one that imagined a coherent and reproductive community of selves secure from penetration, and one that imagined an unbounded site marked by arrivals, departures, profit, and exchange. Anne

Hutchinson's performance of a startlingly modern subjectivity that threatened the very ethos of the Puritan orthodoxy depended on the relations that produced the latter, commercial model of coloniality. Her opponents' rhetoric and fears of infection reveal not only their hostility toward such a model but also a good deal about their own implication within it. It suggests as well the central role that women and their bodies could play in the conflicts that emerged from an emergent world-economy in which women themselves played almost no direct role.

The Economics of Rhetorical Excess

Virtually every record from and account of the Antinomian Controversy is characterized by startling rhetorical moments that, in their excessive outrage and hostility toward the heterodoxy in general and Hutchinson in particular, can only be read as symptomatic. Thomas Weld's fear for the integrity of both individual colonial bodies and the colony itself as a body provides one example. In his preface to John Winthrop's 1644 *Short Story of the Rise, reign, and ruine of the Antinomians*, Weld describes antinomian ideas as a "*Physicke*" secretly administered to unsuspecting strangers in "*stronger & stronger potions, as they found the Patient able to beare*."[2] Prompted by "*a spirit of pride, insolency, contempt of authority, division, sedition*," the antinomians posed a danger that for Weld put at risk nothing less than the political and religious future of the Massachusetts Bay Colony: "*It was a wonder of mercy*," he notes, "*that they had not set our Common-wealth and Churches on a fire, and consumed us all therein*" (*AC* 211). Weld's characterization of New England antinomianism as a menacing and seductive epidemic gone out of control repeats, even several years after the crisis had passed, the tone of panic and urgency evident in earlier descriptions of Anne Hutchinson, her ideas, and her supporters. During Hutchinson's trial, for example, Deputy Governor Thomas Dudley declared himself "fully persuaded that Mrs. Hutchinson is deluded by the devil" and feared that her notions would inspire her "hearers to take up arms against their prince and to cut the throats one of another" (*AC* 343). The Cambridge pastor Thomas Shepard called her "a verye dayngerous Woman to sowe her corrupt opinions to the infection of many" (*AC* 353), who was "likely with her fluent Tounge and forwardnes in Expressions to seduce and draw away many, Espetially simple Weomen of her owne sex" (*AC* 365). John Wilson saw her "*as a dayngerus Instrument of the Divell* raysed up by Sathan amongst us," and he warned against "the Misgovernment of this Woman's Tounge" (*AC* 384). John Cotton, who in the four months between Hutchinson's civil trial and church trial turned from her defender to her opponent, told her that "your opinions frett like a Gangrene and spread like a Leprosie, and infect farr and near, and will eate out the very Bowells of Religion, and hath soe infected the Churches that God knowes when thay will be cured" (*AC* 373). Winthrop himself characterizes her as "the breeder and nourisher of all these distempers," as "a woman of a haughty and fierce carriage, of a nimble wit and active spirit, and a very voluble tongue, more bold then a man," who "easily insinuated her selfe into the affections of many" (*AC* 263). He calls her an "*American Jesabel*" who was given the chance to repent, but instead "kept open a back doore to have returned to her vomit again" (*AC* 310). The verdicts of banishment and excommunication that resulted from the examinations of Hutchinson at, respectively, the court in Newtown in 1637 and the church in Boston in 1638, are certainly reminders that such rhetoric was accompanied by actions that had profound material consequences for Anne Hutchinson as well as many of her supporters. But those verdicts are reminders as well that the Puritan orthodoxy was convinced that the antinomians posed a profound material danger to the colony.

Clearly, the extraordinary hostility and anxiety evidenced in these characterizations are symptomatic of concerns that extended beyond the well-known theological dispute, whose terms were foregrounded in the long lists compiled by Hutchinson's examiners of her so-called "*Erors*" of religious opinion. They objected primarily, of course, to her support of a covenant of grace theology in which assurance for one's salvation was located within oneself, in an internal and invisible experience of grace. She claimed that John Wilson and other "legalist" ministers were preaching instead a covenant of works, which accepted external markers such as moral and law-abiding behavior both as evidence of an individual's salvation and as a way of preparing for the arrival of grace.[3] As several commentators on the Antinomian crisis note, however, Hutchinson's ideas were not so radically inconsistent with orthodox Puritanism as the legal and rhetorical responses to them would suggest. Indeed, she was simply advocating—in part through weekly meetings held in her home—ideas preached by John Cotton, whom she had followed to Massachusetts from England two years before the controversy erupted. Hutchinson repeated and emphasized Cotton's own insistence that works and words were not the same as spirit and grace, and that faith could not be assured without "the seal" of the latter.[4] As Andrew Delbanco explains, "Anne Hutchinson was saying absolutely nothing at odds with Puritan biblicism" and "was in fact speaking firmly within the Pauline tradition" (*Puritan* 135). But if the difference between Hutchinson's ideas and those of other Puritans on both sides of the Atlantic was, as Philip Gura notes, "only a matter of degree" (*Glimpse* 258), why was this woman convicted of conspiring to destroy the stability of the entire Bay Colony and of undermining the most central tenets of its church? Why was she perceived as a danger so extraordinary that only imprisonment, banishment, and excommunication could preserve the commonwealth from the perils that she posed? In other words, how are we to read the striking excess—of anxiety, rage, and panic—in the response of New England's ministers and magistrates to Anne Hutchinson, her weekly meetings to discuss sermons, and her espousal of a covenant of grace?

Antinomian acts of political resistance and rhetorical statements of spiritual resistance can account only in part for the Puritan orthodoxy's fear. The antinomians did express their support for ousted governor Henry Vane and beleaguered minister John Wheelwright by refusing to participate in and support the colony's Pequot War efforts, primarily in protest over the newly elected governor Winthrop and the minister assigned to the Boston militia, John Wilson.[5] Meanwhile, Wheelwright called in his controversial Fast Day sermon for "a spirituall combate," which required that "the children of God, . . . have their swords redy, they must fight, and fight with sprituall weapons" (*AC* 158). If such a battle "will cause a combustion in the Church and comon wealth," Wheelwright insisted, "what then?" He summoned the image of a "Spiritual burning" akin to the "externall burning of Rome" (*AC* 165) and suggested that such conflict was both necessary and justifiable. Winthrop, for one, read Wheelwright's rhetoric literally. He even defended his literalist reading later in the *Short Story* by arguing that the minister consistently referred to material "swords and hammers" as figures for "spirituall weapons" (*AC* 293). Winthrop responded to the sermon by ordering the forcible disarming of all antinomian supporters and instituting a general ordinance against aliens aimed "to keep out all such persons as might be dangerous to the commonwealth" (*History* 1:224), namely those sympathetic to the heterodoxy. Winthrop's interpretation of Wheelwright's language might be read as an instance of what Patricia Caldwell, in her analysis of Hutchinson's trials, has called the "antinomian language controversy." Caldwell perceptively reads the conflict between Hutchinson and her adversaries as a linguistic one, in which "Mrs. Hutchinson was speaking what amounts to a different language" that was incomprehensible to her interrogators (346). But the very words deployed by the Puritan orthodoxy evidence another, related conflict that divided the two groups along more specifically economic lines. Ultimately, the theological, linguistic, and economic dimensions of this crisis cannot be treated in isolation, not only because they each repeat the others' terms, but because together they represent a complex articulation of a crisis in subjectivity that registered its effects in all these domains.

John Winthrop initiates what is arguably the angriest characterization in any account of the controversy when he describes Hutchinson's typological self-alignment with the biblical figure of Daniel as "too too vile": "See the impudent boldnesse of a proud dame," he writes, "that *Athaliah*-like makes havocke of all that stand in the way of her ambitious spirit," and who "vented her impatience with so fierce speech and countenance, as one would hardly have guessed her to have been an Antitype of *Daniel*, but rather of the Lions after they were let loose" (*AC* 275). His account of Hutchinson "vent[ing] her impatience" employs a verb that occurs with remarkable frequency in the texts of the trials and subsequent accounts of the antinomian affair. In fact, the various social, political, and economic tensions that inform the Antinomian Controversy might be said to meet and overlap in the multiple senses of this word. For example, Thomas Weld's description of the arrival from England of those who would eventually make up the antinomian faction invokes an image that, by using a different definition of the verb "to vent," highlights an economic subtext to Winthrop's and others' use of that word. Weld notes that

> *some going thither from hence full fraught with many unsound and loose opinions, after a time, began to open their packs, and freely* vent [emphasis added] *their wares to any that would be their customers; Multitudes of men and women, Church-members and others, having tasted of their Commodities, were eager after them, and were streight infected before they were aware, and some being tainted conveyed the infection to others.* (AC 201–2)

Strategically mixing the metaphors of commerce and disease, Weld associates the antinomians with the infectious relations of mercantile capitalism by classifying their "unsound and loose opinions" as "wares" or "Commodities" sold to "customers." His use of the word "vent" to describe this circulation is particularly suggestive. When this verb appears elsewhere in either the trial records or *A Short Story*, it is invariably associated with Anne Hutchinson: "she had thus *vented* her mind" (*AC* 273), "she *vented* her impatience" (*AC* 275), she displayed "impudency in *venting* and maintaining" her "delusions" (*AC* 309), she "*vented* divers of her strange opinions" (*AC* 317; all emphases added). Among the many usages for this verb in the seventeenth century, two predominated. On the one hand, it meant uttering, discharging, or emitting words. On the other, it meant to sell or vend, to dispose of commodities by sale, by finding purchasers in a market. Often, these two senses of the word mutually inform each other, as in Edward Johnson's description of the antinomians in *Wonder-Working Providence* as "daily *venting* their deceivable Doctrines" (125).

A similar doubling informs the word "estate," which also occurs with extraordinary regularity in accounts and documents of the controversy. Indeed, the dispute between the two camps over the relationship between justification and sanctification hinged precisely on how a "good estate"

(*AC* 263) might be evidenced and apprehended. It is with this sense—of one's condition in relation to the experience of conversion or election—that the word is most often used in writings about Hutchinson. Yet even such pointed references to "spirituall Estates" (*AC* 370) summon up the contemporary resonance of property or wealth, of a more specifically economic condition. Such ambiguity informs, for example, Winthrop's description of Anne Hutchinson's husband William as "a very honest and peaceable man of good estate," particularly considering that on this same page he remembers her son, Edward Hutchinson, declaring in court just before he was fined "that if they took away his estate, they must keep his wife and children" (*AC* 262). The son is clearly objecting to the loss of wealth, but the father is less clearly being described as either wealthy or as a respectable member of the church, as one of the elect. Winthrop, who had cause to be concerned with both his spiritual and material estates throughout his years in New England, regularly employs the word in both contexts. Just before his first reference to Hutchinson and her "dangerous errours" in his *History*, he mentions the burning of a house owned by Shaw, who was discovered to have "concealed his estate, and made show as if he had been poor," despite the fact that he had been "the day before admitted of the . . . [Watertown] church" (1:200). Elsewhere, words with unexpectedly economic import, such as "purchase," "prosper," or "credit," are used to formulate theological questions or to represent relations with the divine. Winthrop accuses Hutchinson of mistakenly believing "that the souls of men are . . . made immortal by Christ's purchase" (*AC* 254), just as Cotton reprimands her for assuming that "*this Imortalety is purchased from Christ*" (*AC* 355). According to Thomas Weld, the antinomians attempted to swell their ranks by convincing others that those who evidenced "their good estate by Sanctification . . . never prospered" (*AC* 205). Weld furthermore accuses them of saying one thing and doing another, and "*By this kinde of Jesuiticall dealing, they did not onely keepe their credit with them, as men that held nothing but the truth; but gained this also, viz. that when, afterwards, they should heare those men taxed for holding errors, they would be ready to defend them*" (*AC* 207). Financial accusations that place the antinomians within scenarios of commercial exchange and monetary accountability echo within such statements and complaints.

Just as these charges of theological error are conveyed in economic language, so is the Antinomian Controversy and its rhetoric undergirded by emergent conflicts over economic ideology. The threat embodied by Hutchinson and her ideas may have been most overtly characterized as theological and political, but those dangers contained and concealed another, almost inarticulable, source of fear: the emergence of a conception of selfhood that was tightly interwoven with the Hutchinsonians' class/

status alignment, particularly their participation in mercantile practice. The vehemence with which her accusers depicted, condemned, and punished Anne Hutchinson can be understood only in the context of the challenge this new articulation of selfhood posed to the dominant modes of ideology and authority in seventeenth-century New England. In other words, the antinomian threat, which became increasingly embodied in the figure of Hutchinson, was the threat of an emergent model of subjectivity—a model constituted in terms of a covenant of grace theology that located religious authority in an invisible experience and, by doing so, divorced the realm of words and works from the world of things and grace. But this selfhood was constituted also in terms of the relatively new world of mercantile capitalism, a world represented by the transcontinental trade relations that characterized the Hutchinson family, among others.

Merchants and Gentry in Massachusetts

When Thomas Weld opened his preface to *A Short Story* with the evocative description of antinomians "venting" their "wares" from open packs, he may very well have intended to remind his readers of the predominant class/status identity of the group who, like the Hutchinson family, consisted in large part of merchants and tradespeople. As Emery Battis notes in his study of the sociology of Hutchinson's supporters, conflicts between merchants and the gentry were particularly tense during the years of the antinomian crisis.[6] But it was differences in economic ideology and practice more than differences in wealth that separated families like the Hutchinsons from those like the Winthrops in 1630s Massachusetts. The two families, who lived across the street from each other in downtown Boston, could both boast signs of affluence such as substantial property holdings and several household servants. What distinguished the Winthrops from the Hutchinsons instead was the means of acquiring and handling wealth and, even more importantly, incompatible attitudes toward social and political authority that followed from their differences in economic ideology. John White's concerned 1636 letter to Winthrop about the "Superfluity of Shopkeepers Inholders etc." in New England suggests the source of these ideological differences. White warns that those who reap a profit by "retailing wares" challenge a production-oriented economy "wherein their labours might produce something for the common good"; merchants instead "drawe only one from another and consequently live by the sweat of other mens brows, producing nothing themselves by their owne endevours" ("To John" 322). White's objection to mercantile commerce and his suggestion "that I should reduce it if I were to advise in the government" reflect the patrimonial economics of the gentry, an ideology to which John Winthrop subscribed. When Winthrop describes being approached in the early years of settlement by the Indian Chickatabot, for example, the governor carefully distinguishes between himself and those who regularly trade commodities when he explains to the Indian "that English sagamores did not use to truck" (*History* 1:53). The Hutchinsons, on the other hand, owned and operated a successful mercer shop, and their economic success depended on a transatlantic network of family ties and mercantile interests in London, the West Indies, Boston, and inland. John Frederick Martin notes that the Hutchinson family participated in the "triangle trade" facilitated by "exporting livestock and provisions to the West Indies" in exchange for "sugar and cotton, which the Hutchinsons then sold for credit in London"; the London Hutchinsons in turn "supplied the American Hutchinsons with manufactured goods for sale in New England" (69).[7] These complex long-distance trade arrangements were of course sustained by equally complex credit arrangements that appeared to fold transoceanic time and space by the overlapping and deferred transfer of goods and payments.

As Darrett Rutman succinctly states, for Winthrop such "commerce was corrupt" (*Winthrop's* 6). Winthrop's wealth as well as his residual class/status as a member of the English landed gentry derived from a very different set of economic relations. In England, he had presided over the family estate at Groton Hall, where he leased land to tenant-farmers, before receiving an office to serve as an attorney in the Court of Wards. Here his duties continued to be fully consistent with the patrimonial economics of the aristocracy, since he most often defended clients who were making claims on family inheritances (R. C. Winthrop 219–20). Only after losing his office, signing on as one of the undertakers for the Massachusetts Bay Company, and emigrating to New England did he have his son sell the Groton estate, for which he received a disappointing sum.[8] John Winthrop has often been accused of having a poor financial sense, of steadily acquiring debts that threatened to outrun his funds, of dying land-poor. But his economic decisions, his adherence to the principle of what John White called "Bonum publicum not Privatum Commodum" ("To John" 322), his application of the benevolent rule of mercy to debts that could not be justly repaid, and his considerable landholdings throughout the commonwealth all appear to be consistent with an established patrimonial rather than an emergent merchant-capitalist ethos.[9]

At the same time, however, Winthrop was himself engaged in the transcontinental investment relations that made up the organizational structure of the Massachusetts Bay Company. Even before leaving England, he entered into the kind of relationship with London merchants that Bradford had established during the 1626 reorganization of Plymouth. Winthrop was one of ten undertakers (half of whom emigrated to New England and half of whom remained in London) who, in exchange for a promise to return the original investors' principal within seven years, accepted the company's assets and debts as well as control over the transport of goods and emigrants, a percentage of the beaver trade, a monopoly on salt manufacture, and control over a magazine of provisions to be sold at fixed prices. Although Winthrop himself did not participate in the fur trade, he shared in the relations of debt and privilege with those who did (see Bailyn, *New England* 19, 26; Brenner, *Merchants* 151). And as Elizabeth Maddock Dillon insightfully argues, his own *Short Story* was produced and printed within the transatlantic investment context that sustained the colony as a company: it was written with "the more immediate aim of reassuring potential investors and immigrants to the colony that Massachusetts Bay remains worthy of their commitments" (71), and published in England at a time (1644) when the economic depression in New England made continued investment and immigration particularly urgent concerns.[10] If the Puritans were, in Stephen Innes' apt phrase, "moving 'crab-like' into the new capitalist world—looking backward in alarm even as they were advancing forward with dispatch"(*Creating* 28), then Winthrop simply appeared to be looking backward more determinedly than most of those with whom he moved forward. It may even be the case that Winthrop's own determined efforts to look back to residual economic models operated in the service of his equally determined efforts to encourage and import colonial investment and interest within the terms of emergent economic models.

The social model espoused by the early modern English gentry not only valued social cohesion and the common good as its preeminent goal but premised that cohesion on a hierarchy that distinguished the governing authority from those it governed. This sociopolitical dividing line was, for Winthrop, precisely commensurate with the line that divided "rich" and "poore," as he expressed it in his famous 1630 lay sermon "A Modell of Christian Charity." But when Winthrop drew the line between the governors and those they governed in New England, even the richest merchants invariably fell into the latter group. For example, although Winthrop allowed deputies to represent the interests of the freemen to the Massachusetts General Court, he insisted that ruling power remain vested in the minority of magistrates. Magistrates, like Winthrop, were invariably members of the gentry and yeoman class, while deputies—one of whom was William Hutchinson—were consistently of the merchant class.[11] The commensurability of this socioeconomic fault line with the theological fault line dividing the Hutchinsonians from the Puritan orthodoxy is striking, and the frequent use of the word "vent" by the latter to describe the antinomians might be seen as a way of inscribing and remarking that doubled line.

According to Battis, proponents of the traditional patrimonial system like Winthrop saw the antinomians' espousal of the covenant of grace as allowing "an anarchistic subjectivism" that "elevated the individual conscience above all external authority and exempted the believer from any considerations of conduct" (286). In this view, merchants were presumably attracted to Anne Hutchinson's theological position since, by rejecting a covenant of works, it permitted them to engage in self-interested profit-seeking without guilt, and provided them religious tenets with which to counteract the censure of ministers and magistrates who, like John Winthrop, advocated government regulation of wages and fixing of prices as a way of maintaining the public good.[12] Battis thus locates the perceived threat of antinomianism in the law-defying opportunities—such as charging prices that exceeded the "common" and therefore just price—made possible by the privileging of justification over sanctification. Yet here, too, the orthodoxy's response seems in vast disproportion to the supposed dangers they sought to control. Rather than locate Hutchinson's threat, as Battis and others do, in her privileging of the internal and the ineffable over the external and the visible, I locate it instead in her more radical alienation of these two realms from each other. That splitting introduced a gap between the internal and the external self, just as her comments in court presumed a gap between the words and the spirit of scripture. What emerges from the texts of Hutchinson's trials therefore is a contest between a form of selfhood that acknowledges—indeed, is founded on—that gap, and one for which that gap is a source of terror and confusion. The labeled portrait of the merchant Lewes Roberts that appears in his *Merchants Mappe of Commerce* (fig. 2), published for the first time just as the Antinomian Controversy was concluding, points toward this suggestive interval between internal and external versions of the self. Below the image of Roberts "CIVIS & MERCATOR" (citizen and merchant) is the poetic warning that "th'effigies" or representation of Roberts does not contain or covey "his real worth," which can be discerned only in the contents of "this his work." The pictorial image only "speaks him outward, But his inward parte / is best expresst, within this Booke of Arte." The claim gives a kind of inscrutability not only to the merchant who gazes out from the page, but to the one whose very "inwardness" is contained in a work described as "art." If Winthrop and his allies responded to the inscrutability of Hutchinson and her cohorts with such vehemence, it may be because they saw in her performance of such a "monstrous" form of selfhood a version of themselves.[13]

FIG. 2. Engraved portrait of Lewes Roberts, merchant and author, from Roberts' *Merchants Mappe of Commerce* (London, 1638). By permission of the Syndics of Cambridge University Library.

Subjectivity and Mercantile Theory

It has generally been acknowledged that the climactic moment in Hutchinson's first trial is her claim to have received "an immediate revelation" that arrived to her "[b]y the voice of [God's] own spirit to my soul" (*AC* 337). But despite the surprised "How!" with which Thomas Dudley responds to her announcement, the court as a whole only gradually, and over the course of several pages of further testimony, works itself into a horrified consensus about the danger represented by this claim and therefore the necessity of banishing the defendant. The movement toward that verdict begins when Winthrop clarifies that

> the ground work of her revelations is the immediate revelation of the spirit and not by the ministry of the word, and that is the means by which she hath very much abused the country that they shall look for revelations and are not bound to the ministry of the word . . . and this hath been the ground of all these tumults and troubles. (*AC* 341–42)

The profound error here, for Winthrop, is not just that Hutchinson experienced a revelation but that "it is impossible but that the word and spirit should speak the same thing" (*AC* 342). To claim otherwise, he rather melodramatically insists, "overthrows all" (*AC* 343). Though several speakers subsequently came to her defense, none was able to avert the tide of opinion against Hutchinson following the governor's assertion.

Emphasis on the defendant's "revelation" in the 1637 courtroom has tended to obscure the climactic moment in Hutchinson's second trial, which followed her intervening imprisonment at a home in Roxbury. If the admission of her revelations was the climax of the Newtown trial, then Hutchinson's curious retraction of an earlier statement marks the turning point in the Boston trial. Here, too, Hutchinson's own words appear to invite, almost to necessitate, her conviction. But in both cases, it is not Hutchinson's words that condemn her so much as the failed relation that she posits between words and their referents. The momentum that ends with John Wilson's pronouncement of excommunication begins pages earlier, when Hutchinson is asked to respond to a series of "errors" with which she has been charged. She accepts Thomas Shepard's correction to her understanding of the "*Inherence of Grace*" (*AC* 378) by responding that "I doe not acknowledge it to be an Error but a Mistake. *I doe acknowledge my Expression to be Ironious but my Judgment was not Ironious*, for I held befor as you did but could not express it soe" (*AC* 361). Much later in the examination, she responds similarly to a question put to her by Shepard: "*I confess, my Expressions was that way but it was never my Judgment*." When asked to clarify, she repeats: "My Judgment is not altered though my Expression alters" (*AC* 378). Her defense in both instances relies on the same principle as her theological distinction between the spirit and the word; that is, for Hutchinson, words are representations or "Expressions" that cannot be equated with "Judgments," with the things they represent. It is this alienation of a thing's representation from the thing itself that leads Shepard, despite the fact that Hutchinson is conceding to him at these moments, to take her response as evidence that she is after all "a Notorious Imposter" (*AC* 383), while Wilson declares "This you say is most dayngerous" (*AC* 378). They do so not because she retains the heretical misunderstanding of grace they thought she held but because she has torn signs loose from that which they signify.

By insisting on a potentially radical distinction between "Expression" and "Judgment," Hutchinson here insists that her words could and did misrepresent her self. As Patricia Caldwell has argued, this examination reveals a conflict between what amounts to two different and incompatible notions of language. But those differences correspond also to two profoundly different models of selfhood.[14] When Anne Hutchinson insists that her words bear no necessary or organic relationship to her ideas, she speaks within the terms of a remarkably modern subjectivity, and by doing so she throws into crisis the terms in which New England's Puritan orthodoxy have defined themselves. Her understanding of language remains, however, perfectly consistent with her theological position and with the economic ideology associated with merchants.

Hutchinson continued to argue, in both trials, that the word and the spirit could, indeed, speak different things, an argument not unlike that advanced by writers on commerce that the weight and the value of a coin need not correspond. Such a notion undercut the most fundamental assumptions of the premodern worldview articulated by the religious and political orthodoxy in seventeenth-century New England, who defended Winthrop's refusal to separate the word from spirit as well as his periodic refusals, by instituting fixed prices, to allow prices to fluctuate by unseen market forces. What emerges in the documents of these debates is a portrait of Hutchinson as a subject whose distinctively modern depth and interiority derives from her introduction of a potentially irreconcilable gap between an external, social self on the one hand and an internal, invisible self on the other. It is above all against this "monstrous" subjectivity that the anxiety and hostility of her examiners is directed.

Contemporary economic debates both in England and New England reveal the emergence of economic principles, derived from the operation of mercantile capitalism, that coincide with the radical innovation of subjectivity I have identified with Anne Hutchinson and New England antinomianism. The massive expansion of commerce, facilitated largely by an exploding Atlantic trade and attendant colonizing ventures, led over the course of the early seventeenth century to the emergence of a new economic paradigm, which—in ways that strikingly paralleled Anne Hutchinson's religious notions—appeared to challenge the sovereign authority of the king as well as traditional principles of social cohesion and the common good. Joyce Appleby's history of seventeenth-century economic thought locates the development of these ideas in a series of pamphlets written by merchants such as Thomas Mun and Edward Misselden. In Mun's and Misselden's discussions, the sphere of economics became divorced from that of the state just as monetary values became divorced from a presumed "order of real things" (Appleby 44). Against the views of an economic writer in the patrimonial tradition like Gerald de Malynes, for example, who defended the sovereign's power to set prices and emphasized the metallic value of coin, Misselden emphasized instead the fluctuating price of commodities determined only by the buying and selling of goods, and implied that the laws of the market were distinct from the laws of the king. As Appleby notes, these pamphlets described a world in which "a sinuous course of things real, felt, imagined, and calculated had replaced the *terra firma* of weight, purity, and sovereign statement" (46). Another way of describing this shift is to emphasize that these writers had, like Anne Hutchinson, introduced a split into a once-organic system, and that split opened up a troubling gap between, for example, the static value of a coin as measured in metallic weight and its fluctuating value in the marketplace. What was troubling about this split was the hidden dynamics that inhabited this new fissure.

As a result, the new mercantile world seemed a world of secrets, secrets that resided in this gap and that were all but invisible to the common observer, who consequently needed experts to discern and explain the workings of commerce (Appleby 49). At the same time, the moral imperatives behind a merchant's economic decisions became equally invisible. Adherents of patrimonialism, for whom the production of goods had the virtuous and evident role of sustaining the general good of the commonwealth, saw such invisibility as cause for alarm, as John White's 1636 letter reveals. The case of Robert Keayne, a successful New England merchant, illustrates precisely those fears expressed by White and others. Convicted of price gouging in 1639 for selling a bag of nails above the just price, Keayne was accused of exploiting economically the disjunction between price and value, a disjunction analogous to the one that Anne Hutchinson seemed also to be exploiting when she insisted that her expressions did not always or necessarily match her judgment, and that works and words could not be taken as evidence of grace or spirit.[15]

The rhetorical excess in the New England orthodoxy's response to antinomianism cannot be understood outside the contemporary developments and effects of mercantile capitalism, particularly when one considers that conflicts between Massachusetts' merchant and gentry groups over issues such as the General Court's regulation of prices and wages coincided with, as well as bore striking parallels to, the theological conflicts associated with Anne Hutchinson. When Hutchinson proclaims in the Newtown courtroom that "having seen him which is invisible I fear not what man can do unto me" (*AC* 338), she places herself—as one whose seal of grace gives her privileged access to the invisible world—in a position analogous to that of a commercial expert. More importantly, by doing so she robs her questioners of authority, just as market experts were perceived as challenging and usurping the authority of the king.

As a result of this splitting of word and spirit, of external and internal selves, possibilities for secrecy, deception, and dissimulation suddenly loom large. For example, in a particularly revealing description, Weld claims that "*it was so frequent with* [the antinomians] *to have many darke shadowes and colours to cover their opinions and expressions withall, that it was wonderfull hard matter to take them tardy, or to know the bottome of what they said or sealed*" (*AC* 207). As a result of this sense of bottomless depth—a striking description of the interiority of the modern subject—he ascribes to them generally the habit of "*fearfull lying*" (*AC* 216), which they share with Hutchinson herself. Winthrop too argues that "shee cunningly dissembled and coloured her opinions" (*AC* 263), while Shepard accuses her of playing "a Tricke of as notorious Subtiltie as ever was held in the Church" (*AC* 383). Wilson, too, notes that "she sayth one Thinge to day and another thinge to morrow: and to speake falsely and doubtfully and dullye wheras we should speake the Truth playnly one to another" (*AC* 384). These expressions of frustration indicate her examiners' failed attempts to locate and fix Anne Hutchinson as a subject. Because her speech is "dull" and "doubtful" rather than clear and "plain," she herself seems to slip in and out of view, as if she were blurring and changing shape. While these statements are made in the specific context of her self-defense at the Boston trial, they might also be read as characteristic concerns of early seventeenth-century society generally in response to emergent principles and practices derived from the expanding global market—whose intricate and mysterious workings are both reflected and deciphered in such texts as Lewes Roberts' voluminous *Merchants Mappe*. Dangers of dissimulation were associated with the world of commerce, and Hutchinson, repeatedly accused of "venting," is portrayed also as a liar holding secrets from the court. John Wilson's outraged rejection of Hutchinson's explanation exemplifies the orthodoxy's response, as he urges the church "to Ease our selves of such a member, Espetialy for her untruth or Lyes, as that she was allways of the same Judgment, only she hath altered her Expressions. Therefor I leave it to the Church to consider how safe it is to suffer soe eronius and soe schismaticall and soe unsound a member amongst us, and one that stands guiltie of soe foule a falshood" (*AC* 385). In his verdict of excommunication, Wilson proclaims her guilty, not just of holding erroneous opinions, but of lying.

Reproduction and Colonialism

While investors in many of the larger early modern merchant adventurer companies tended to come from the gentry and nobility and to respect patrimonial social relations, a group of smaller and newer merchants emerged during the seventeenth century who took advantage of the increase in commerce and who did not subscribe to traditional socioeconomic principles such as the limitation of trade. Robert Brenner traces the shift in power, during the decades preceding the outbreak of Civil War in England, from large merchant companies such as the East India Company that relied on government favor, to an emergent group of new merchants—many of them shopkeepers, artisans, or small producers—who tended to take greater economic risks and, when successful, to enjoy rapid social and economic advancement (Brenner, *Merchants* 112). Investors in the Massachusetts Bay Company were also characterized by this same shift (150–51). According to Appleby, these more adventurous merchants were often described as "promiscuous" (106), a term that resonates with certain characterizations of Anne Hutchinson.

Amy Schrager Lang has argued that the figure of Hutchinson marks the first site in American culture in which dissent becomes associated with female empowerment, and more specifically with the speaking public woman. Indeed, Hutchinson's gender figures prominently in the rhetoric of her opponents, who accuse her of stepping out of her place, of encouraging other women to do so, and even of practicing a promiscuous sexuality that, they suggest, must certainly accompany such behavior.[16] Therefore Hutchinson is accused of circulating not only her ideas but her body too freely and too publicly. Cotton warns her that "though I have not herd, nayther do I thinke, you have bine unfaythfull to your Husband in his Marriage Covenant, *yet that will follow upon it*" (*AC* 372). Thomas Weld similarly compares the antinomians' seductive strategies to the "*Harlots*" in Proverbs 7.21: "*with much faire speech they caused them to yeeld, with the flattering of their lips they forced them*" (*AC* 205). Descriptions of Hutchinson's circulation often betray an economic subtext in their diction as well as their figures. Weld notoriously equates her religious ideas with her so-called "monstrous birth," for example, explaining that *"God fitted this judgement to her sine every way, for looke as she had* vented [emphasis added] *mishapen opinions, so she must bring forth deformed monsters; and as about* 30. *Opinions in number, so many monsters"* (*AC* 214). Here the corruptive force that John White and others associated with commerce and the practice of "venting" leaves its marks on Hutchinson's body as well as on her theological ideas. For Weld, these multiplied monsters embody the damaging effects of excessive circulation on an economy of (re)production. Similar fears are expressed in Edward Johnson's *Wonder-Working Providence*, where antinomian "Errours" are described as "their bastardly brat" (126), as a "bastardly brood" (146), and as the multiplying heads of "Hidra," of which "as fast as one is cut off two stand up in the roome" (125).

Various seventeenth-century definitions of venting were associated with emissions from the body, but such definitions resonated also in the civic realm, where the nation was often figured as a body.[17] The years of the Antinomian Controversy in New England were years of economic crisis in Old England, when poverty rates were high and wages low. The literature advocating emigration tended to highlight, for English wage laborers in particular, the possibilities for improved prosperity in New England. Interestingly, the word "vent" and variations on it often appear in texts encouraging emigration to the colonies. An early report submitted to the House of Lords, for example, offers the "deducing of colonies" as one means by which to "vent the daily increase" in population that will otherwise "surcharge the State." Failure to do so, the author of the report warns, will mean that in England, "as in a full body, there must break out yearly tumours and impostumes as did of late" (Thirsk and Cooper 109). This image of the state as a body that overpopulation will drive to disease helps to put into context the language of disease and infection used by Weld, Cotton, and others to describe the antinomian threat to the Massachusetts commonwealth. This same report advocates, in defense of land enclosures in England, that "[l]eaving the employment of the ground to the discretion of the occupants" will improve opportunities for "the vent of such their commodities" (108).[18] In the rhetoric of colonization, expelling people comes into linguistic alignment with the market circulation of goods. The 1648 promotional piece *Good news from New-England*, which mixes poetic with prose form, likewise mixes its descriptions of emigration and trade. It specifically invites those readers whose "earnings are but small" to "*venter* to this new-found world, and make amends for all" (1, emphasis added). A page later, the poem pictures these "poore Christians" as they "packe to Sea-ports ships to enter, / A wonderment, in streets they passe, dividing their strange *venter*" (2, emphasis added). This same tract goes on to tell a brief history of the antinomian affair, indicating that those who supported Hutchinson and her "grosse errors" included "certain persons more affecting trade than truth" (20).[19]

While cloth merchants in England were having a difficult time finding a market or "vent" for their product, in New England the prices of goods and wages were soaring, as Winthrop's journal entry for September 1636 notes: "Cattle were grown to high rates;—a good cow, £25 or £30; a pair of bulls or oxen, £40. Corn was now at 5*s*. the bushel, ... Bread was at 9 and 10*s*. the C.; carpenters at 3*s*. the day, and other workmen accordingly" (*History* 1:206). Such inflation represented the dangers of relaxed wage and price controls while permitting the economic advancement of those new merchants who flourished during the 1630s, provoking considerable resentment among others in New England. In 1637, after Winthrop ousted Henry Vane in the election for governor, he immediately passed an order that required any persons arriving in Massachusetts to receive the magistrates' approval. A strategy for ensuring that the antinomian faction would not receive additional reinforcements, this alien law was also defended by Winthrop as an attempt to seal the borders of the commonwealth to prevent strangers from penetrating and violating "the wellfare of the body" (*History* 1:224) of the colony. Edward Johnson turns to similar metaphors of boundary building when he opposes those who remove to New England for "the increase of Trade, and traffique" (146) to those magistrates who functioned as "stones" to "build up the walls of Jerusalem (that his Sion may be surrounded with Bulworkes and Towres)" (141). Winthrop's notoriously bizarre description of Hutchinson's "monstrous birth" as "twenty-seven several lumps of man's seed" (*History* 1:271) suggests the dangers to reproduction posed by circulation among and penetration by strangers, dangers linked consistently in contemporary accounts of the Antinomian Controversy with the mixed economic, theological, and social associations of venting.

Narratives of the crisis and its place in New England history written by Johnson, Winthrop, and Weld tell similarly anxious but insistent stories of a religious and communal enterprise whose success was briefly threatened by a "Master-piece of Womens wit" (Winthrop, *History* 1:132). But these histories also reveal that Hutchinson and her followers challenged dominant social, economic, and spiritual authority in New England by invalidating the significance of visible evidence, undercutting the covenant of works preached by authorized Puritan ministers as well as the organic social and economic models subscribed to by the ruling authorities in Massachusetts. By locating authority instead in an internal and invisible self, and by insisting and demonstrating that this self could be inconsistent with and misrepresented by the visible self (as would some of those accused of witchcraft in Salem several decades later), Anne Hutchinson performed in her trials a very early and extremely modern notion of selfhood—one crucially linked with the relations of mercantile capitalism and one that provoked panic among the orthodoxy perhaps especially because they were, in fact, "infected" with precisely the "disease" whose symptoms they so urgently projected onto Hutchinson. As Stephen Innes and others have observed, the attitudes and practices of seventeenth-century New Englanders reflected a profound ambivalence toward emergent capitalist relations. Indeed, economic practice in Puritan New England tended to disable the social order whose stable hierarchy it was meant to support, thus producing the very things many orthodox Puritans most feared (*Creating* 101). The hostility aimed at the Hutchinsonians by dominant magistrates and ministers was thus a function at least as much of the likenesses—including economic similarities—between the two groups as it was of the differences between them. This ambivalence helps to account for the excessive hostility that characterizes so many accounts of New England antinomianism. Hutchinson herself almost seems to be suggesting that those who exiled her played a role in producing her ideas, when she insists under examination in Boston that she "*did not hould any of thease Things*" (*AC* 372) prior to the imprisonment imposed on her by the magistrates following the Newtown trial. The orthodoxy's exile of Hutchinson aimed to banish the "monstrous" possibilities set loose by the world of trade and commerce in which colonialism necessarily situated them, even while repeating the gesture of venting, which they otherwise sought to curtail. A rather different story—of class/status tensions, commercial profit, and mercantile interests—presses within and against the narrative of religious community and freedom these texts anxiously tell, a narrative that has been perhaps too easily repeated in subsequent literary histories of colonial New England. If the discourse of exceptionalism, to which some of those literary historical narratives are committed, has its origins in the anxious rhetoric of Hutchinson's accusers, we might begin to suspect exceptionalist discourse itself of exiling the nation's own folded participation within the terms and history of global commerce.

Chapter Five

EQUIVALENCE: ROGER WILLIAMS AND THE TYPOLOGY OF TRADE

WHEN ANNE HUTCHINSON left Massachusetts Bay Colony in 1638, she went, along with many other of the antinomian exiles, to Aquidneck, located outside Providence in what would later be called Rhode Island. She followed more or less in the geographical footsteps of fellow dissenter Roger Williams, who had likewise been banished from Massachusetts only two years previously for failing to relinquish a series of positions that were perceived as a threat to the colony.[1] Whereas Hutchinson was condemned for her antinomian heresies, however, Williams was convicted on the basis of his radical separatism and the contentious opinions to which it led him. A list included in Williams' 1644 *Mr. Cottons Letter Lately Printed, Examined and Answered* includes the following four points of disagreement raised during his 1635 trial: his insistence that the king's patent did not entitle English settlers to Native American land; his objection to oath taking; his refusal to hear ministers in New England who attended services in nonseparating churches while in England; and his appeal for the separation of church and state in order to preserve liberty of conscience and to eliminate religious persecution.

All these dissenting positions are consistent with Roger Williams' developing attitude toward historical time—an attitude that emerged even more clearly in the years after his trial and banishment, when his already radical separatism became extended even further. W. Clark Gilpin describes Williams' move during the early 1640s toward an idiosyncratic millenarianism that led him to identify not with any earthly church but instead as a witness and hopeful apostle who awaited a pure form of the church to emerge in the world with Christ's second coming. Unlike other contemporary millennialists, however, Williams insisted on the unpredictability and discontinuity of time's advance: no one in this world could anticipate either the arrival of this future church or the form it would take. This radical insistence on temporal discontinuity marks Williams' best-known writings of the 1640s, including his extended pamphlet debate with John Cotton.

Despite the differences between their alleged heresies, the dissenters Williams and Hutchinson can both be seen to have created or exposed a division within categories that their orthodox opponents viewed as organically unified wholes. The previous chapter argued that Hutchinson maintained a disparity between the inner and outer self, a subject position consistent not only with her theological beliefs but with her linguistic practice and her economic ideology. This chapter likewise locates Williams' dissent within the nexus of his theology, his language, and his economics. But whereas Hutchinson's trials expose a constitutive split between the interior and exterior self, the disagreements between Williams and his opponents circulate instead around the split he posited between the present and the future. Williams maintained an absolute and unsurpassable separation between the historical present and the millennial future, and he saw any practice that falsely equated or linked these two temporal realms—that read the present in terms of an unknowable and unpredictable future—as doomed to violence and disaster.

In contrast to the prematurity that he accused Cotton and others of practicing, Williams advocated a kind of restless patience, an anxious hopefulness in expectation of what is *not yet here*, and therefore *not yet known*. As Truth declares in *The Bloudy Tenent*, "[t]he Vision yet doth tarry . . . but will most surely come: and therefore the patient and believing must wait for it" (*BT* 353).[2] While he awaited the arrival of this future, Williams engaged in print dialogue, producing writings that, in their content as well as in their style, were characterized by perpetual seeking, repeated revision, and purposeful extension. Keith Stavely identifies this quality of prolonged self-perpetuation, for example, in Williams' argument for liberty of conscience, which, he observes, "chased its own tail. Liberty of conscience was needed to protect conscience against itself; but once the conscience thus protected began to express itself, it reproduced the conditions of tyranny, violence and illegitimate human invention from which it had originally needed to be protected. And at that point, the cycle had to begin all over again" (87).

Williams the pamphleteer and fur trader depicted dialogue and commerce in the same way: the arrival at truth was as perpetually deferred as the pursuit of truth was perpetually sought, and the result was a strategy of negotiated searching that took on the "prolix" and "gnarled" qualities so often used to describe his prose.

Anne G. Myles has provocatively suggested that as a dissenter Williams spoke an altogether different language, that he was moving "toward a language of affect significantly at odds with the orthodox vocabulary of New England" (134)—a claim that positions Williams, along with Hutchinson, at the fold where premodern and protomodern sensibilities overlap within the consolidating capitalist world-system. The incipient interiority that Myles locates or senses in Williams' prose results, I suggest, from the inaccessibility of the self in the present because, for Williams, the authentic self is located instead in an unarrived and unimaginable future. The interim self is represented over and over again, in and by Williams' writing, as one carved out through a relentless and prolonged process of dialogue and negotiation that will not be finalized until the millennium arrives. Authentic self is for Williams deferred, awaited. And until it arrives, self is uncertain—an effect of the inequivalence that besets the changeability of the present world, and that was represented perhaps best in the experience and language of trade.

The Ministerial Marketplace

In 1643, Williams departed for England to obtain from Parliament a charter for Providence Plantations. During the subsequent year he spent in England, Williams published the books for which he is best known, including *A Key into the Language of America* (1643), *Mr. Cottons Letter* (1644), and *The Bloudy Tenent of Persecution* (1644). Of these three texts, only *A Key* explicitly addresses issues of trade and the market, but a language of trade—and an awareness of language as itself an object of exchange—characterizes all three of these otherwise very different texts, which share a kind of traffic in and between economic and religious discourses. While spiritual concerns certainly shape Williams' approach to and view of trade, economic concerns appear also to have influenced, or at least intersected with, his theological positions. *A Key* was literally written on the ship to England, as a record for himself and others of what he had learned in his years spent negotiating political matters, religious concerns, and economic goods with the Narragansett Indians. Intended at first "as a private *helpe* to my owne memory, that I might not by my present absence [from New England] *lightly lose* what I had so *dearely bought* in some few yeares *hardship*, and *charges* among the *Barbarians*" (*K* 83), the *Key* aims to make some return on an experience that, he admits, was purchased at a very high price.

This language is at once figurative and literal. Williams is remembering, of course, the spiritual rewards of the material suffering he experienced after his banishment. But upon his return to New England, he would also move to consolidate and extend his trading contacts among the Indians by establishing a trading post in Narragansett Bay—so that he is also, by writing the *Key*, literally remembering the details and language of commercial exchange for future use. Williams' description of his book—as the product for which his experience (of suffering, of trading) has been cashed in—points to an economic sensibility that not only runs throughout the *Key* but marks Williams' other, more explicitly theological, writings as well. Williams often, for example, turns to the language of the marketplace to comment on ministerial practice. He warns in *The Bloudy Tenent* against incompetent trading in the spirit, arguing that "having bought Truth deare, we must not sell it cheape" (*BT* 13), and goes on famously to compare the church to a merchant company when he remarks, "The *Church* or *company* of *worshippers* (whether true or false) is . . . like unto a *Corporation, Society, or Company* of *East-Indie* or *Turkie-Merchants*, or any other *Societie* or *Company* in *London*" (*BT* 73).[3] He rails, in the later *Hireling Ministry None of Christs* (1652), against those "misticall *Merchants*" (*HM* 170) or ministers who see their office as a "*Trade* . . . of *Spirituall merchandize* . . . of all sorts of *spices* and precious things, the precious sweet *Truths* and *Promises* of holy *Scripture*; yea . . . a trade of selling *God* himself" (*HM* 171).

But perhaps his most developed discussion of the ministry in market terms appears in *Mr. Cottons Letter*. John Cotton, in a letter written shortly after Williams' 1635 banishment (but not published until 1642), defended the colony's decision by chastising Williams for his refusal to preach to those who had not fully and publicly separated from the Church of England. To support his case, Cotton cites Proverbs 11.26: "he that with-holdeth the Corne (which is the staffe of life) from the people, the multitude shall curse him" (Cotton, *Letter* 13). Williams' 1644 reply counters Cotton's criticism by developing a far more extended analogy between preaching and the marketplace. He notes: "Doth not even the common civill Market abhorre and curse that man, who carries to market and throws about good corn, against the owners mind and expresse command, who yet is willing and desirous it should bee sold plenteously, if with his consent, according to his order, and to his honest and reasonable advantage? This is the case of the true and false Ministery" (*MC* 46). A false ministry like Cotton's that would preach to nonseparating Puritans and even to the unregenerate in the hopes of converting them is, in Williams' figure, comparable to an open and unregulated market, in which ministers, as merchant-agents responsible for selling the corn owned by God, disregard the owner's express instructions for how and to whom that corn (a figure here for the Lord's word) should be sold. It is not that bad ministers are like merchants, for all ministers are likened to merchants here; it is just that bad ministers are comparable to bad merchants. He equates the false minister with an incompetent or deceitful trader who violates the rules of honest mercantile exchange in his too-eager pursuit of immediate profit.

This analogy is interesting for a number of reasons, not the least of which is that Roger Williams spent a good portion of his daily life in New England quite literally selling corn—as well as furs and other goods—to the Indians, the English, and the Dutch. He turned to selling corn as an economic necessity after refusing payment for his ministerial services, and continued to expand the practice both before and after his banishment. The passage becomes yet more meaningful when one considers the incredible importance of corn in New England, not only as a source of food for the early colonists but—because it was one of the only commodities in relative abundance—its early use by them as money. The unequal balance of trade between North America and Europe during the early years of colonial settlement meant that other commodities—most commonly tobacco in the South and wampum and corn in the North—were used as currency in the perpetual absence of coin. Therefore while Cotton and Williams are carrying out a debate about Puritan separatism and the proper role of the ministry, they are doing so in terms that simultaneously suggest a debate about the circulation and exchange of commodities and money. Williams the trader implies that, like the marketplace, the ministry requires tight regulations and standards to prevent the contamination, misrepresentation, and greed that an "open" ministry, like an unregulated market, would invite.

Such ideas may have had dual origins in theology and economics. The passage on selling corn in *Mr. Cottons Letter* betrays Williams' knowledge of market relations as much as it articulates his Separatist position, and it furthermore points to implicit concerns with exchange, equivalence, market deceptions, and materialist greed that run throughout Williams' writings and his conflicts with Massachusetts Bay authorities. Like many of the Puritans who settled in New England, Williams brought a familiarity with mercantile exchange and the marketplace with him from England. That knowledge would have been supplemented by his entrance into the New England economy as a farmer and trader. As an active trader, Williams was familiar with the difficulties of commercial exchange, and devotes significant sections of his *Key* to making both spiritual and material sense of the challenges of Indian trade in New England. But outside these sections, there are surprisingly few direct descriptions by Williams of his trading experience, considering his involved and ongoing engagement in it.

Unfortunately, that absence has been perpetuated by virtually every study of Roger Williams, which collectively, from at least Perry Miller onward, have confined Williams within exclusively theological boundaries. Even if Williams did not spend much time literally writing about trade, his writings are frequently marked by the language of trade, as the examples above suggest. His economic practice, his idiosyncratic theology, and his literary style all depended on a belief that, in the world that still awaited Christ's second coming, truth (much like economic value and linguistic meaning) could be negotiated only in a process of exchange. Until this future arrival, truth remained uncertain, just as subject to shift and change as were market values. Any premillennial claims for an absolute, fixed, or certain truth had to be suspended and deferred. Churches, nations, and even selves therefore had always to await Christ's anticipated arrival to find out who they really were, and had to be content with negotiating unfinished identities until then.

Cloth, Scales, and Fur

Although Roger Williams never entered into mercantile practice in England, his father and older brother were both members of London's Merchant Tailor Company, one of the oldest English trading guilds. His father kept a shop where he sold cloth in the front of the Williams house, and his brother Sydrack became a transnational merchant engaged in trade and travel to Turkey and Italy (Ernst 17). Moreover, Williams grew up in Smithfield, a section of London that hosted livestock and hay markets four days of the week, and where St. Bartholomew's cloth fair, made famous by Ben Jonson, took place every year. Despite Williams' opposition to the "pleasures and pastimes" associated with the life of the market and the fair, James Ernst suggests that both were nevertheless important sources for many of Roger Williams' "vivid figures of speech" (12; 10 n.8). At such markets, it was the task of guild merchants like Williams' father to regulate the sale and purchase of cloth goods so as to prevent deception and fraud—as Williams later suggested ministers should be similarly guided in their preaching. Although the older guilds were quickly being surpassed by newer joint-stock companies like the one that would finance the Massachusetts Bay project, the Merchant Tailor Company was still responsible for enforcing accurate measurements and weights, and maintaining quality standards for merchandise sold at the cloth fair (Brockunier 8).

Regulation to ensure the accuracy of both the quantity and quality of trade goods is an ongoing concern in seventeenth-century economic tracts. In the second, "Corrected and much Enlarged," edition of his international

Merchants Map of Commerce (1671), for instance, Lewes Roberts adds discussions of garbling and the office of the alneger, both devoted to assuring that a product's actual quality and quantity were consistent with its proclaimed value. Garbling, Roberts explains, is the activity of "cleansing, severing, sorting and dividing of the good from the bad" in a commodity such as spices or drugs, separating the better from the inferior (or even counterfeit) product (42). The alneger (or alnager) likewise is appointed to measure and attest to the quality of imported cloth, to "view and prevent the false making of all sorts of Woollen Clothes." Such functions are needed because merchants are so often tempted to privilege profit over truth, and Roberts mourns those earlier days when such an office was, he indicates, unnecessary, because deceit was "hatefully loathed" (44–45).[4] Edward Misselden, in his 1623 tract on free trade, contrasts the office of the alneger, usually filled by "so *Noble and Honourable a Personage*" (44), to that of the searcher, who is responsible for inspecting and then "sealing" the cloth. But when the searchers are "silly Countreymen . . . not expert in the *mystery* of making of Cloth," corruption follows, and they often "set the seales of their office, to Clothes they never search't nor saw" (46).

Thus, when Roger Williams in his reply to Cotton's letter compares scripture to a set of "scales" (*MC* 75) and argues for a true ministry in terms of the proper selling of corn, he is employing not only the terms but the logic of a seventeenth-century marketplace with which he was surely familiar. For Williams, claims to religious truth have to be placed on the scales and weighed against the scriptural standard. Of course, this process is just as subject to imperfect human interpretation as are market measurements, but for Williams no less than for Roberts or Misselden, nothing is worse than a falsely applied seal or a falsely balanced scale: "how abominable in his [God's] eyes are a *waight* and a *waight*, a *stone* and a *stone* in the bag of *waights*! one waight for themselves when they are under Hatches, and another for others when they come to Helme" (*BT* 205). The figure of Truth who holds the scales in *The Bloudy Tenent* promises not to be "tyred with holding the *balances* of the *Sanctuarie*," and to "weigh as in the presence of Him whose pure eyes cannot behold *iniquitie*" (*BT* 221). The role of the minister or witness is as a kind of garbler or merchant-middleman between God and the congregation. What is so fascinating about this analogy in Williams' writing is that sometimes, in order to be as honest and accurate as possible, the holder of this office produced a language that appeared garbled (in the more modern, linguistic sense of confused) precisely in order to perform well his charge of garbling (in the now obsolete, mercantile sense of selecting out elements of value or truth).

Long before his 1652 tract *A Hireling Ministry None of Christs*, Williams made clear his opposition to clergy who accepted payment for their services, a position that eventually led him to occupy a class/status position different from that of other Puritan New England divines. In *A Hireling Ministry*, he urges those drawn to the ministry to take up another trade (whether the law, the military, medicine, education, or farming) while continuing to prophesy, rather than to "*live under the* slavery . . . *and the* censure . . *of a mercenary and* Hireling *Ministery*" (*HM* 153). While preaching at Plymouth, Williams refused to be paid, but was provided with a house and farmland. He supplemented his farming income by trading with the Indians and the Dutch, and later brought this trading business with him when he went to preach at Salem, where he also continued to work the land (Ernst 70, 98–99). What distinguished Williams from fellow ministers like Skelton, Hooker, Cotton, Shepard, Eliot, and Peter was, biographer John Garrett observes, that they had chosen "not to soil their hands with toil" (108). Some of his contemporaries felt that Williams, by choosing to work as a farmer and trader, betrayed the class/status that his birth and university degree entitled him to, and aligned himself instead with common laborers (Garrett 109).[5] If Thomas Morton argued for socioeconomic promotion by foregrounding the easy profitability of colonial and transcontinental trade, Roger Williams appears to have invited social demotion through his participation in such trade, though perhaps because he foregrounded instead the difficult cultural and linguistic dialogics of colonial commerce.

Eventually Williams soiled his hands primarily by working at the trading post he had established, at least as early as 1637, at Cocumscussoc (on Narragansett Bay, near present-day Wickford), and from which he conducted extensive trade with the Indians and the Dutch.[6] Williams frequently resided at the post between 1645 and 1651, in a trading house that he finally deeded to Richard Smith (Chapin, *Trading* 13, 14) in order to pay for an upcoming voyage to England (LaFantasie, "Day" 109). The Cocumscussoc post was clearly a response to the sudden and surprising poverty that met Williams almost immediately after his banishment from Massachusetts when, after being "unkindly and unchristianly (as I believe) driven from my howse and land, and wife and children" through "Winter snow wch I feele yet" (*C* 610), he found it necessary to build shelter, plant fields, and support his family while denied access to the market in Boston and his former trade contacts. As Williams vividly and bitterly remembers in this 1670 letter, even after his initial exile he was asked to leave the land on which he had "begun to build and plant at Secunk" (*C* 610) after being advised by Winthrop that it fell within the Massachusetts patent, only to learn that the land he moved to on the other side of the river belonged to Plymouth. "[B]etween those my Friends of the Bay and Plymmouth," he remarks, "I was sorely tost for one 14 weekes (in a bitter Winter Season) not knowing what Bread or Bed did meane. Beside the Yearly losse of no small matter in my trading with English and Natives, being debard from Boston (the chiefe Mart and port of N. Engl.) God knows that many thouhsand [*sic*] pounds can not repay the very temporary Losses I have Sustained" (*C* 611). Glenn LaFantasie suggests that it was such "financial hardship" and "persistent indebtedness" that prompted Williams "to devote so much of his time and energy to the trading post," although the remote Cocumscussoc location also facilitated his spiritual reflection, his missionary activity, and his "tireless search for pure forms of worship based upon the model of Christ's primitive church" (LaFantasie, "Day" 99, 103; see also Brockunier 184).

His trading post did quickly become a crucial means toward economic survival in his Providence exile—it eventually netted him £100 per year—and, by gathering the few details that do appear in his own writings together with other accounts of the New England fur trade, it is possible to get a fair sense of what his trading post experience entailed. As fur trade scholars invariably note, the New England fur trade demanded a combination of Old and New World commercial contacts, since it was part of a "far-reaching economic system" that "spanned the Atlantic and reached even to Russia" (DePaoli 177, 195). Spurred largely by European desire for beaver hats, the fur trade was the most profitable trade in early New England, and it was a favored means by which colonial merchants could make payments to their creditors in London (W. Roberts li). To get beaver furs and other animal skins from Indians, however, colonial traders had to have a stock of appealing goods available for exchange, and the Indians preferred practical items such as cloth, cooking utensils, tools, or firearms (see W. Roberts 29, 32, 51–53; DePaoli 177). Especially in the early years of the New England trade, these goods were typically advanced to New England traders by London merchants, who accepted furs in exchange (W. Roberts 72), although later Massachusetts Bay became an equally important supplier of goods and buyer of furs. Several Boston merchants maintained warehouses in remote fur-trading areas, which they kept stocked with English goods for trading purposes (W. Roberts 106), and Williams' storehouse likely contained such typical trading items, since, as LaFantasie reports, "it appears that the Indians came freely and frequently to Williams's post to trade their wampum, pelts, corn, and other items for English goods, such as kettles, metal tools and utensils, and cloth" ("Day" 101). Williams also owned a canoe, a shallop, and a pinnace used to transport tools and cloth to exchange for Indian furs (Brockunier 186).[7]

While both Plymouth and Massachusetts Bay controlled access to the fur trade in their colonies, in Rhode Island trade was open to all (Moloney 101). Through the Dutch, who competed with Williams for trade in the Narragansett Bay, wampum was introduced to create what Lynn Ceci describes as a trade triangle in the Northeast. Cloth and other goods were shipped from Europe to the American Northeast where they were exchanged for wampum, which was transported upriver and exchanged for furs, which in turn were shipped back to investors in Europe who sold them for great profit (Ceci 58). Eventually, as the number of traders increased, many began to seek a competitive advantage by granting goods to Indians in the autumn, in advance of the furs they were to bring in during the winter (W. Roberts 67), a practice that Williams clearly engaged in. Even while the natives depended on this credit, they also frequently ran into debt, and a few traders were known to demand in exchange a "mortgage on Indian land" (Moloney 58). The New England fur trade—in which Roger Williams participated and prospered for many years—was therefore a site of complex linguistic, cultural, and economic transactions. His trading experience, while hardly the only key, is nevertheless an important key to understanding the temporal logic that supported Williams' various dissenting arguments about land rights, religious tolerance, oath taking, separation, and eschatology.

Converting Value

Williams repeatedly decried the error of predicting in the present the form of a future that had not yet arrived. His central metaphor for this position in *The Bloudy Tenent* is the opposition between "the *Garden* and the *Wildernesse*, the *Church* and the *World*," as two utterly distinct realms that Cotton has impatiently made "all one" (*BT* 233). By imagining the present as an anticipatory version of the future, Cotton collapses the vital distinction between them and ushers violence into the breach. Only when the present and the future are accurately recognized as discontinuous does the world avoid "shedding the *blood* of such *Hereticks*, &c. whom *Christ* would have enjoy longer *patience* and *permission* untill the *Harvest*" (*BT* 416). Because the pure church or garden is for Williams located altogether outside the wilderness of earthly temporality, its purity cannot be contaminated by the chaos and mixture that characterizes the world. Punishing heretics as if they were weeds (rather than patiently waiting for them to mature until the harvest) is therefore utterly misguided, for "a false *Religion* out of the *Church* will not hurt the *Church*, no more then *weedes* in the *Wildernesse* hurt the inclosed *Garden*" (*BT* 198).[8]

In her analysis of Williams' garden-wilderness opposition, Lisa Gordis astutely recognizes his use of the language and principles of agriculture, particularly in his introduction of fields as a liminal site between the wilderness and the garden. Such fields represent "areas of potential growth in need of careful cultivation" in preparation for the coming harvest whose time and shape will be determined only by God (127). But while Williams does mention fields, he also explicitly prohibits their cultivation, insisting that "the *ministers* or *messengers* of the *Lord Jesus* ought to let them [the tares] alone to live in the world, and neither seeke by *prayer* or *prophesie* to pluck them up before the *Harvest*" (*BT* 118). Such cultivation would misunderstand the field as a premature garden, and "turne the *Garden* and *Paradice* of the *Church* and *Saints* into the *Field* of the *Civill State* of the *World*, and to reduce the *World* to the first *chaos* or *confusion*" (*BT* 415). At the very point where agricultural knowledge and language fall short, then, Williams turns instead to the language and experience of trade, for until "the *Harvest* or end of the World" (*BT* 110) does come, humans must abandon cultivation and weed pulling for negotiation and trade, using the currency of language as they would corn, wampum, and coin. In fact, contemporary economic writers used similar metaphors to encourage their readers to think about economic decisions in terms of long-term investments. The English economic writer Thomas Mun argued in his 1664 treatise on foreign trade, for instance, that "if we only behold the actions of the husbandman in the seed-time when he casteth away much good corn into the ground, we will rather accompt him a mad man than a husbandman: but when we consider his labours in the harvest which is the end of his endeavours, we find the worth and plentiful encrease of his actions" (19).

Before he left for England in 1643 to procure a charter, Williams' Providence farm was the primary means of support for himself and his family, but his trading activity among the Narragansetts continued to grow. Following his return to New England, he employed an agent at Cocumscussoc and moved to the post himself in 1647. His shift in orientation from public affairs to private finances around this time was certainly prompted by the need to maintain his large family in the wake of his unremunerated expenses associated with obtaining the charter, but his turn to trade may also have been facilitated in part by the book he wrote on the ship to England. *A Key into the Language of America* is introduced to readers in the context of contemporaneous travel and promotional writing by "Others of my Country-men [who] have often, and excellently, and lately written of the *Countrey* (and none that I know beyond the goodnesse and worth of it)." Williams offers his *Key*, or dictionary, of "the *Native Language*" (*K* 83) as a linguistic addition to this body of descriptive writing, and suggests that those with purposes of "*Travell, Discourse, Trading &c.*" (*K* 90) will benefit in particular from his Narragansett-English glossary. David Murray—perhaps the only reader of *A Key* to recognize the central role of trade in the book—accurately identifies its engagement with commercial, religious, and linguistic forms of transformation, with "the overlapping terms of exchange, conversion and translation" (237).

But even as *A Key* promises a kind of practical access to knowledge in all these arenas, it also resolutely questions the certainty of the knowledge it shares. Murray reads Williams' central metaphor of the "key" as providing epistemological access that proliferates and branches (since this "little *Key* may open a *Box*, where lies a *bunch* of *Keyes*" [*K* 83]), thereby opening up "a treasure in the form of resources, as well as souls for conversion" (Murray 238). But we might also read in Williams' description of a key that uncovers only more keys a metaphor not of multiplied but of deferred access, a description of knowledge expected (through the "Key" that opens a "Box") and then denied or, rather, suspended further (since the box contains only "a bunch of Keyes"). And indeed the book suggests that the certainty of religious conversion and the accuracy of linguistic translation are ultimately just as indeterminate as the truth of economic value.

As several scholars note, Williams' representation of New England trade inverts the conventional trope of English superiority and Indian ignorance.[9] The Indians themselves he portrays as masterful and clever traders; at one point he describes them as being "as full of businesse, and as impatient of hinderance (in their kind) as any Merchant in *Europe*" (*K* 120). As a result, Indian-English trade emerges as a challenging process of establishing economic equivalencies across radical differences in culture and language. If Thomas Morton's inflated pastoral occludes the bodies and voices of indigenous laborers and traders, the condensed dialogism of Williams' book emphasizes them. The following dialogue, presented in the form of a bilingual glossary in the chapter "Of buying and selling," represents one such negotiation over the quality and value of a piece of cloth:

Aumpachunnish.	*Open it.*
Tuttepacunnish.	*Fold it up.*
Mat Weshegganunno.	*There is no Wool on it.*
Tanogganish.	*Shake it.*
Wuskinuit.	*New Cloth.*
Tanocki, tanocksha.	*It is torne or rent.*
Eatawus.	*It is Old.*
Quttaunch.	*Feele it.* (*K* 216)

Like most of Williams' accounts of trading dialogue, this one involves the commodity of cloth, so central to colonial Indian trade as well as to the Williams family's own mercantile history. In addition to providing cloth traders with useful Narragansett phrases and terms, this exchange represents the act of trade as a tense linguistic encounter and debate that centers around the determination of the economic value of a product like cloth.

After this debate about its quality, negotiation continues when the buyer asks, "Tahenauatu? *What price?*" (*K* 216).

Cosaúmawem.	*You aske too much.*
Kuttíackqussaûwaw.	*You are very hard.*
Aquie iackqussaúme.	*Be not so hard.*
Aquie Wussaúmowash.	*Doe not aske so much.*
Tashin Comménsin?	*How much shall I give you?*
Kutteaûg Comméinsh.	*I will give you your Money.*
Nkèke Comméinsh.	*I will give you an Otter.*
Coanombúqusse Kuttassokakómme.	*You have deceived me.*

> *Obs.* Who ever deale or trade with them, had need of Wisedome, Patience, and Faithfulnesse in dealing: for they frequently say *Cuppànnawem*, you lye, *Cuttassokakómme*, you deceive me. (*K* 217)

Repeatedly in these prolonged dialogues, Williams characterizes the scene of exchange as a site of potential deception and misrepresentation, since the threat of fraud prompts such elaborate and extended debates. Because the Indians are "very suspicious that *English* men labour to deceive them" (*K* 217–18), they will travel long distances in order to "beate all markets" (*K* 218) or "to save six pence" (*K* 218), and "are marvailous subtle in their Bargaines to save a penny" (*K* 217). The wampum that serves as Indian currency is another source of potential fraud, since it is sometimes authentic and sometimes counterfeit. But Williams admits that "I never knew any of them [the Indians] much deceived, for their danger of being deceived (in these things of Earth) makes them cautelous [cautious]" (*K* 217). The Indians' skepticism prolongs and complicates their commercial exchanges, but it also, literally, pays off, since their distrust enhances their gain.

As Williams records it, the process of economic exchange requires a vigilance against not only the potential for deception but the constant changeability of value. Just as both goods and currency can be misrepresented, value also shifts, depending on such forces as supply and demand, currency exchange rates, and trends within transcontinental markets. For example, Williams explains that "one fathom" of wampum is "now worth of the English but five shillings (sometimes more) some few yeeres since was worth nine, and sometimes ten shillings *per* Fathome" (*K* 211). Such profound fluctuation is, he explains, "occasioned by the fall of Beaver in *England*," an explanation that the Indians have trouble accepting. They "are very impatient, when for English commodities they pay so much more of their money, and not understanding the cause of it; and many say the English cheat and deceive them, though I have laboured to make them understand the reason of it" (*K* 211–12). The *Key* represents economic value as determined through a difficult and elaborate establishment of equivalency between product and price, but it also makes clear that this negotiated value can never be counted on as fixed; value has to be negotiated anew—often with radically different results—at different moments in time or space. There is, therefore, no "true" value, since all value is negotiated and contingent.

Linguistic truth is subject to the same uncertainty, and Williams appears equally skeptical of (while remaining absolutely dedicated to) linguistic commerce. When he first introduces the subject of Indian conversion, Williams emphasizes just how much conversation he has had with the natives on this topic ("I have run through varieties of *Intercourses* with them Day and Night, Summer and Winter, by Land and Sea"; "Many solemne discourses I have had with all *sorts of Nations* of them, from one end of the Countrey to another"). But despite laying claim to some knowledge resulting from these exchanges ("I know there is no small *preparation* in the hearts of Multitudes of them"; "I know strong *Convictions* upon the *Consciences* of many of them"), Williams takes up a position of hopeful reticence that is based finally on what he does not know: "I know not with how little *Knowledge* and *Grace* of Christ, the Lord may save, and therefore neither will *despaire*, nor *report* much" (*K* 87). The one example Williams does include—his deathbed dialogue with the Pequot Wequash—refuses to offer the certainty of Native conversion that the English so "longed for" and that the New Englanders "so much pretended" (*K* 87), but only "mine owne Hopes of Him (though I dare not be so confident as others)" (*K* 88). After reporting Wequash's discussion of his family, his sickness, his imminent death, and his soul, Williams records Wequash's dying words and his own understanding of them: "*Me so big naughty Heart, me heart all one stone! Savory expressions* using to breath *from compunct and broken Hearts*, and a sence of *inward hardnesse* and *unbrokennesse*" (*K* 88). Picking up on Wequash's own imagery of hearts and stones, Williams refuses to claim an access to the man's interior, to his conscience. If his linguistic ability does offer Williams a "key" into the "box" of Wequash's self, all he finds there are, indeed, more "keys." Barely distinguishing between Wequash's and his own words, Williams relates not proof and knowledge of conversion but only the hopeful uncertainty of expressive language, the end product of a long negotiation.

Williams makes a similar point about the paired uncertainties of language and conversion in the pamphlet *Christenings Make Not Christians*, written during the same trip to England that produced the *Key*, but not published until 1645. In it, Williams continues his practice of challenging the conventional or perceived meanings of words—in this case, "Heathen" and "Christian"—and deconstructs, in his own way, the opposition between them.[10] He positions the truly converted self at a site of inaccessibility, and cautions against interpreting exterior transformation as evidence of interior change. Turning once again to the commodity and metaphor of cloth so important to *A Key* and his own trading network, he explains that

> it is not a suite of crimson Satten will make a dead man live, take off and change his crimson into white he is dead still, off with that, and shift him into cloth of gold, and from that to cloth of diamonds, he is but a dead man still: For it is not a forme, nor the change of one forme into another, a finer, and a finer, and yet more fine, that makes a man a convert I meane such a convert as is acceptable to God. (*CM* 37)

Such changes in drapery, such false conversions, are analogous to the deceptive use of words, and "woe be to me, if I call light darknesse, or darknesse light; sweet bitter, or bitter sweet; woe be to me if I call that conversion unto God, which is indeed subversion of the soules of Millions in *Christendome*, from one false worship to another" (*CM* 37). The only true conversion, Williams maintains, "(whether of *Americans* or *Europeans*) must be such as those Conversions were of the first pattern, either of the Jewes or the Heathens" (*CM* 39). But the purity of this first pattern is made by turns illegible and inexpressible through the wilderness language of the present world, for "In matters of Earth men will helpe to spell out each other, but in matters of Heaven (to which the soule is naturally so averse) how far are the Eares of man hedged up from listening to all improper Language?" (*CM* 40). The work of converting commodities, like that of converting souls, was therefore not only subject to continual change but depended on an imperfect earthly language unable to access certain truth or value. Roger Williams' representation of commerce and conversion shared with his theology this unwavering commitment to human uncertainty and changeability in the premillennial world.

Lexicography and Linguistic Value

Several of the columned glossaries in the chapter "Concerning their Coyne" look less like linguistic translations than like the currency conversion tables that often appear as a supplement at the end of economic handbooks like Lewes Roberts' *Merchants Mappe of Commerce*, and that inform readers of the relative value of one national currency in the terms of another. For instance, when Williams introduces the Narragansett words for different quantities of wampum, he produces this list:

Nquittómpscat.	1 *peny.*
Neesaúmscat.	2 *pence.*
Shwaúmscat.	3 *pence.*
. . . .	
Piuckquaúmscat nab nèes, &c.	12 *pence.*

Obs. This they call *Neèn*, which is two of their *Quttáuatues*, or six pence.

. . . .

Quttatashincheck aumscat, *or, more commonly* *used* Piúckquat.	5s. 10 quttaúatues, *or,* 10 six pences.

Obs. This Piúckquat being sixtie pence, they call *Nquittómpeg*, or *nquitnishcáusu*, that is, one fathom, 5 shillings. (*K* 210–11)

This multiplying series of equivalences within and between languages and currencies exposes the complex overlapping of economic and linguistic exchange, and it even more pointedly aligns exchange with conversion and translation. But just as in his cloth-trading dialogues, these lists, too, insist on the various and changeable terms of conversion—whether monetary, linguistic, or religious. Indeed, Williams recognizes language as itself a kind of currency in his exchanges with the natives, and he explains that his first purchase of land from the Narragansetts was conducted "(not by monies nor payment, the Natives being so shy, And jeloues that monies could not doe it, but by that Language, Acquaintance, And favour with the Natives" (qtd. in Chapin, *Documentary* 27–28).[11]

Indeed, Williams' position on the Massachusetts Bay patent makes most sense when we recognize just how closely the registers of language and trade overlapped for him. Although Williams' original tract on the patent does not survive, John Winthrop's record of it makes clear that Williams rejected the Englishpeople's claim to represent "Christendom" in the patent, and therefore rejected their right to land granted them on that basis. To describe any current people or nation as "Christendom" was a misuse of the word, which, for Williams, could accurately describe only a future condition that would come in a form and a time determined by

God. The English colonists possessed North American land only on the basis of a misuse of language that stemmed, in turn, from a falsely continuist or anticipationist understanding of time. English settlers in New England had no more right to claim prematurely the title of "Christendom" than did the natives, and Williams maintained, here as elsewhere, that until the millennium set language and truth straight, all that could be done was to negotiate with each other in worldly trade.

The lexicon of Narragansett words and phrases that makes up so much of *A Key* suggests that, just like commodity values, linguistic meaning is renegotiated over time. The translations, presented in two columns, clearly match English with Narragansett words or phrases to which they are equivalent. Williams explains, however, that many different Indian terms could be equivalent to a single English term: "sometimes there are two words for the same thing (for their Language is exceeding copious, and they have five or six words sometimes for one thing)" (*K* 90–91). Therefore the glossaries, which often record multiple ways of understanding or articulating analogous claims (*You aske too much . . . You are very hard. . . . Be not so hard . . . Doe not aske so much*; or Quttatashincheck aumscat [=] Piúckquat [=] *Nquittómpeg* [=] *nquitnishcáusu* [=] 10 quttaúatues [=] 10 six pences [=] one fathom [=] 5 shillings), document not just linguistic (or monetary) equivalents but the variability within such equivalence.

Whatever temporary certainty of meaning the individual entries within these glossaries might promise is furthermore unsettled by their function as small dialogues or linguistic exchanges in which meaning is less predetermined than it is negotiated between parties, much like exchange value. In the chapter "Of their Warre, &c.," for example, one listing-dialogue begins with the phrases "Niss-níssoke. *Kill kill.* / Kúnnish. *I will kill you.* / Kunnì shickqun ewò. *He will kill you*" before moving to the phrases "Neene núppamen. *I am dying.* / Cowaúnckamish. *Quarter, quarter.* / Kunnanaumpasúmmish. *Mercy, mercy*" and finally ending with "Cowauôntam. *You are a wise man.* / Wetompátitea. *Let us make Friends*" (*K* 238). This protracted exchange gradually undoes its initial depictions of Indian (and/or English) aggression through the shared work of physical and linguistic renegotiation. Williams also sometimes singles out hybrid words—such as "*Cuppaimish* I will pay you" (*K* 216) and "*Moneash* from the English Money" (*K* 210)—that have emerged out of the cultural and linguistic encounter between English and Indian, and that demonstrate language's capacity to mutate in unpredictable ways. Not surprisingly, most of these hybrid terms are economic ones. Like value, meaning is negotiated for Williams in a complex and tense process of exchange, and, like value, meaning shifts and develops as a result of movement in time or across space.

Monetary conversion tables were sometimes also included along with linguistic translations in early modern English dictionaries, such as Thomas Elyot's 1542 *Biblioteca*, which "declared the ancient coynes, weyghtes, and measures, conferryng them with those whiche be currant and vsuall among vs" (Elyot, qtd. in Hayashi 19). By the time Williams published *A Key*, there were a number of dictionaries in print that were dedicated to explicating in English what were called "hard" English words (typically those derived from Latin or borrowed from foreign languages) for an audience that did not have access to formal education, especially upper-class women and members of the merchant or craftsmen classes.[12] The vocabulary sections of Williams' *Key*, however, follow rather the principles established in earlier, multilingual dictionaries or vocabularies of both Latin and modern languages. John Withals' *Shorte Dictionarie for Yonge Begynners*, for example, first published in 1553 and frequently reprinted until 1634, arranged in columns its entries of Latin-English equivalents, and grouped words not alphabetically but according to topics such as "Building" or "Water."[13] Williams would have been familiar with manuals like Withals', which were commonly used by schoolboys, and with Latin-English dictionaries generally, which were used by those studying for the ministry. Williams also had experience in language instruction, and while in England he taught Dutch to, among others, John Milton when he served as Secretary of Foreign Tongues. In a 1654 letter to John Winthrop, Jr., Williams explains that language is best taught not through "Grammar rules," which "begin to be esteemed a Tyrannie," but "by words phrazes and constant talk &c." (*C* 393), and this privileging of protracted and variable dialogue over succinct and exact equations is clearly at work already in his 1643 *Key*.[14]

As both a lexicographer of the Narragansett dialect and a trader of Narragansett goods, Roger Williams is engaged in the process of establishing equivalencies that, he emphasizes, are binding at the moment of agreement but are subject to (and indeed likely to) change over time. Even the visual form of the bilingual glossaries presented in the *Key* resembles the form of double-columned account books maintained by seventeenth-century merchant traders. Such traders' books recorded all exchanges in parallel columns of debits and credits, better known as double-entry bookkeeping. Numerous manuals appeared in print during the seventeenth century that offered instruction in this bookkeeping method. Richard Dafforne's popular *Merchants Mirrour* offered its instruction through a dialogue in which a schoolboy answers a series of questions designed to test his bookkeeping knowledge. The volume also includes concrete examples of the various forms of account books, including the ledger book, in which a merchant's debits and credits are arranged on facing pages whose totals are required to match or "mirror" each other (see figs. 3 and 4). While each individual entry represented a binding agreement, that record hardly guaranteed the stability of those prices or values in the future; in other words, the content of such account books had a documentary rather than a predictive function. Furthermore, although an account book could be balanced to determine a merchant's current net value at any synchronic moment, these books—as an ongoing record of exchanges, debts, and credits—were fundamentally diachronic, and any final "meaning" or "value" was therefore held in a kind of perpetual suspense.

In his chapter devoted to "Debts and Trusting" in the *Key*, Williams begins by providing the following translations and observation:

Noónat.	*I have not money enough.*
Noonamautuckquàwhe.	*Trust me.*
Kunnoonamaútuckquaush.	*I will owe it you.*

> *Obs.* They [the Indians] are very desirous to come into debt, but then he that trusts them, must sustaine a twofold losse:
>
> First, of his Commoditie.
>
> Secondly, of his custome, as I have found by deare experience: Some are ingenuous, plaine hearted and honest; but the most never pay, unlesse a man follow them to their severall abodes, townes and houses, as I my selfe have been forc'd to doe, which hardship and travells it hath yet pleased God to sweeten with some experiences and some little gaine of Language. (*K* 221)

Once again, his experience among the Indians has been costly (or "deare") for Williams, and he hopes his book will lessen that expense by allowing future traders to benefit from his "little gaine." Whereas the Indians were earlier presented as skeptical traders wary of English deception, the English emerge here as gullible victims of Indian dishonesty or, rather, cultural confusion (since the trading difficulty Williams recounts here is the result of the practice of English traders advancing goods on credit to Indians in anticipation of the furs they will bring in later in the season). These chapters underscore the limitations and losses that result when Englishmen presume a too-easy equivalence between English and New England marketplaces. Like the false ministers Williams warns about in his letter to Cotton, these merchants eager for profit are likely to "throw about good corn" to any and all buyers and to lose any "honest and reasonable" profit they might have made on it as a result. In such cases, ministers and merchants alike make the mistake of assuming a lasting equivalence where there is instead an inexpressible difference.

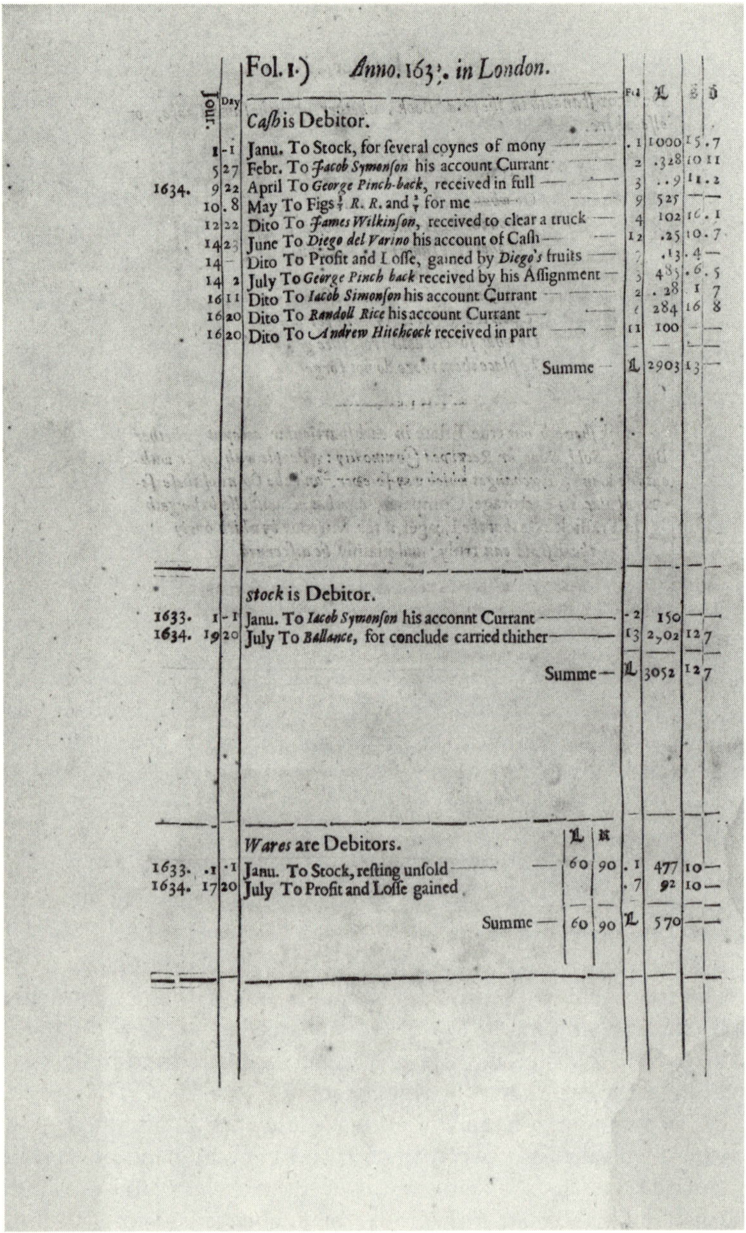

Fol. 1.) *Anno.* 163¾. *in London.*

	Jour.	Day		Fol.	£	s	d
			Cash is Debitor.				
	1	1	Janu. To Stock, for several coynes of mony	1	1000	15	7
	5	27	Febr. To *Jacob Symonson* his account Currant	2	328	10	11
1634.	9	22	April To *George Pinch-back*, received in full	3	9	11	2
	10	8	May To Figs ⅞ *R. R.* and ⅞ for me	9	525	—	—
	12	22	Dito To *James Wilkinson*, received to clear a truck	4	102	16	1
	14	23	June To *Diego del Varino* his account of Cash	12	25	10	7
	14	—	Dito To Profit and Losse, gained by *Diego's* fruits	7	13	4	—
	14	2	July To *George Pinch back* received by his Assignment	3	485	6	5
	16	11	Dito To *Iacob Simonson* his account Currant	2	28	1	7
	16	20	Dito To *Randoll Rice* his account Currant	6	284	16	8
	16	20	Dito To *Andrew Hitchcock* received in part	11	100	—	—
			Summe	£	2903	13	—

	Jour.	Day		Fol.	£	s	d
			stock is Debitor.				
1633.	1	1	Janu. To *Iacob Symonson* his acconnt Currant	2	150	—	—
1634.	19	20	July To *Ballance*, for conclude carried thither	13	2,902	12	7
			Summe	£	3052	12	7

	Jour.	Day		L	R	Fol.	£	s	d
			Wares are Debitors.						
1633.	1	1	Janu. To Stock, resting unsold	60	90	1	477	10	—
1634.	17	20	July To Profit and Losse gained			7	92	10	—
			Summe	60	90	£	570	—	—

FIGS. 3 AND 4. Facing "Debitor" and "Creditor" pages in sample ledger book, from Richard Dafforne's *Apprentices Time-Entertainer Accomptantly*, 3rd ed. (London, 1670). Courtesy of Princeton University Library. Rare Books Division. Department of Rare Books and Special Collections.

	Jour.	Day	*Cash* is Creditor.	Fol.	L	S	D
	2	4	Janu. By *George Pinchback*, payd in part	3	144	—	—
	2	9	Dito By *James Wilkinson*, payd in part	4	120	—	—
	3	30	Dito By *George Pinckback*, payd him	3	135	19	8
	4	9	Febr. By *Iac. Symons.* his account of Couchaneille, payd	3	5	5	4
	4	21	Dito by Voyage to Lisborn, consigned to *Diego dell Varino* for company $\frac{1}{7}$, and $\frac{6}{7}$ payd	5	59	—	—
	5	13	March by Dansick-exchange for *Arth. Mump.* and me $\frac{1}{2}$	8	200	—	—
	5		Dito By Kersies in comp $\frac{1}{3}$ *Iac. Symonson*, $\frac{2}{3}$ for me	4	2	2	6
	9		Dito By *Iacob Symonson* his Cambrix-cloth	8	4	7	—
	6	21	Dito By *Iacob Symonson* his account Currant	2	9	7	6
	6	—	Dito By Figs in company $\frac{1}{3}$ *R.R.* $\frac{2}{3}$ for me	9	8	7	9
1634.	6	29	Dito By *Hendrick vander Linden*, and Company their account of commodities, for charges	10		12	5
	7	7	April By Silver, for charges of 8. Barrs	10	4	7	2
	10	8	May By *Randoll Rice* his account Currant	6	99	19	1
	11	13	Dito By Amsterdam-exchange $\frac{1}{2}$ for *Jacob Symonson*	11	504	19	6
	12	7	June By *Diego del Varino* his account of Cash	12	25	10	7
	12	7	Dito By Figs in Company $\frac{1}{3}$ *R R.* $\frac{2}{3}$ for me	9	23	8	9
	12	7	Dito By *Andrew Hitchcock* payd him	11	73	16	8
	13	15	Dito By *Iacob Symonson* his account of Cambrix-cloth	8	1	7	—
	19	20	July By *Ballance*, transported thither to conclude this	13	947	2	1
			Summe	L	2903	13	—

	Jour.	Day	*Stock* is Debitor.	Fol.	L	S	D
1633.	1	1	Janu. By Cash, for several coynes of mony	1	1000	15	7
	1	—	Dito By Wares for sundry sorts unsold	1	477	10	—
	1	—	Dito By Kettles for 5. Barrels unsold	2	55	—	6
	1	—	Dito by *Jean du Boys* at Roan my account Currant	2	240	—	—
	1	—	Dito By *Jacob Symonson* my account by him in company	2	229	—	—
	1	—	Dito By *Jacob Symonson* his account of Couchaneille	3	3	17	8
1634.	19	20	July By Profit and Losse, gained by this handle	7	1046	8	10
			Summe	L	3052	12	7

	Jour.	Day	*Wares* are Creditors.	L	B	Fol.	L	S	D
1633.	2	13	Janua. By Kersies in company, by me layd in	..	90	4	270	—	—
	6	21	March By *Jacob Symonson*, sold to him	60	..	2	300	—	—
			Summe	60	90	L	570	—	—

Dissent and Typological Equivalence

Repeatedly in Williams' writing, economic and religious lessons and language reinforce and clarify each other—such as when the final poem in his chapter "Of Debts and Trusting" parallels debt to sin and warns against the danger and terror of dying with "*sinnes unpaid*" (*K* 223). Most Williams scholarship, however, has divorced his theology from his economics in the attempt to understand the source of his dissent. Sacvan Bercovitch initiated a significant shift in Williams studies when he insisted long ago that what differentiated Williams from other Puritans was not, as Miller had argued, his use of typology but the kind of typology he used. Cotton and other orthodox Puritans employed a historical or "horizontal" form of typology, which not only established parallels between Old Testament types and their antitypes in the New Testament, but which extended a "literal parallel between the biblical chosen people and the children of Israel in New England" (Bercovitch, "Typology" 173). Williams rejected this latter extension of typology to secular history, maintaining that once the Old Testament type was fulfilled in the New, it was effectively completed and could not validly be used to predict the future or interpret the present.[15]

Jesper Rosenmeier locates the Cotton-Williams dispute not in typology but in the two men's contrasting views on Christ's incarnation, setting Cotton's assertion that the flesh and spirit must remain united in anticipation of Christ's coming against Williams' claims that they must remain separate, that, for him, "flesh and spirit, spoke completely different languages" ("Teacher" 421). Reiner Smolinski turns instead to the two men's "conflicting eschatological theories on Christ's Second Coming" (63), explaining that whereas Cotton believed in "the continuity of the Church throughout the centuries, Williams insisted on nothing less than complete disjuncture" (85). Cotton's continuity permitted him to work to anticipate the pure church in a way that Williams rejected for the purely divine will that would usher in the millennium. Thus, whereas Cotton wanted to "implement in New England the prophetic exemplum in anticipation of the New Earth" (89), Williams refused to spell out what he could not see.[16]

It is, of course, worth noting here the ways in which typology itself is a form of hermeneutics that relies on establishing equivalencies, and Williams' typology may finally reveal a sensibility as trade-oriented as it is Bible-oriented. Clearly, all three theories oppose Williams' disjuncture and separation to Cotton's continuity and union; all share Williams' insistence on a temporal inequivalence that rejects Cotton's inclination to, as Smolinski puts it, "misread temporal as eternal institutions" (73). Bercovitch calls Williams' approach allegorical, Augustinian, or "vertical" typology, and this latter term emphasizes a synchronic temporality that refuses incorporation into a "horizontal" or progressive narrative. But while Williams may have distinguished himself from the Puritan orthodoxy by reviving Augustinian typology, he more obviously distinguished himself from other Puritan New England divines by engaging in colonial trade. Indeed, Roger Williams' representation of economic equivalence is surprisingly homologous to his views on typological equivalence. Typology was, for Williams, documentary rather than predictive, just like the exchanges in traders' account books or the translations in his *Key into the Language of America*. The continuity and predictability of economic value, linguistic meaning, and religious truth were equally subject to unpredictable forms of historical, cultural, linguistic, and geographical inconstancy.

For Williams the former-minister-become-witness, the continuity and predictability of religious truth was just as limited; in *The Bloudy Tenent* especially he frequently notes the changeability of both the church and individual believers. Using the biblical parable that was central to his debate with Cotton, he explains that

> they who now are *Tares*, may hereafter become *Wheat*; they who are now *blinde*, may hereafter *see*; they that now *resist* him, may hereafter *receive* him; they that are now in the *devils snare*, in *adversenesse* to the *Truth*, may hereafter come to *repentance*; they that are now *blasphemers* and *persecutors* (as *Paul* was) may in time become *faithfull* as he; they that are now *idolators* as the *Corinths* once were (1 *Cor*. 6.9.) may hereafter become *true worshippers* as they; they that are now *no people of God*, nor under *mercy* (as the Saints sometimes were, 1 *Pet*. 2.20) may hereafter become people of *God*, and obtaine *mercy*. (*BT* 30–31)

Although its paragraph form differs from the bilingual columns of *A Key*, we might read this lengthy sentence as similarly offering a series of equivalent statements that all insist, in slightly different terms, on the possibility of future transformation. Later, Williams comments again on human changeability and unpredictability, for "he that is a *Briar*, that is, a *Jew*, a *Turke*, a *Pagan*, an *Anti-christian* to day, may be (when the Word of the *Lord* runs freely) a member of *Jesus Christ* to morrow cut out of the wilde *Olive*, and planted into the true" (*BT* 94). God is the only authorized cultivator in this field where briars may become fruitful plants, tares may become wheat or corn, pagans may become Christian.[17] Against Cotton's argument that when the difference between tares and wheat is clear, the latter can and should be removed, Williams retorts that any good minister, like any self-respecting farmer, can easily distinguish between a weed and a crop, but that tares nevertheless should never be removed because—quite outside of the control of any minister—tares may not always remain tares.[18] The minister must then turn in his farming skills for trading skills, just as Williams turns in his agricultural language for the language of trade, and just as Williams would, in the years just after *The Bloudy Tenent* was published, turn his attention from his Providence garden increasingly to his Cocumscussoc trading post.

He adopts the example of trade, for instance, to explain that just as usury is permitted in order to prevent the greater evil of ceasing commerce altogether, so must "the *Tares* . . . be permitted in the *World*, because otherwise the *Good wheat* should be indangered to be rooted up out of the *Field* or *World* also, as well as the Tares" (*BT* 169).[19] In a world of perpetual and unpredictable changeability, mixture and impurity have to be tolerated until the "*Harvest* or end of the World" (*BT* 110), when the standard for judging purity will become clear. Williams was fond of pointing to recent English history for evidence of just how much and how quickly change can come:

> within a few scores of yeeres, how many wonderfull *changes* in *Religion* hath the *whole Kingdome* made, according to the *change* of the *Governours* thereof, in the severall *Religious* [*sic*] which they themselves imbraced! *Henry* the 7. finds and leaves the *kingdome* absolutely *Popish*. *Henry* the 8. casts it into a *mould* half *Popish* halfe *Protestant*. *Edward* the 6. brings forth an *Edition* all *Protestant*. Queene *Mary* within few years defaceth *Edwards* worke, and render the *Kingdome* . . . all Popish. *Maries* short *life* and *Religion* ends together: and *Elizabeth* reviveth her Brother *Edwards* Modell, all Protestant. (*BT* 136–37).

He returns later to this historical changeability and asks, in the context of insisting on the impossibility of finding a true example or antitype of Israel in the present world, "Who knowes not how easie it is to turne, and turne, and turn again whole *Nations* from one *Religion* to another?"(*BT* 325).

Unlike Cotton's expectationist temporal logic, Williams' typology is one *without* a future whose terms can be anticipated in the present. Like the travel writers who described New England for English merchants, Cotton encourages a kind of investment in the present with the hopeful promise of future spiritual returns. Williams rejects this progressivist investment narrative. But even if he refuses to invest, he does advocate the necessity of ongoing exchange in the present—of goods as well as language—while he prophesies and waits for the indeterminate future to arrive. Roger Williams practices not the uncertain certainty of mercantile investment—the silent importation of an imagined and profitable future into the present—but commits instead to relentless negotiation in the face of an utter uncertainty. This indeterminacy energizes his religious identity as a seeker, committed to witnessing and prophesying the twists and turns of truth and error. These motivations help to determine what might be called the seeking quality of his prose, its tendency to list synonymic series rather than settle for a single word, its ceaseless rhetorical pursuit of an as yet unpossessable truth through the rigorous exchange of words.

Prolix and Gnarled

Lisa Gordis finds in Cotton's sermonic style a practiced inevitability that, she argues, appears to represent "the Spirit working through the minister"—a strategic "illusion" that masks the presence of the minister and his own "artistry and argumentative strategy" (55). Cotton's "interpretive inevitability" (58) parallels the predictive temporal logic of his typology; both his style and his eschatology purport to know what is to come, and they import the terms of that anticipated future into the present. In contrast, Williams maintains the fundamental impossibility of interpretive certainty in the earthly realm. As Reiner Smolinski puts it, "[w]here Cotton frequently expressed certainty, Williams admitted doubt" (81). And Williams' stylistic idiosyncrasies—his long sentences and exhaustive arguments, his use of the dialogue form and multiplying metaphors—are every bit as consistent with his hermeneutic uncertainty as Cotton's are with his "interpretive inevitability." The very complexity of Williams' writing seems to insist on his presence, as much as Cotton's masks his.

Virtually every text that Williams wrote, of course, is in the form of a dialogue, a conference, a linguistic exchange, an epistolary correspondence. He published letters (such as *Mr. Cottons Letter*) that replied to previous letters; he constructed linguistic glossaries (in *A Key*) that have been read as dialogic; he organized lengthy books (like *A Bloudy Tenent*) in the form of extended dialogues. And as Ivy Schweitzer has argued, Williams' use of dialogue corresponds to his "notion of fallen epistemology: until further divine revelation, truth is merely provisional, in this world engaged in a continuous dialogue with peace" (*Work* 199). Like the protracted negotiations and extended pursuit of truth associated with dialogue, for Williams economic exchange is characterized by extended linguistic bargaining in search of an always impermanent value. In a passage that evokes Williams' experience of using wampum shells for Indian trade, he remarks on this fugitive quality of truth and value: "Precious *Pearles* and *Jewels*, and farre more precious *Truth* are found in muddy shells and places. The rich *Mines* of *golden Truth* lye hid under barren hills, and in *obscure* holes and *corners*" (*BT* 180). Williams saw his task as witness to search out truth in such "obscure holes and corners," using the tool of language.

But as many of his colleagues and correspondents in the seventeenth century (like many of his twentieth- and twenty-first century readers) complained, his linguistic exchanges had an exhausting and inaccessible quality to them. John Winthrop, commenting in a letter to John Endicott on Williams' now-lost treatise on the patent, complained that "if he allowe not allegoryes, he must condemn his owne writings and speeches, seeinge no man vseth them more than him selfe: and this verye treatice of his, exceeds all that ever I haue read (of so serious an Argument) in figures and flourishes" (*Winthrop Papers* 3:147). Williams himself acknowledged in a 1638 letter to Winthrop that "my lines are as thick and over busie as the Muskeetoes" (*C* 159). More recently, Glenn LaFantasie, editor of Williams' correspondence, reports on his opaque and "prolix" style, his use of "[r]ambling sentences," "cryptic allusions," "torturous syntax," and "gnarled and convoluted" prose ("Introduction" xxvi). Robert McCarron reports that the average sentence length in *The Bloudy Tenent* is 47 words, with some sentences as long as 215 words (72). And while several commentators attribute to him a "plain" (Pooley 196) or "clear" style (McCarron 79) that eschews difficult words or elaborate ornamentation, most acknowledge that his complex syntax and overextended metaphors make his prose unusually difficult and challenging. In contrast to Cotton's self-effacing style, Williams' would almost seem to insist on the messiness of his mediating presence.

As noted in the previous section, Williams' sentences are often extended by their tendency to list multiple versions or equivalents of a single word or idea. In passages from *The Bloudy Tenent* quoted earlier, for example, Williams offers a series of terms ("a *Briar* . . . a *Jew*, a *Turke*, a *Pagan*, an *Antichristian*" and "they who now are *Tares* . . . *blinde* . . . in the *devils snare* . . . *blasphemers* and *persecutors* . . . *idolators* . . . *no people of God*") that emphasize at once the changeability of language within and over time, and its fundamental inadequacy. The multiplying synonyms and alternatives might be read as evidence of a determined but hopelessly asymptotic quest for linguistic certainty. Language takes on, for Williams, the task of seeking the truth, much as the faithful seek the pure church form, or a trader seeks absolute certainty of value. But this search entails a continuous exchange and dialogue, and we often find in Williams' writing what seems like deliberately confusing reversals of original meaning, as if in an effort to resist the temptation of certainty. Consider, for example, Williams' much-cited poem that concludes the section "Of their paintings" in *A Key*. In his careful reading of the poem, David Murray points out that Williams begins by privileging Indian over European forms ("*Truth is a Native, naked Beauty*"), only to complicate this claim in the second line ("*Lying Inventions are but Indian Paints*") and to reverse this new position altogether in the second verse ("*Fowle are the* Indians *Haire and painted Faces*, / *More foule such*

Haire, such Face in Israel. / England *so calls her self*"), before once again privileging the nakedness first associated with the natives (*K* 241; Murray 239). The value attributed to Indian and European, to nakedness and ornamentation, is constantly being reversed, unsettled, and complicated in the poem. Murray goes on to suggestively read Williams' vocabulary lists as themselves poems that—read down rather than across (as they must be by the vast majority of readers without a knowledge of Narragansett)—"form almost random metonymic connections" (240), as it sometimes seems Williams' long, serial lists in prose do, as well.

This repetition that emphasizes variability and reversal is consistent, too, with Williams' insistence in the *Key* and elsewhere on the changeability of translations (see *CM* 32), on the "multiplicity of names and the differential and conventional, rather than essential, nature of them" (Murray 244). In a wilderness world of constant changeability and deception, "the question of any fixed or proper value is thrown into doubt" (Murray 246). If anything, Williams was even more suspicious of language's imperfection and capacity for deceit than other Puritans, and his writing reveals an urgency to witness against linguistic error as much as against religious error. In his patent tract he challenged English use of the term "Christendom," in his print debates with Cotton he accused his opponent of reading figurative language literally, and in *Christenings Make Not Christians* he insisted that the words "Heathen" and "Christian" had been mistranslated and misused. As Roger Pooley observes, Williams' position certainly allows the lively and accessible use of "an image-rich discourse," but it also resists "the kind of intellectual smuggling that such a discourse tends to permit" (197). If certain linguistic meaning, like certain religious truth, could not be determined yet in the present, Williams saw it as his duty to witness against improper or corrupt meaning, but also to avoid false claims to certain meaning, as a way of making the wilderness ready for the coming millennium.

After his voyage in the early 1650s to England to secure his Providence patent, Williams apparently abandoned both his trading post and publication—with the one exception of his 1676 condemnation of Quakerism, *George Fox Digg'd out of his Burrowes*. But this literary history overlooks Williams' correspondence during the intervening years, where he continues his engagement with intertwined economic, linguistic, and religious debates. In fact, Williams spent these years embroiled in the fierce and tumultuous arguments about landownership then gripping Rhode Island, centered largely on the figure of William Harris. One 1669 exchange of letters with John Whipple, an ally of Harris, was prompted by these battles about land boundaries; but what remains of this epistolary exchange reveals an equal (and equally contentious) attention to each other's linguistic style. Williams recalls twice in one letter Whipple's description of Williams' "clamorous toung," and defends his so-called "clamours and crying" by comparing them to "A woman that [*torn*] can not but cry when she is forct and ravished: she that cries not, she is a whore before God and Men" (*C* 587, 588). Whipple in reply clearly faulted Williams "for padling in Such Stuff: viz in Rapes and crying out etc.," but Williams—subtly accusing Whipple of reading his figural language too literally—warns him to "take heede how you speake so slightly and reproachfully of your Langwage of the Spirit of God in Scripture" (*C* 600). Williams is even more explicit about his views of language in a heated exchange of letters with John Throckmorton—another of William Harris' supporters—in July 1672. In these letters, which concern the Quakers, Williams accuses Throckmorton of reading too much like "[t]he *Papists*" or "the *Generalists*" who "catch hold upon the *Letter*" and take it literally, rather than recognizing that the "*Sence* and *Meaning* is in all *Speech* and *Writing*, (in our own and other *Languages*) the very *Speech* or *Writing* it self." Objecting to the Quaker belief in divine light derived from what he sees as their literalist interpretation of John 1.9, Williams insists that scriptural language, just like "our own and other *Tongues*," is "often used *figuratively*" (*C* 657). He objects here once again—as he did with Massachusetts Bay authorities during the 1630s, and with Cotton during the 1640s and '50s—to readings that locate in the material world equivalents to events, figures, or experiences described in the language of scripture. Linguistic meaning cannot be prematurely fixed—in the same way that land was, for Williams, possessed in the present only in a kind of trust for the future.

Even these brief epistolary instances go a long way toward explaining the quality as well as the quantity of Williams' writing, for what is interesting in Williams' replies—to Throckmorton and Whipple as much as to Cotton earlier—is not just that he rejects the easy equivalence of literalist reading but that he sustains that rejection with a rhetorical energy that seems almost deliberately prolonged. In a 1651 reply to John Endicott, Williams maintains the necessity of voicing one's conscience in language, insisting that even while he was banished for his opinions, "my Letters are not *Banished!*" (*C* 337). And repeatedly in his exchange with Throckmorton, he appears perturbed or disappointed at his opponent's curtailed engagement with him. Williams objects, for instance, that Throckmorton's accusations of "'*Lyes and Slanders*'" are unaccompanied by even "one *Scripture* or *Reason* to prove them so" (*C* 662). It is as if Throckmorton is engaging in linguistic trade without using the balancing scales of scripture to ensure the fairness of the exchange, as if he is attempting to deceive Williams in order to make a false profit too quickly. In explaining and defending himself, Throckmorton replies that Williams should "Lay thy hand upon thy mouth and Consider thy Windings and Turnings, in thy Judgment and Practice"—

a warning that points to Williams' own changes in position, but that clearly comments also on his "winding and turning" linguistic style. Williams seems disappointed that Throckmorton does not engage him in the kind of exhaustive print debate he once had with John Cotton, but Throckmorton seems equally determined to avoid precisely such an exchange, apparently cutting off the correspondence after Williams' third letter, which outlines and counters in detail twelve items in Throckmorton's previous response.

Religious history was, for Williams, not unlike an open account book that recorded a series of difficult and fractious negotiations, none of which, however, could reliably be assumed to predict the final form of the true church. To make false predictions based on a knowledge that was temporary at best risked dying with debts outstanding or "sinnes unpaid." Therefore dissent was for Williams, as Lisa Gordis perceptively argues, "normative" (10), even an obligation, and one that took place through language. Roger Williams awaited, with a kind of anxious patience, the millennium and the arrival of Christ and truth; until then, he engaged in a style that emphasized his ongoing interpretive search, a process of exchanges whose final meaning or value had as much to be pursued as it had to be deferred, held in a kind of hopeful suspense.

Dispossessive Selfhood

It sometimes seems that, for Williams, the continuist collapse of the present into the future promotes corruption. If present nations proceed as if they are the antitype of Israel, and collapse the civil and spiritual realms by putting "to death all, both men and women, great and small, . . . What a world of hypocrisie from hence is practised by thousands, that for feare will stoope to give that God their bodies in a forme, whom yet in truth their hearts affect not?" (*BT* 329). Intolerance—bred by falsely equating the present with the unseeable future—encourages hypocrisy, the performance of outward forms that are discontinuous with inward truth. But at other times this causality seems inverted, so that material corruption promotes this temporal collapse. Williams often accuses his interlocutors, for example, of contamination by the temptations of the material world, such as accepting payment from unconverted church members: "Compell them to *Masse* (say the *Papists*:) compell them to Church and Common prayer, say the *Protestants*: Compell them to the *Meeting*, say the *New English*. In all these *compulsions* they disagree amongst themselves: but in this, *viz*. Compell them to pay[;] in this they all agree" (*BT* 300). Truth maintains that although ministers, like laborers, are entitled to economic support, that support must first of all come only from "them that hire him, from the *Church*, to whom he laboureth or ministereth, not from the *Civill State*: no more then the Minister of the Civill State is worthy of his hire from the Church" (*BT* 304), and even then such support must represent "the free and willing contribution of the Saints" (*BT* 304–5). Williams believed that ministers should be laborers who "must not thinke much at, but rejoyce in *poverties, necessities, hunger, cold, nakednesse*, &c." (*BT* 305).

In the struggle for truth to which Williams was fully committed, the biggest challenge was resisting the idolatrous desire for riches and property:

> For a little puffe of credit and reputation from the changeable breath of uncertaine sons of men. [:]
>
> For the broken bagges of Riches on Eagles wings: For a dreame of these, any or all of these which on our death-bed vanish and leave tormenting stings behinde them: Oh how much better is it from the love of Truth, from the love of the Father of lights, from whence it comes, for the love of the Sonne of God, who is the way and the Truth, to say as he, *John* 18.37. For this end was I borne, and for this end came I into the World that I might beare witnesse to the Truth. (*BT* 13)

Williams positions the act of bearing witness here against the temptations of credit, reputation, and riches, implying that witness bearing entails earthly poverty and painful suffering.

In Roger Williams' rather complex theology, the self engages in the present through protracted and negotiated exchange, but in a very real sense his is also a self that does not possess itself, that instead belongs and is beholden to an indeterminate future. Conscience emerges in the Whipple letter as evidence of this dispossessed self—not in the form of a definitive guarantee of truth, but as an uncertain and hopeful credit toward the future. As most of his commentators and biographers note, Williams clung to and made much of his experiences of dispossession—of health, of favor, of property—almost as if such suffering and pain provided him with a kind of somatic proof of the certainty of his selfhood. This understanding of self seems to have come up against an incipient possessive individualism during the Rhode Island land disputes, for he accused William Harris not just of worshiping God Land but of worshiping God Self—of valuing both land and his self as if both were God.

The arguments about linguistic style in Williams' letters to John Whipple, seen together with the economic and religious accusations made there against William Harris, expose a conflict over competing models of selfhood. Williams begins his first letter to Whipple with a sustained reflection on conscience, subtly urging the young man to reconsider his allegiance to William Harris, who sought to expand his own and Pawtuxet's landholdings through a series of legal and political maneuverings that included challenging the terms of Williams' original grant of land from the Narragansetts. In a sense, Williams remains concerned in this letter with his perennial theme of liberty of conscience, but here his worry is more explicitly that conscience remain free not just from the threats of others but from one's own material desires.

Williams compares Harris "and his Disciples" to

> Thieves and cheatours Selling a Silver Cup, a gold ring or a Watch they are content with 20s for 20 pounds etc. (according to the proverbe, Light Come, Light goe). Alas what is 20 miles to thouhsands of thouhsands without bound or limit? just like the Generalists who make Gods Mercy and Justice by their wresting of Some Scriptures (as they doe our writings) to be Nonsensicall Whimsies without any Bounds or Order? (*C* 587)

Harris is simultaneously accused here of parallel economic, religious, and linguistic crimes: of underselling stolen goods for whatever profit he can get, of being a Generalist Baptist (who, Williams claims elsewhere, give themselves permission to act as they will on earth because they deny the existence of heaven and hell [*C* 598]),[20] and of freely misreading sacred and scriptural language. Harris and his allies are illicit traders—in goods, spirit, and words—because they are absolutely unregulated by anything outside their own selves; they function without any external standards or scales. If Cotton made the mistake of collapsing the millennial future into the present, Harris has made the mistake of denying a millennial future altogether, with the result of claiming a virtually limitless self represented by its possessions. Williams articulates this charge through his outraged attack on Harris' claim to a twenty-mile tract of land on the basis of a land grant that entitled him to "Boundles Bounds," a concept that Williams likens to "a monstrous Beast above all other Beasts and Monsters," and that has caused "all the Storms and Tempests Factions and Devisions in our litle World amongst us" (*C* 587). Calling Harris a "Machivilian Land monger" in league with other "Extortioners, Cheatours and Lyers," concerned only with "private Ends, designs and plots" (*C* 599), Williams seems aghast at the apparent limitlessness of Harris' possessiveness, depicting him as one "who maketh Selfe his God and End" (*C* 602).[21]

If Williams accused Harris of having too much self, Harris ascribed to Williams almost no self at all, or perhaps a self so unreadable as to seem inaccessible. According to Glenn LaFantasie, William Harris apparently called out at one public meeting the phrase or question "What is Roger Williams," reportedly to suggest that the founder of Rhode Island had no greater power or influence than anyone else. The statement seems to have become, however, a kind of rallying cry for Williams' opponents, and Williams himself clearly became preoccupied with the sentence and its implication. He repeated it in his 1669 letter to John Whipple, where he describes it as "that Envious Voice" asking "What is Ro. Wms:" (*C* 594–95), and later in a 1677 letter to the Special Court of Commissioners, where he remembers those "Envious and ungratefull Soules" who "cried out What is R. Williams" (*C* 743). But Williams might be stunned less, perhaps, by the stab to his importance than by the apparent denial of his self altogether, for his mention of the phrase always occurs in the context of the suffering he experienced in negotiating with the Narragansetts. Williams reminds Whipple of the "great expence of time, my labours and travells (having no horse) my hazards in Canows and by Pequts and Monhiggins" (*C* 595), and he reminds the court of the "deare bought rate" (*C* 743) with which he purchased the favor of Canonicus. Such suffering and loss is, for Williams, the only meaningful evidence of self-identity in the present, for the true self will otherwise be revealed and determined only in an inaccessible future. It is this dispossessive form of selfhood that Harris and his backers appear to deny with their dismissive claim, but which Williams offers in contrast to the apparent limitlessness of Harris' own possessiveness.[22] Thus even while he maintains a rigorous fundamental human uncertainty, Williams offers his accumulated suffering as a potential credit toward a future reckoning. "No question but all humans Affaires, (the most Righteous and most righteously caried) are subject to Errours and Mistakes," he affirms, "Yet my humble hope is, that God will more and more vindicate my Righteousness." He offers as hopeful evidence his prior "testimonie" of "what I have forsaken and Suffered for his Names Sake," hoping that he will remain "able to retract any mistake as gladly as to be saved by Jesus from the Wrath that is to Come. I have bene used to beare Censures and Reproaches for Truths Sake for reproving and witnessing agnst the Worcks of Darkenes above these 50 Yeares" (*C* 601–2). Williams clings to the experience of his suffering as perhaps the only material foundation on which his selfhood rests in the present, and as evidence of the conscience he hopes will sustain him in the face of continuing human uncertainty.

Chapter Six

DEBT: SALEM WITCHCRAFT AND PAPER MONEY

SALEM, LIKE PLYMOUTH and Massachusetts Bay, began as a joint-stock company. First named Naumkeag, the settlement at Salem was funded by investors in a joint-stock venture called the New England Company, and was first settled by Roger Conant, one of those "Particulars" at Plymouth whom William Bradford criticized for their self-interested lack of commitment to the "General" good of the company. After abandoning Plymouth, Conant first spent time at a fishing and trading settlement called Cape Ann, an enterprise that was funded by the joint-stock Dorchester Company. After that economic venture failed, he joined the New England Company project and moved to Naumkeag. One of the principal stockholders in both the Dorchester and New England Companies was the West Country minister John White, who was also an active advocate for both colonial projects.[1] As part of his efforts to gain settlers and investors for Naumkeag, White published a promotional tract in 1630 called *The Planters Plea*, a defense of colonization in general and an attack on critics of the new venture.

Addressing his reader-investors in the tradition of colonial promotional travel writing, White begins *The Planters Plea* by carefully classifying its contents as either "*Fact*," derived from "*knowledge*," or "*Opinion*," deemed "*most probable*." By advancing his text's arguments as both accurate and provisional, he advocates in turn a kind of cautiously engaged reading that is neither wholly naive nor blindly dismissive. Characterizing his printed words as precious metal and himself as a kind of mint master, White promises readers that he will "*receive backe any light golde that hath passed from him unweighed, and to exchange it for that which will be weight*" ("To the Reader" n.p.). He goes on to represent the failure of the Cape Ann project and the Dorchester Company as a past loss foundational to future success: "as in building houses the first stones of the foundation are buried under ground and are not seene, so in planting Colonies, the first stockes employed that way are consumed, although they serue for a foundation to the worke" (42). The tract concludes by encouraging his "Marchant" or "Gentleman" readers to invest "twentie-fiue pound or fiftie pound" in this colonial and christianizing endeavor in exchange for "an hundred or two hundred acres of Land" and the promise of greater returns in the future. White assures such investors that "their posteritie (if not themselves) may have cause in time to come, to acknowledge it a good purchase that was made at so low a rate: but if they lend, looking for nothing againe, wee know the promise *Luk*. 6. 35. he is no looser, that hath made God his debter" (47). Gold that might or might not be worth its weight, stock that has vanished yet remains as solid as stone, a debt that may or may not be repaid: for all its stylistic plainness and directness, White's prose is nevertheless filled with phantom-like figures. Like so many colonial towns and plantations, Salem began in the folded rhetoric of investment writing that asked readers to imagine the possession of future returns (both material and spiritual) in the place of present loss.

In this chapter, I argue that the spectral qualities of commercial credit relations and the experience of colonial debt form a critical and overlooked context for the historical event for which Salem became best known—the 1692 witchcraft accusations and trials. Just two years before the witchcraft "epidemic" began, the Massachusetts colony found itself heavily indebted as a result of its failed military expedition to Canada during the Second Indian War (or King William's War). The colony responded to this debt crisis by printing and issuing the very first publicly sponsored paper money to circulate in the Western world (Newman 7).[2] This paper money was in many ways analogous to the bills of exchange that had for so long made transoceanic trade possible, but it nevertheless appeared to many colonial subjects a representational conundrum: it was a relatively worthless object of great value that was simultaneously debt itself and its repayment. Like John White's phantom foundation stone, it both was and was not there. The Salem witchcraft trials and their peculiar preoccupation with the matter of spectral evidence allowed for a concentrated performance of anxieties that registered across the domains of subjectivity, language, and economics, and that were associated with the colony's sudden and explicit assent—evidenced by the paper money experiment—to the spectral terms of a mercantile credit culture.

A number of excellent studies already suggest in different ways the importance of economic concerns to the events at Salem.[3] Carol Karlsen, while focusing on the important category of gender, indicates the centrality of economics to witchcraft accusations when she observes that the women who were tried and convicted as witches in New England tended to be those who owned property, engaged in commercial exchange, inherited money that might in other cases have gone to male heirs, or otherwise took up economic roles and practices traditionally reserved for men. Paul Boyer and Stephen Nissenbaum, in their classic study *Salem Possessed*, locate the witchcraft crisis at the intersection between an emergent "pre-industrial capitalism" (*SP* 105) practiced by the wealthy merchants of Salem Town and their supporters, and the "pre-capitalist patterns of village existence" (*SP* 88) favored by an increasingly residual class of husbandmen in Salem Village, many of whom had failed to adapt to or succeed at commerce.[4] More recently, Phyllis Whitman Hunter has argued that the crisis in 1692 was sparked "not only from resistance to capitalism but also from those marginalized for reasons of nationality, religion, or cultural practices" whose "'foreignness,' their difference, threatened the social order built on both a capitalist and a Puritan foundation" (69). Hunter suggests that it was the tension between this "mobile and multicultural commercial economy" and the community's commitment to "a fixed social and religious order" (69) that set the stage for the witchcraft crisis in Salem, where those accused were often those members of the community who "were in motion socially and geographically" (63).[5] But Hunter offers this division between sociocultural fixity and fluidity only after deconstructing Boyer and Nissenbaum's own division between Salem's economic traditionalists and its merchant capitalists, accurately pointing out that many Puritan traditionalists committed to a stable social order were also merchants engaged in the mobilities of transnational overseas trade.

By recognizing the transregional, transcontinental, and transatlantic dimensions of Salem's and New England's economic identity at the end of the seventeenth century, Hunter's study initiates an important shift away from earlier studies of Salem that focused on the intricacies of geographic and social relations at the local level. But her own analysis repeats, in the end, the tendency of earlier Salem scholarship to overdetermine the opposition or division between accusers and trial supporters, on the one hand, and the accused and trial critics, on the other. The unusual intensity and anxiety that characterized the witchcraft scare at Salem might in fact be attributed to the disturbing similarities as much as to the stark differences between those two groups. As the recent issue of paper money had made explicit, all colonial subjects were to varying degrees increasingly implicated in the complex credit arrangements that demanded understanding money—as well as language and selves—less as objects (like a metal coin) that had inherent value and more as objects (like paper money) that had representational value. In Salem in 1692, the spectral qualities identified in others were therefore also folded within, and such mutual implication may explain why those possessed and afflicted by witches could in some cases become those accused and convicted of witchcraft.

A similar dynamic of enfolding and projection characterizes the earlier episodes of dissent studied in this book, and I maintain that Salem must be situated within the same context of the early modern world-system that I have identified throughout *Folded Selves* as crucial to understanding this earlier history of colonial New England dissent. The witchcraft affair exposes—even more dramatically than these earlier instances do—the structural, global, and economic rather than the merely personal, local, and theological character of such dissent. Because dissent has been so identified with individuals (and their religious disagreements), scholars have missed the operation of dissent within the witchcraft affair, which is generally referred to instead as a crisis or conflict because of the difficulty of assigning disagreement or resistance to particular individuals (or to clearly religious matters). Yet in Salem—as earlier in Plymouth, Ma-re Mount, Boston, and Providence—dissent emerges not as an individualized expression of idiosyncratic difference but as a complex response of resistance to the folded terms of the seventeenth-century modern/colonial world-economy by subjects embedded within those very terms.

The documents and narratives of the witchcraft trials repeatedly perform dissenting anxieties fueled by the spatial and temporal folds, suspensions, and delays of transcontinental mercantile capitalism and its credit culture. Nothing represented these fears better than spectral evidence, evidence of wrongdoings that were performed not by the accused witch herself but by devils who had replicated her form (and who could replicate her form because she had reputedly covenanted with them). In most cases, this specter was moreover invisible to all but the one who was possessed and afflicted by it. Indeed, spectral evidence is the unseen center of the Salem witchcraft affair, which differs from other witchcraft outbreaks in either New England or Europe because it was ultimately less about witches than about the community's use of, response to, and debate about spectral evidence. Spectrality provided an ideal vehicle by which to explore the possibilities, articulate the dangers, and test the limits of a representational economy. It is no surprise therefore that once spectral evidence was barred from consideration in the trials, the Salem witchcraft affair was over.[6]

Paper Money

Questions about spectral representation had already been raised in the very different but surprisingly analogous context of the money shortage experienced in Massachusetts only two years before the witchcraft scare erupted at Salem. After Governor William Phips' failed military expedition in Canada, the colony sustained considerable debt that rendered it unable to pay the soldiers, sailors, and merchants who were owed money after the war. Paper money was printed in response to this crisis, a solution recorded by Cotton Mather in the same chapter of *Magnalia Christi Americana* that recounts the witchcraft affair, and that was also published separately as a biography of Phips under the title *Pietas in Patriam: The Life of His Excellency Sir William Phips*. As Mather and later historians note, paper money provoked considerable suspicion among New Englanders, who doubted the ability of such an ephemeral substance as paper to carry the value printed upon it. Bernard Bailyn notes, for example, that this paper money "was received with distrust and rapidly depreciated. Some of the recipients were so eager to get rid of the bills that, despite the General Court's pledge to receive them at a premium of 5 per cent, they sold them for only 60 per cent of their face value. They were still in circulation, badly worn and heavily discounted, as the century closed" (*New England* 189). Most colonists perceived paper money as somehow insubstantial and unreal and refused to trust it as they might have coin or other money of account.

Not until the nineteenth century in America would such a debate become framed in terms of "paper money men" versus "gold bugs," but the characterizations of paper money and its dangers that circulated in the mid-1800s are already evident in the context of New England's money shortage of the late 1690s. Marc Shell remarks on this perceived difference between metal coins and paper notes in *Money, Language, and Thought*:

> The widespread use of coins, which are both symbols and commodities, may precipitate some conceptual misunderstanding of the relationship between signs and things, but it does not encourage its users to believe that symbol and commodity, or word and concept, are entirely separable. . . . Paper money, on the other hand, does appear to be a symbol entirely disassociated from the commodity that it symbolizes. (105)

Paper money was seen therefore as a misleading and deceptive entity, "an appearance or shadow," that called into question the relationship between reality and appearance, between substance and sign. This association has historically led paper money to be aligned with other figures that suspend the coherence of signs with things, including figures such as ghosts and phantoms and specters. Indeed, as Derrida suggests in *Specters of Marx*—an essay on debt, ghosts, and grief—money is, for Marx, itself a specter, an entity that, like a ghost, represents that which is invisible or absent: "this spectral virtue of money" aligns it with "ghosts, illusions, simulacra, appearances, or apparitions" (45). For Marx, Derrida notes, "When the State emits paper money at a fixed rate, its intervention is compared to 'magic,'" and "This magic always busies itself with ghosts, it does business with them" (45–46). In some ways, those who were "possessed" by demons or shapes can be seen as testing the limits of this new representational economy, of seeing what it might be like to do business with ghosts.

Two pamphlets that circulated together in Massachusetts in 1691 defended the issue of paper money and encouraged their clearly reluctant readers to accept the bills with the conviction with which they were used to handling coin or other money of account. The first of these pamphlets, *Some Considerations on the Bills of Credit Now passing in New-England*, is attributed to Cotton Mather and addressed to Mather's father-in-law John Philips, though intended "for the Information of the Inhabitants" (*Some* 13). In it, Mather condemns and questions those "who Refuse to accept that, which they call *Paper-mony*, as pay of equal value with the best *Spanish* Silver" (13). The pamphlet maintains that the only function of "*Coyned Silver*" is "to furniss a man with *Credit*, that he may obtain from his Neighbours those Commodities, which he hath occasion for" (27) and asserts that paper bills of credit are "less *Troublesome* & *Cumbersome*, then Silver would be; and more *Safe*" (29). Captain John Blackwell, reputed author of the companion pamphlet *Some Additional Considerations*, likewise sought to collapse the distinction between paper and metal money when he scoffed at "the foolish Flout of some, in the Name they put upon these Bills, calling them *Paper-mony*; when all know that a *Paper* signed and sealed may be worth many Pounds of Silver" (31). Both writers repeated an argument made in an earlier 1682 pamphlet titled *Severals Relating to the Fund* that the "Instrinsic value" of coin "is not essential to a thing, [but] meerly good for Exchange," a function that "*Bank-bills*, or payments therein, will effect, to all Intents, as well as plenty of Coin" (*Severals* 7).

Mather's and Blackwell's arguments for accepting paper money as if it were coin hinges on convincing their readers to think and behave like merchants who, Mather reminds them, already traffic in bills of exchange, which "Transmit to Remote Parts, vast summs without the intervention of *Silver*" (*Some* 15). He even goes so far as to recast the relationship between colonial subjects and magistrates as one between factors and merchants, encouraging readers to imagine their governing leaders as trusted merchants with whom they are doing business:

> 'Tis strange that one Gentlemans Bills at *Port-Royal* for divers years, and that among Forreigners; or another Gentlemans *Bills* in the Western Parts for as many or more years should gain so much Credit as to be current pay, among the Traders in those places; yea, that the Bill (as *I* have heard) of any *one Magistrate* in the *Western English Plantation*, shall buy any Commodities of any of the Planters; and yet our People (in this pure air) be so sottish as to deny Credit to the Government, when 'tis of their own *Chusing*: Had the *single Gentlemen* (above named) a good bottom for their Credit in their *Ware-houses*, and are not the whole *Estates* of the *Massachusets* as good? Is the Security of one Plantation-Magistrate, better than that of *All* the *Massachusets Representatives*? (15–16)

Mather seeks to make paper money appear substantial and enduring rather than ephemeral by insisting that such paper has a "bottom," a material foundation, in the very land possessed by New Englanders. Blackwell similarly maintains that "there are no men *of business* through the world, who do not *use* as well as *know* the way of dealing by *Bills of Credit*: How many Credible Merchants are there, whose *Bills* do Pass as *ready mony*, with hundreds of People with whom they have had no immediate Concernment? And shall not the Government of this Colony, have much Credit with a people that *choose* all, and *make* part of it?" (28). Mather and Blackwell alike call on all colonial subjects to behave as if they were long-distance traders, to enter into the network of relations that already sustains the credit culture of overseas mercantile exchange, by using and accepting this new form of money.[7]

But the issue of government-backed paper money in 1690 Massachusetts nevertheless generated not only considerable economic anxiety but an epistemological conundrum for much of the colonial population, as Jennifer Jordan Baker notes: whereas historically metal money was perceived as "real" and paper money as "imaginary," the new public bills constituted "an erasure of this classic distinction. Bills of credit were paper that acted *as money itself*, an 'imaginary' that staked a claim to the 'real.'" Moreover, this money was itself a "communal debt" since it "promised something the government did not, at the moment, have in its possession," and it constituted a "deferred promise . . ." since it operated as "a measure to buy time until the colony could procure funding" ("'It'" 4). Unlike coin, paper money that was not backed by metal paradoxically promised to *alleviate* debt at the same time that it *was* debt. It asked colonists to place sufficient trust in its present representation as to make that representation become real in the future. It encouraged its possessors to fold time, to imagine that they possessed already what an unarrived future promised to bring. Like earlier colonial travel writers addressing their doubting investor-readers,

Cotton Mather and John Blackwell charge New Englanders with an unnecessary and harmful skepticism. They attribute this skepticism, however, to the unusual political situation in Massachusetts, which was still awaiting the issue of a new charter following the revocation of its original charter by the king in 1684. Mather, for instance, asserts that "there would not be the least Scruple in accepting your Bills as Currant Pay" if it were not the case that "peoples Heads [are] Idly bewhizled with Conceits that we have no *Magistrates*, no *Government*, And by Consequence that we have no *Security* for any thing, which we call our own" (*Some* 16). Blackwell, too, criticizes those who "plead we have no *Government*, and so have no power to *raise mony*," indicating that it is nothing "less than a *Treason* against the Crown of *England*, for any to intimate, that we have no Government" (24). In other words, political authority in Massachusetts itself appeared to be spectral, to have no material foundation or "bottom," and this phantom quality of the interim government seemed perhaps confirmed rather than erased by the act of issuing what to many appeared to be a phantom and spectral form of money. Mather's dedication to both paper money and spectral evidence can be seen, therefore, as paired efforts to reestablish that foundation or bottom, as an ironically uncertain method to resecure lost or damaged certainty.

Before he was appointed by the king as the first royal governor of Massachusetts, William Phips—who originally hailed from the Maine frontier—was best known for his daring and successful expedition to recover treasure on a sunken ship in the West Indies. Phips returned from his poorly planned but audacious treasure-seeking mission with what Cotton Mather estimated to be an astonishing £300,000 of silver in coins, bars, and plate. Phips' 1687 boatload of bullion is only one of the episodes in which the West Indies factor into the Salem witchcraft affair, however. Samuel Parris—the embattled minister of Salem Village seen by many as responsible for fueling the witchcraft accusations—had also come to Boston from the West Indies several years earlier after failing as a plantation owner and selling what was left of his inherited estate. Parris brought with him from Barbados the servants Tituba and Indian John, whose respective confession and testimony were so critical in launching the witchcraft crisis. Once he arrived in Boston in 1681, Parris set up shop as a merchant and engaged in local and transatlantic trade. But he fared little better in this pursuit than he had in plantation management and soon found himself in debt, and was sued in 1683 for failure to repay a loan (Gragg 31–32). Robert Calef, the successful merchant and critic of the witchcraft trials for their reliance on spectral evidence, would describe the then-indebted minister Parris as failing to meet "with any great Encouragement, or Advantage in Merchandizing, to which for some time he apply'd himself" (Calef 3:4).

It may seem ironic that Phips moved from an association with recovered West Indian bullion to an association with Massachusetts printed money. On the one hand, both the sunken treasure expedition and the paper money experiment promised to generate quantities of money out of nothing, and both seemed fabulous and risky schemes.[8] But while the former pursuit of wealth was pursued on behalf of the English king, the latter response to debt was in many ways the result of Phips' relationship with New England merchants, who exercised increasing political authority in New England during the late seventeenth century. As Bernard Bailyn notes, long before Phips' arrival, merchants gained considerable control in the colony; they "came into immediate control of the colony's Council" (*New England* 175) in May 1686, and their power strengthened after the April 1689 rebellion against Andros, particularly when—following the new 1691 Massachusetts charter and the appointment of a royal government in New Hampshire—the council was reinstituted "as the political voice of the merchants in the centers of New England commerce" (176). Because they tended also to control so much of the colony's very limited supply of money (most of which returned to England, where it helped to foster a positive balance of trade), these merchants also exerted considerable power over credit terms and prices (Gragg 25).

In fact, most of the silver that came into New England came from the Caribbean islands, where New England merchants engaged in a profitable fish market. As Ian Steele observes, at the end of the seventeenth century most of the ships trading to Barbados came from the New World, predominantly from New England (26). Thus while ships left from Salem carrying fish and other goods to the West Indies, ships also arrived in New England bringing silver and bills of exchange as well as people like Samuel Parris and his slaves. The paper money experiment replicated the instruments of such long-distance mercantile commerce in an attempt to repay debts that were due, in part, to merchants, who had been strong supporters of Phips' military expeditions. Phips' first campaign at Port Royal, for instance, had been funded by merchants eager to gain greater control over a region where they had experienced great trade losses to the French (Barnes 289). His success at Port Royal in turn prompted support for the bolder plan of conquering Canada, an expedition that ended, however, with the profound losses that the paper money plan attempted to recoup.

Even Cotton Mather saw the fates of New England and the West Indies as intertwined in shared spiritual and economic ways during these years. In a passage from *Wonders of the Invisible World* that betrays his own transregional consciousness, Mather remarks on the "*Earthquake* that has lately happened at *Jamaica*; an horrible *Earthquake*, whereby the *Tyrus* of the English *America* was at once pull'd into the Jaws of the Gaping and Groaning

Earth, and many Hundreds of the Inhabitants buried alive. The Lord sanctifie so dismal a Dispensation of his Providence unto all the *American* Plantations!" (*W* 78).[9] He later worries about "how much the way of living in many parts of *America*, is utterly inconsistent with the very Essentials of *Christianity*" (*W* 97), a concern perhaps that the reputation of the West Indian islands as sites of great wealth and great dissipation might be penetrating and infecting New England as well. Mather repeats this worry in a 1692 letter to John Cotton included in his *Diary*, where he describes the Jamaican earthquake as erupting "on a fair day" when "the sea suddenly swell'd, and the Earth shook, and broke in many places; and in a Minutes time, the Rich Town of Port-Royal, the *Tyrius* of the whole English America, but a very Sodom for Wickedness, was immediately swallow'd up." He notes that "Some of our poor N.E. people are Lost in the Ruines, and others have their Bones broke," and interprets the event as "an Accident speaking to all our English America" (*D* 143). The witchcraft accusations then spreading in Salem were evidence that an earthquake of another kind had erupted in his own English American colony, threatening the destruction of New England.

Border and Body Violations

When he sought investors for it in 1630, John White had imagined Salem as a farming community, but by the end of the seventeenth century the town had become an important commercial site within an extensive and far-ranging network of trade that, as Phyllis Whitman Hunter explains, "extended to and from the West Indies, Spain, Portugal, France, and England, as well as up and down the colonial coastline" (33). Fish along with fur and timber were regularly exported from Salem to Europe and the Caribbean in exchange for imported raw materials, finished goods, and currency, as well as indentured servants and slaves. Salem had become a significant node within a circumatlantic trade circuit where ships, goods, people, and money constantly arrived, exchanged hands, and departed. In his descriptions of the witchcraft crisis, Mather's language repeatedly suggests that it was precisely by means of such perforations that the devil had entered the colony.

In his 1693 account of the witchcraft outbreak, *The Wonders of the Invisible World*, Cotton Mather frequently describes the devil's attack on the promised land of New England in the dramatic terms of penetration.[10] He writes, "The usual *Walls* of defence about mankind have such a Gap made in them, that the very *Devils* are broke in upon us, to seduce the *Souls*, torment the *Bodies*, sully the *Credits*, and consume the *Estates* of our Neighbours, with Impressions both as *real* and as *furious*, as if the *Invisible* World were becoming *Incarnate*" (*W* 101). Mather employs similar language in his earlier *Memorable Providences* when he proclaims that "hellish Witches are permitted to break thorough [*sic*] the Hedge which our Heavenly Father has made about them that seek Him" (*MP* 131), and in his later report on the possession of Margaret Rule when he announces that the "Devils have with most horrendous operations broke in upon our Neighborhood" (Calef 2:46). The body of the colony has been penetrated and occupied by foreign invaders, such that "the present Sufferings of the Country are the effects of *horrible Witchcrafts*" (*W* 162). Mather bemoans the descent of "The Body of the People" into "*Swearing, Sabbath-breaking, Whoring, Drunkenness*, and the like" (*W* 12) and warns that devils inhabit witches with the design of "sink[ing] that Happy Settlement of Government, wherewith Almighty God has graciously enclined Their Majesties to favour us" (*W* 25). He urges readers to resist the descent into disunity and division by maintaining a charity that is necessary to keep "our Body Politick" from being burned, and without which even "giving our [individual] Bodies to be burned would profit nothing" (*W* 28).

The devil has entered New England through cracks in its otherwise impenetrable borders, and the language that Mather uses here suggests that what is happening at the edges of the colonial community is being replicated on the skins of individual bodies. The decadent town of Port Royal in Jamaica had been reduced to rubble and the bones of bodies there had been broken. In New England, the integrity of the body of the colony, like the bodies of its inhabitants, has been violated by mysteriously unseen outside forces. These bodies rendered porous by surrendering to temptation become open to inhabitation by nefarious others who cloak themselves in the shape of their host. Those practicing witchcraft, Mather explains, allow the devil to be "evermore invited" into their "Service" until he might "become at last a *Familiar* to them, and so assume their *Livery*, that they cannot shake him off in any way" (*W* 24). And despite becoming what Mather calls the "Owners of *Spectres*" by virtue of this possession, these witches also become owned by the specters themselves, who "require . . ." and "compel . . ." (*W* 104) the bodies they inhabit to afflict and torment individuals against whom they may well have neither grievance nor desire for revenge. These images of penetration and infection recall the language of the Antinomian Controversy half a century earlier, and the events at Salem suggest again the ways in which the bodies of women could become sites for the expression and disciplining of the dangers and fears associated with mercantile exchange.

The testimony of those who claimed to be assaulted by these witches makes clear that their bodies were subject to penetrations that they struggled to resist. The afflicted commonly complained of physical symptoms similar to the ones Mather ascribes to the violated body of the colony and its inhabitants. It is hard to find a page from the many collected narratives and documents from Salem that is not filled with complaints by the afflicted about being pinched and bitten by invisible beings, and pricked or scratched or pecked at by such objects as pins, nails, or the beaks of birds. Several of Bridget Bishop's accusers, for instance, claimed that the shape of the defendant "did oftentimes very grievously Pinch them, Choak them, Bite them" (*W* 164), and Mather notes more generally that the afflicted "are miserably scratched and bitten," that "Invisible Furies do most visibly stick Pins into the bodies of the afflicted" (*W* 103). Ann Putnam, Elizabeth Hubbard, Tituba, Abigail Williams, Sarah Bibber, and Susannah Shelden all testified that "the apparition of Sarah Good" (Boyer and Nissenbaum, *SVW* 3) tortured them by "pricking and pinching me" (*SVW* 4), by "pinching me and almost choking me to death, and pricking me with pins after a most dreadful manner" (*SVW* 12), by "biting, pricking, and pinching me" (*SVW* 13). Virtually identical charges are made in virtually identical language by many of the same witnesses against accused witches Rebecca Nurse, Bridget Bishop, and John Willard. A good number of victims also lose control of their mouth and jaws, which are alternately forced open or sealed shut against their will. Mather, for instance, records that Mercy Short's mouth was forcibly opened by invisible specters so that poison could be poured into her body ("Brand" 265). His *Memorable Providences* records the earlier case of siblings whose "Tongues would be drawn down their Throats; another-while they would be pull'd out upon their Chins, to a prodigious length. They would have their Mouths opened until such a Wideness, that their Jaws went out of joint" (*MP* 101). In his testimony against Bridget Bishop, Samuel Gray declared that "he felt something come to his mouth or lips, cold, and thereupon started and looked up, and again did see the same woman [Bishop] with something between both her hands holding before his mouth" (*SVW* 42). Margaret Rule also had "her Jaws forcibly pulled open, whereupon something *Invisible* would be poured down her throat" according to Cotton Mather (Calef 2:32).

These afflictions share as their dominant description fear of the forced puncturing and entering of the body by a foreign object. And the accusers repeatedly offer up their bodies or verbal descriptions of their bodies to demonstrate these attempts at corporeal entry, such as "the marks of Teeth both upper and lower set, on each side of her wrist" (Lawson 153). The accused in turn are subject to having their own bodies inspected, usually for evidence of an extra teat or a "preternatural excrescence of flesh" (*SVW* 31) reputedly used to nourish the body of the devil who feeds from the accused—proof that her body is not entirely her own, that it is inhabited and owned also by another. These accounts of the body's collapsed integrity indicate that formerly sealed boundaries, of both the flesh and the state, have sustained "Gaps" or openings whose penetration has caused New England's people to become "infected and infested" (*MCA* 1:206). The devil convinces his victims that "tho' the *Laws* of God were so many *Walls* of Stone, yet we shall break through them all" (*W* 222–23), and Mather's language evinces a fear of bodies thus become porous and open to invasion from without. He warns against any further "Widening of our Breaches" (*W* 33) and worries that New Englanders, through their sinfulness, have had "too much of an hand in letting of the Devils into our Borders" (*W* 121). Once the walls of the community and of the self yield to these outside forces, not only the spiritual but the economic condition of both community and self are at risk, for once these walls are broken, "Doubtless the *Devil* makes good Earnings of" the results (*W* 226).

The symptoms of those afflicted by witches at Salem were consistent with those reported in other and earlier witchcraft cases in Europe and New England. But those same symptoms—of the loss of self-possession as a result of violation, temptation, and penetration—led to a different kind or measure of anxious dissent in Massachusetts in 1692. Placed in the context of the transatlantic trade and credit relations so vital to Salem's mercantile population, the language of Mather and others suggests an alliance between these suspected witches and those merchants who were repeatedly penetrating the borders of the commercial port town of Salem, establishing often confusing credit contracts with local producers, and profiting from those relations. The problem for those seeking to convict accused witches was therefore similar to those seeking to escape indebtedness: if the agents of this spiritual/economic penetration seemed able to shift shape, take on the bodies and forms of others, even become invisible, how could such indeterminate selves be identified and held accountable? How could economic or spiritual security be regained in the face of such uncertainty? Cotton Mather had just appealed for public faith in the insubstantiality of paper money in an effort to solve the colony's debt crisis. He would repeat that gesture in his qualified support for the trials and their use of insubstantial spectral evidence in an analogous effort to solve the colony's spiritual crisis. And as if they were replicating the practice of printing paper money to fix the problem of debt, contemporary commentators on the Salem affair would produce volumes of printed pamphlets and books in which they sought to establish or refute the certainty with which they understood such evidence and each other.

Money and Possession

Mary Beth Norton's *In the Snare of the Devil* makes a convincing case that the events at Salem must be understood in the context of warfare with the

Northeastern Wabanaki, who were quite literally violating the geographic borders and corporeal bodies of English settlers during the Second Indian War.[11] As Norton shows, a surprising number of figures involved in the witchcraft affair—whether they were among the afflicted, the accused, or the judges—had ties to the Maine frontier where the Wabanaki were raiding villages, destroying property, killing settlers, and torturing captives. The devil who appeared in the visions of the afflicted was often described as an Indian, or in terms that allied him with the Indians, and the devil's threats often resembled the results of Wabanaki attacks on the northern frontier. In the course of her account, however, Norton also makes frequent mention of English merchants who visited the northeastern frontier region in order to profit from trade with the Indians—despite fears that the natives were using the guns and ammunition gained in such trade to kill English settlers. Several of these traders would be among those accused of witchcraft at Salem.[12] By insisting that the 1692 witchcraft affair must be understood "as intricately related to concurrent political and military affairs in northern New England" (5), Norton significantly repositions Salem's events within a broader geographical context that includes all of Essex County and the Maine frontier. Yet given the position of that region and its inhabitants within a transatlantic commercial network, we might press Norton's geographical recontextualization of Salem much further still.

Phyllis Whitman Hunter notes that a "concern with boundaries had become increasingly evident throughout Essex County in the decade preceding the trials," which also saw an increase in the number and intensity of lawsuits over land possession. Witches were accused of violating the borders that secured the community, much like the French, Anglicans, or Quakers, whose language, religion, or social status marked them as outsiders (Hunter 63–64) . But these borders were most consistently transgressed by merchants of varying religious, national, and ethnic backgrounds who did business in coastal towns such as Salem and who were sometimes perceived as gaining money and advantage through deceptive forms of trade, credit, or outright theft. As many of the region's settlers lost their land, their property, and their families in the northeastern Indian raids, visiting traders gained fur that would be shipped to Europe for substantial profits. This commerce was equally vital to the English and French traders who depended on the returns they made in Europe, and to the Wabanaki who depended on the goods and guns they received in exchange for furs.

But this fur trade continued to be "a source of constant friction, for each side regularly suspected the other of cheating" (Norton 86). According to an account reported by John Gyles in his captivity narrative, when a group of Pennacooks and Sacos arrived to raid Major Richard Waldron's trading post at Cocheco (now Dover, New Hampshire), they paused while stabbing him to demand that he "order his book of accounts to be brought and cross out all the Indian debts (for he had traded much with the Indians)" (Gyles 101 n.8).[13] As observed in the previous chapter on Roger Williams, traders typically advanced on credit to Indian hunters the guns and ammunition they needed to capture animals for both furs and food. As a result, the Indians were constantly in debt, and this perpetual time lag in account balancing (as well as the inscrutable price fluctuations determined by changes in the transcontinental demand for fur) frequently led to Indian accusations against their English fur-trading partners of cheating.

The fishing industry centered in Salem operated on a similar credit system that left laborers indebted for much of the year. Merchants offered credit in the form of outfitted and leased ships to fishermen, while allowing their families at home "to purchase supplies on credit" in return for the promise of the catch that would be brought home from each voyage. These merchant creditors would later distribute to the fishermen the profits from the sale of those fish in ports around the Atlantic rim, and begin the process of credit distribution once again (Hunter 42). As Hunter notes, the amounts involved in this system steadily increased, and as early as the 1660s the merchant George Curwen "carried over one thousand pounds in debit balances for eighty men involved in fishing 'to the Eastward' off the coast of Maine. This investment ensured Curwen and other merchants an ample inventory of fish to supply their own creditors in London and their customers in the Caribbean" (43). But just as the northeastern Indians challenged English traders, Salem fishermen often rebuked the merchants to whom they were indebted. Non-English or non-Puritan merchants in particular could be identified by their debtors as unintelligible cheats who "threatened to invade the very heart of Salem" (Hunter 45). Such was the case, for example, with the wealthy Salem merchant Philip English, who was accused of witchcraft in 1692 and who had followed the practice common to his home on the French Isle of Jersey of suing debtors quickly for repayment. Such behavior gained him and other Jersey French merchants "a reputation not only of sharp legal practice and clannish conniving, but also of lying and theft" (Hunter 64).

As Hunter notes, these local credit networks circled within the transoceanic credit relations between colonial merchants and their London backers, who likewise fronted to Salem merchants goods or money that would be repaid once the fish were sold to customers in the West Indies and elsewhere. In a sense, most everyone within these interlocking networks had some kind of almost continuous outstanding debt, but not everyone experienced or understood that debt in the same way. As their complaints suggest, the Salem fishermen or Indian fur traders often perceived their repeated indebtedness as a kind of fraud or trickery: always promised profitable returns in the future, they nevertheless seemed always to experience an absence of money in the present. They were constantly borrowing against a future that never seemed to arrive. The merchants, on the other hand, constantly treated this future *as if it had arrived*, and therefore treated money that was not there *as if it were there*. A tract on trade and money published in London in 1691, on the eve of Salem's witchcraft outbreak, explains this dynamic when its trader-author observes that "The Merchant and Gentleman . . . instead of having Ten Thousand Pounds in Cash by them, as their Accounts shew they should have, of other Mens ready Money, to be paid at sight, have seldom One Thousand in Specie; but depend upon a course of Trade, whereby Money comes in as fast as it is taken out" (*Discourses* 535). A merchant's account book frequently represented a sum that was possessed but could not be seen, a sum that existed but could not be felt. This invisible yet real money could—especially for those unfamiliar with accommodating the lags of time and distance that constituted the early modern transcontinental credit system—look decidedly spectral.

Those afflicted by accused witches repeatedly testified that the invisible beings who pinched, bit, and pricked their skin would proceed to offer and urge them to sign a book. Sarah Good's "apparition," for instance, begged Ann Putnam "to write in her book" (*SVW* 3), and Rebecca Nurse reportedly brought to Putnam "a little red book in her hand and a black pen, urging me vehemently to write in her book" (*SVW* 19). Mercy Lewis accuses John Willard of "threatening to kill if I would not write in his book" (*SVW* 57), while John Hathorne asks Bridget Bishop why she or her "likeness" approaches victims and "tempts them to write in the book" (*SVW* 38). Much has been made in analyses of the Salem witchcraft affair of this spectral book offered to the afflicted for their signatures to seal their covenant with the devil. This book has conventionally been understood in religious terms, as an inversion of the Bible or of the church covenant book, or sometimes as a French Catholic treatise.[14] Others suggest its evocation of contemporaneous books on the occult. Mary Beth Norton, citing the work of Jane Kamensky, remarks as significant that the devil offered a book rather than merely a piece of paper, suggesting an "obsession with books (especially small, easily concealed ones) evident in the Salem records" that corresponded with "an explosion in the availability of such volumes after the mid-1680s," including popular imported volumes on astrology and fortune-telling (Norton 52).[15]

Yet no one has noted the possibility that this devil's book might also correspond to another kind of book that would have been very familiar to colonial inhabitants: the account books of traders like Richard Waldron. It was only a few years after the enraged Indians in 1689 demanded that their names and debts be erased from Waldron's book that reports began to circulate and multiply about the devil's efforts to get Salem-area residents (many of whom were dispossessed wartime refugees from the northcountry region where Waldron lived) to inscribe their names in his book. And at the same time, the colonial issue of paper money emphasized the entrance of all colonial subjects into relations of long-term indebtedness that they were urged to perceive as financial stability. While it is the case that the devil was often described as an Indian, it might also be the case that those possessed by witches at Salem saw themselves, like Waldron's Indian fur trappers did, as defrauded debtors who had in some sense lost possession of their very selves, who had become inhabited by the insubstantiality of paper credit, and who then projected onto others the representational shiftiness long associated with merchant-investors. Consider Cotton Mather's significant description of the devil who tempts and taunts the possessed Mercy Short by offering her a "Book, [that is] somewhat long and thick (Like the wast-books of many Traders)" ("Brand" 262). Waste books were one of several types of account books used by early modern merchants, and were specifically designed to be used by merchants as a means of quickly recording all of a day's transactions as they occurred, in a series of notes that would be discarded once the information was transferred to the more systematic journal at the end of the day (see Jordan 20–21).[16] The waste book was therefore the first place in which a mercantile transaction would be written (see figs. 5 and 6). Those like Mercy Short are of course being encouraged to enter into a moral or spiritual transaction, but it is striking that her would-be creditor arrives with a trader's waste book in which to record and seal that debt.

This instance is not the only one in which Mather's language reveals suggestive links between merchants or traders and those demons who are invading the visible world of New England. In his testimony against Susanna Martin, for example, Joseph Ring reports that "there often came to him a Man, who presented him a *Book*, whereto he would have him set his Hand; promising to him, that he should then have even what he would; and presenting him with all the delectable Things, Persons, and Places, that he could imagin [*sic*]" (*W* 187). Mather's account of the devils entering the colony also highlights their damaging effect not only on the "*Bodies*" and "*Souls*" but also on the "*Credits*" and "*Estates*" of New Englanders. He observes in *Wonders of the Invisible World* that "These *Witches* have driven a Trade of Commissioning their *Confederate Spirits*" to disturb and destroy "the Bodies and Estates" of the community (*W* 18–19). These witches have also attempted to buy the souls of New Englanders by "steal[ing] several quantities of Mony from divers people, part of which Money, has . . . been dropt out of the Air into the Hands of the Sufferers, while the *Spectres* have

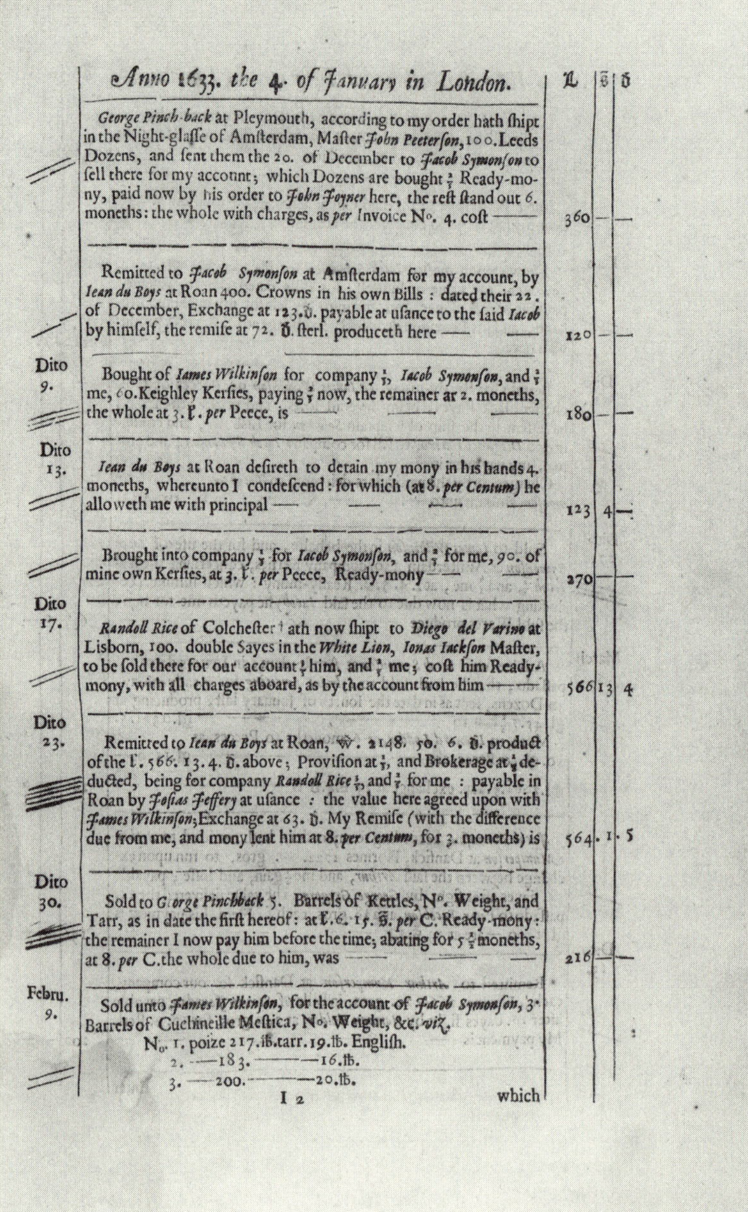

	Anno 1633. *the* 4. *of January in London.*	l.	s.	d.
	George Pinch-back at Pleymouth, according to my order hath shipt in the Night-glasse of Amsterdam, Master *John Peeterson*, 100. Leeds Dozens, and sent them the 20. of December to *Jacob Symonson* to sell there for my accomnt; which Dozens are bought $\frac{2}{3}$ Ready-mony, paid now by his order to *John Joyner* here, the rest stand out 6. moneths: the whole with charges, as *per* Invoice N°. 4. cost ——	360	—	—
	Remitted to *Jacob Symonson* at Amsterdam for my account, by *Iean du Boys* at Roan 400. Crowns in his own Bills : dated their 22. of December, Exchange at 123.d. payable at usance to the said *Iacob* by himself, the remise at 72. d. sterl. produceth here —— ——	120	—	—
Dito 9.	Bought of *Iames Wilkinson* for company $\frac{1}{3}$, *Iacob Symonson*, and $\frac{2}{3}$ me, 60. Keighley Kersies, paying $\frac{2}{3}$ now, the remainer ar 2. moneths, the whole at 3. l. *per* Peece, is —— —— ——	180	—	—
Dito 13.	*Iean du Boys* at Roan desireth to detain my mony in his hands 4. moneths, whereunto I condescend: for which (at 8. *per Centum*) he alloweth me with principal —— —— —— ——	123	4	—
	Brought into company $\frac{1}{3}$ for *Iacob Symonson*, and $\frac{2}{3}$ for me, 90. of mine own Kersies, at 3. l. *per* Peece, Ready-mony —— ——	270	—	—
Dito 17.	*Randoll Rice* of Colchester hath now shipt to *Diego del Varino* at Lisborn, 100. double Sayes in the *White Lion*, *Ionas Iackson* Master, to be sold there for our account $\frac{1}{3}$ him, and $\frac{2}{3}$ me; cost him Ready-mony, with all charges aboard, as by the account from him ——	566	13	4
Dito 23.	Remitted to *Iean du Boys* at Roan, w. 2148. 50. 6. d. product of the l. 566. 13. 4. d. above; Provision at $\frac{1}{3}$, and Brokerage at $\frac{1}{8}$ deducted, being for company *Randoll Rice* $\frac{1}{3}$, and $\frac{2}{3}$ for me : payable in Roan by *Josias Jeffery* at usance : the value here agreed upon with *James Wilkinson*; Exchange at 63. d. My Remise (with the difference due from me, and mony lent him at 8. *per Centum*, for 3. moneths) is	564	1	5
Dito 30.	Sold to *George Pinchback* 5. Barrels of Kettles, N°. Weight, and Tarr, as in date the first hereof: at l. 6. 15. s. *per* C. Ready-mony: the remainer I now pay him before the time; abating for $5\frac{1}{2}$ moneths, at 8. *per* C. the whole due to him, was —— —— ——	216	—	—
Febru. 9.	Sold unto *James Wilkinson*, for the account of *Jacob Symonson*, 3. Barrels of Cuchineille Mestica, N°. Weight, &c. *viz.* N°. 1. poize 217. lb. tarr. 19. lb. English. 2. —183. ——16. lb. 3. —200. ——20. lb.			

I 2 which

FIGS. 5 AND 6. First and last pages of sample waste book, from Richard Dafforne's *Merchant Mirrour,* 2nd ed. (London, 1651). Courtesy of Princeton University Library. Rare Books Division. Deaparment of Rare Books and Special Collections.

Anno· 1624. the 11. of July in London	l.	s.	d.
Transported by order of *Jacob Symonson* to *James Wilkinson* the debts due to him upon his account Currant (which I effect) receiving of the said *James* to clear the account l. 28. 1. 7. d. the whole debts being	405	—	—
Dito 20. Assigned *Andrew Hitchcock* upon *James Wilkinson*, of whom he receiveth (lesse l. 3. 6. 8. d. being forbearance of 250. l. payd 2. moneths before the time) the sum of	51	6	8
Diego del Varino ordereth me to pay unto *Pedro del Varino*, such monies as are in my hands for his account: unto whom I deliver an Assignation upon *Randoll Rice* for l. 161. 4. 9. d. the rest I pay to *Pedro*; and then receive of the said *Randoll* to clear account, his whole debt being	446	1	5
Sould to *Andrew Hitchcock* to pay 100. l. Ready-mony, these Wares following received in date 29. March. 160. Peeces of Figs, poize 40. C. at 45. s.—l. 90. 4. Bales of Pepper, poize 1468. lb. at 17. d.-l. 103. 19. 8. The remainer at 6. moneths.	193	19	8

End of the Waste-book
A.
ANNO 1634. in
London.

THE

been urging them to subscribe their *Covenant with Death*" (*W* 105). Of course, such economic seduction was hardly a new element of witchcraft cases. Increase Mather's 1684 *Essay for the Recording of Illustrious Providences*, for example, tells the story of a young French scholar in "want of Money" who is led to sign the devil's contract in order to continue receiving the money supplied to him by the devil (I. Mather 9–10). A demon who inhabits an English home in 1662 makes—in addition to knocking and beating sounds—"a noise like the jingling of Money, the occasion of which was thought to be, some words spoken the night before, by one in the Family; who said that Fairies used to leave money behind them, and they wished it might be so now" (I. Mather 32). In New England, Elizabeth Knapp's symptoms of possession in 1671 included "sometimes weeping, sometimes laughing, sometimes roaring hideously, with violent motions and agitations of her body, crying out Money, Money, etc." (I. Mather 22).[17]

Money appears and disappears with equal unexpectedness in a good many witchcraft accounts, but the Salem accusations seem particularly concerned with the spectral quality of individual and collective debt. In his testimony against accused witch Bridget Bishop, William Stacey reported that Bishop "got him to do some work for her, for which she gave him three pence, which seemed to this deponent as if it had been good money. But he had not gone not above 3 or 4 rods before he looked in his pocket where he put it, for it, but could not find any" (*SVW* 41). What should be a simple financial transaction becomes illegible and phantasmic, almost as if the conventional temporal progression of such an exchange has been folded over upon itself. Samuel Shattuck likewise reported that he offered Bishop an item at "little" price for which she had expressed "pretended want" but that she then refused to buy it. She later did pay him for dyeing some sleeves and lace, although he subsequently discovered that "the purse and money was gone out of the box" in which they had been locked, "he could not tell how, and never found it after" (*SVW* 43). Susanna Sheldon reported in her testimony against accused witch Elizabeth Colson that she "proferred me a black purse of money and said I might touch it and I shall be well" (*SVW* 56). Those accused of witchcraft appear in these cases to subvert conventional monetary transactions or to generate unexpected ones, defrauding their accusers of rightful gain by giving them income that proceeds to magically vanish. The unbalanced financial accounts that result could be seen as a consequence of poor trading in spiritual matters. John Goodwin, in his 1688 account, explains his children's possession as the result of his own spiritual auditing: "the more God hath been doing for me, the less I have been doing for Him. My Returns have not been according to my Receivings" (Mather, *MP* 130). In the documents and narratives of the witchcraft affair, the invisible demons tormenting New England often appear aligned with those investor-merchants who were comfortable with the prolonged and folded relations of debt and credit and whose participation in and profit from both domestic and overseas trade made them guilty of consistently penetrating the borders of places like New England, of entering "Gaps" in the borders around the colony—much as the witches that Mather and others feared entered the gaps between their world and his.

In their collection of materials related to the events at Salem, Boyer and Nissenbaum remark that colonial New England culture as a whole was remarkably litigious and that "New Englanders of this period went to court a great deal" (*SVW* 137). They caution, therefore, against overreading the evidence of earlier court appearances by those accused of witchcraft in 1692. It is nevertheless interesting, however, that so many of these earlier court appearances concern matters of unpaid debt. Sarah Good, for instance, had appeared a decade earlier in court with her siblings, demanding her unpaid inheritance from her father's estate in the form "of a parcel of land which our father bought at a very dear rate for his convenience" (*SVW* 142). She was sued a few years later by John Cromwell for an outstanding debt from her deceased first husband and was required to pay in "corn and cattle, and cost" the "debt of about seven pounds due by book or account" (*SVW* 145). Eventually, the court seized land owned by the Goods to satisfy this unpaid debt. Court records demonstrate that Rebecca Nurse inherited both land and debts left by her deceased father (*SVW* 152), and Bridget Bishop was forced to sell land inherited from her deceased husband in order to pay some of his outstanding debts (*SVW* 159). George Burroughs was arrested for failing to pay his debts to others, a result of the failure of Salem Village inhabitants to pay his salary (*SVW* 175, 178). The vast majority of these court appearances constituted attempts to settle long-unbalanced accounts, to satisfy outstanding debts. Moreover, when an individual like Rebecca Nurse or John Willard or George Burroughs was convicted of witchcraft, their property and possessions were promptly seized by the court.[18] As a result, the families of many of those convicted of witchcraft ended up themselves in debt, and were forced to petition the court for money in recompense for their sufferings and loss of estate.[19] Those making or supporting accusations were just as likely as those accused to be indebted in one way or another, suggesting the extent to which late seventeenth-century Salem was a debt culture in which one's possessions were likely to be insubstantial or unrealized or deferred. Indeed, Cotton Mather himself struggled with personal as well as collective debt anxiety for much of his life.[20]

Cotton Mather's image of the broken wall of defense around New England, with which I began this section, describes the violated boundary between the visible and invisible worlds. The results of that violation are chaos and disorder of an almost unimaginable magnitude, for once the border between the visible and invisible dissolves, otherwise incorporeal devils can "appear in the shape of an innocent and a virtuous person" (*MCA* 1:211) at the same time that "the most *corporeal* things in the world" are shrouded "with a *fascinating mist* of *invisibility*" (*MCA* 1:206). Elements in the material world become unseen, while elements in the invisible world become material. In other words, the danger posed and fear inspired by this broken boundary wall is not just about invading devils but about the representational disaster their invasion brings. It is a world in which visible signs can no longer be read with confidence, where the readability of signs has disintegrated because signs are torn loose from the things they represent. Mather's descriptions of specters convey both the frustration and the fear of failed readability. He notes that witches "have plotted the Representations of *Innocent Persons*, to cover and shelter themselves in their Witchcrafts" (*W* 21). Those who were tormented by these witches maintained "that the spectres which afflicted them, did exactly resemble" the accused persons, who had been "*represented*" by demons "with a marvellous exactness" (*MCA* 1:208). When the distinction between the visible and the invisible dissolves, how is one to tell the difference between a self and its specter, between a body and its representation by a devil, between, say, Bridget Bishop and the replicated "*Shape*" (*W* 164) of Bridget Bishop? The debate over spectral evidence during and after the Salem witchcraft trials raised precisely such troubling questions about the nature of representation.

Linguistic Deception and Spectral Selves

Samuel Parris decried the increase of fraudulence in his culture in a 1690 sermon when he proclaimed that "[t]here are too many in this guileful and deceitful age who live as if they had drunk in that heretical notion together with their mother's milk, *Qui nescit dissimulare, nescit vivere* [He who cannot manage to dissimulate cannot manage to live]" (43). As Joyce Appleby notes in her study of seventeenth-century economic thought, because merchants were able to manipulate the otherwise invisible workings of new and complex markets to their own advantage, they were typically seen as agents of deception—very much like those witches who seemed to have uncanny access to the secrets of others. Carol Karlsen has noted that of all the charges brought against those accused of witchcraft, one of the most common and persistent was the charge of deception. Witches were guilty of practicing linguistic as well as visual trickery. But the lies of witches more specifically marked a use of language that brought into question its presumed transparency, that exposed a gap rather than a coherence between words and the things they represented. Just as witchcraft in Salem blurred the distinction between individuals and the specters masquerading as their shapes, it blurred the distinction between words that represented the truth and words that merely masqueraded as truth. The difficulty of separating pretense from truth is revealed in Mather's own confused account of witches who "in their Confessions *pretend* [emphasis added], that they are sometimes Masters of" the "trick of rendring themselves *Invisible*." He goes on to claim, however, that this "pretend" confession "is the more credible, because there is Demonstration, that they often render many other things utterly *Invisible*" (*W* 162). It is difficult to distinguish between falsity and sincerity in the verbal and visual performances of witches, and this difficulty seems to infect Mather's own linguistic efforts to report the truth.

If witches shared a reputation with early modern merchants for deception, they were also accused, like merchants, both of keeping secrets and of having access to the secrets of others. In the trial of George Burroughs as Mather records it in *Wonders of the Invisible World*, it was testified that Burroughs "used all means to make his Wives Write, Sign, Seal, and Swear a Covenant, never to reveal any of his Secrets" (*W* 160). But though Burroughs forced others to secrecy, no secrets appeared inaccessible to him. Burroughs reportedly knew the contents of a conversation between one of his wives and her brother despite the fact that he was nowhere near them when the conversation took place. Burroughs claimed to have such knowledge because "*My God makes known your Thoughts unto me*," although the Court suspected that he instead "put on his *Invisibility*" with the help of "the *Black Man*" (*W* 161). Mather's record of the questions answered by Susanna Martin during her trial suggests that this capacity for secrecy often coincided with a kind of remote reservoir within the self of the witch. After refusing three times to respond substantively to the magistrate's questions about what is causing the ailments of her accusers, the magistrate asks her to "Tell us your Thoughts about them then." Martin replies "No, my thoughts are my own, when they are in, but when they are out they are anothers" (*W* 176). Her interrogators believe that she is confessing here to being bewitched by the devil, admitting that the devil speaks through her words. Martin might, however, instead be making a startling declaration about language and its relation to selfhood. Much like Anne Hutchinson's differentiation between judgment and expression in her trial over half a century earlier, Martin's careful distinction between her unspoken thoughts and their conversion into words suggests that there is a failed correlation between her psychological and corporeal self, that her words fail to represent accurately the thoughts they are meant to convey, that her spoken language does not give access to her interior self. Like Hutchinson's opponents in her trial, Martin's appear unable to conceive of a self that is split or doubled in such a way and instead—by collapsing the two versions offered by Martin into a single self—interpret her claim as an inadvertent confession of guilt.

Sarah Good's examination depicts a similar distinction between her internal and external selves as well as a similar effort on the part of the judges to collapse that distinction. When the children testifying against her begin to exhibit signs of torment, the judges ask her:

> Q. Sarah Good, do you not see now what you have done? Why do you not tell us the truth? Why do you thus torment these poor children?
> A. I do not torment them.
> Q. Who do you employ then?
> A. I employ nobody. I scorn it.
> Q. How came they thus tormented?
> A. What do I know? You bring others here and now you charge me with it. (*SVW* 5)

While on its face a simple series of accusations and denials, this dialogue also produces a kind of doubling of the interrogated self. In these questions and answers it is as if the self to whom the judges refer ("you") and the self to whom Sarah Good refers ("I") are two separate selves who happen to be identified by the same name and body. Good repeatedly distinguishes her self from the body that her opponents name and accuse, while the judges insist on the shared identity of the defendant and her shape. Many charges of lying brought against accused witches generate a similar effect of self-doubling or self-splitting. The court records note in the trial of Bridget Bishop that "[t]wo men told her to her face that they had told her" about the confessions made by other accused witches, a testimony that Bishop denies. Her accusers vehemently assert that "[h]ere she is taken in a plain lie" (*SVW* 38) and later they remark again that "you are taken now in a flat lie" (*SVW* 39). When Bridget Bishop herself, however, denies ever having heard the account that others insist she was told, she is not only disputing the claims of such witnesses but offering a version of her self that cannot be brought into alignment with the court's version of her self. The judges' recourse to spectral evidence theory allowed them not only to explain that discrepancy as the work of the devil but to use such evidence to marshal the certainty they needed in order to convict the accused. In defending themselves, however, the accused rejected such certainty.

Nancy Ruttenburg argues that the afflicted performed a new kind of selfhood during the Salem affair that found cultural authorities "struggling to understand what modern society terms personality: an individuality which, lacking a transcendent referent, reveals itself in and as a series of representations, each of which might plausibly support the claim to constitute the truth about the self" (82). Indeed, in their ability to mutate, to shift shape, and to transform, the possessed at Salem offered multiple representations of a single self. Ruttenburg argues that defenders of the value of spectral evidence therefore "found themselves committed to a view of human personality as diabolically multifaceted," and were suddenly confronted with a multiplying population of individuals who appeared "endowed with a revolutionary power of dissemblance drawn from their ability to maintain a vital—and, in terms of character, a contradictory—presence in the visible and invisible domains simultaneously" (37). She maintains that those who rejected the value of spectral evidence, on the other hand, held onto a more traditional and premodern conception of selfhood as stable and fixed. But a careful reading of the dialogue between these two sides of the debate suggests a less simple opposition between their positions. In the end, the debate itself may have spawned an understanding of human subjectivity more startling even than that which Ruttenburg attributes to Mather and other supporters of spectral evidence, for it raised the possibility not of a multiple and contradictory but of a single and uncertain self, whose inconsistencies existed but simply could not be explained, even by the intervention of the devil.

Writings by those opposed to the trials and their use of spectral evidence make it very clear that Cotton Mather and other trial supporters were making the mistake, not of recognizing multiple versions of a single self, but rather of conflating into a single self what were really two different versions of the accused witch—the defendant herself and the defendant's "shape," which had been borrowed and manipulated by the devil. Trial critics such as Thomas Brattle and Robert Calef—both of whom were also merchants—argued that any conviction based on a conflation between these two versions of the accused self was not only potentially but inevitably wrong, because there was finally no certain way for human beings to distinguish confidently between the two, between, for instance, Sarah Good and the specter of Sarah Good. Such critics essentially charged Mather and the judges of using spectral evidence to claim certainty where there was none, and what was radical about their own position was their willingness to adopt and admit such indeterminacy.

These critics also turned the charges of deception and lying around, attributing the evils of dissemblance not to those accused of witchcraft but to those making the accusations. The wealthy Boston merchant and Royal Society member Thomas Brattle challenged the court's reliance on spectral evidence in a 1692 letter that promises to "communicate my thoughts unto you, and in plain terms to tell you what my opinion is of Salem proceedings" (170). Brattle characterizes not the accused but the afflicted as unreliable witnesses who have been caught telling "flat lyes, or contradictions" and whose testimony cannot be accepted as "evidences either against themselves, or any one else" (173). He maintains that the witnesses in Salem have failed to distinguish verbally and visually between "the appearance and shape of such an one (say G. Proctour)" and the person represented by that shape, "as tho' there was no real difference between G. Proctour and the shape of G. Proctour" (174). For Brattle, therefore, the "you" identified by Sarah Good's interrogators and Sarah Good's own "I" must be recognized as two different entities—one is Sarah Good's appropriated "shape" and the other is Sarah Good herself. By collapsing the critical distinction between a spectral self and a real self, Brattle maintains, juries and justices repeat the same grievous misreading as the afflicted whose testimony falsely condemns those on trial.

Unlike the accusers or the judges, Brattle insists on registering the vital distinction between the person and his or her spectral representation. In doing so, he does not necessarily exculpate the accused witch so much as he renders it impossible to determine her guilt and therefore to convict her on the basis of spectral evidence. He makes an even more complicated distinction in the case of those who appear to have confessed to witchcraft. Brattle argues that by virtue of being possessed by the devil, these people are no longer *themselves*—because they are possessed "they are not their own men" (173), he says—and their words therefore can neither be credited to them nor accepted as true, since their words properly belong to the devil who is known to "represent false ideas" (174) and to lead them to "lye, [or] at least speak falsely" (188). A confession spoken by a possessed person could very well be the devil speaking falsely through the appropriated shape and voice of his victim. For Brattle then, the legal and judicial authorities of Salem have fallen into the very clutches of the devil by convicting defendants on the devil's own false testimony.[21] Throughout Brattle's letter, the central distinction between his position and those he challenges is his insistence on the potential lack of correlation between a person and her visual or verbal representation, whereas the "Salem gentlemen" collapse this representation into the person herself. For Brattle, the person is not necessarily the same as his or her shape, just as real and direct suffering (for instance, when "the bodies of the said afflicted were really pined and consumed") is not the same as the indirect appearance of suffering (such as those "afflictions as naturally *tended* to their being pined and consumed") (188–89). While everyone involved with the Salem trials agreed that spectral evidence existed, opponents of the trials objected to the court's acceptance of such evidence as true—or even as indirect confirmation of the truth of other testimony (as Cotton Mather insisted such evidence should be used).

Another way of putting this distinction is to say that for Mather and other trial supporters, spectral evidence provided one means toward arriving at certainty, whereas for Brattle and other trial critics, spectral evidence confirmed human uncertainty. Interestingly, both groups turned to the emergent discourse and methods of science in order to make their radically different claims. The debates about truth and the credibility of evidence and testimony gathered during the trials themselves were replicated in the letters and narratives about the trials, which sought to discredit each other by opposing their own "truth" to the "lies" of their opponents. Brattle asserts, for instance, that what he has to say "is truth, and that I can bring you many credible persons to witnessse it, who have been eye and ear wittnesses to these things" (173). Deodat Lawson, author of the 1692 *Brief and True Narrative*, insists that the information in his volume was "made by a Credible Eye-witness" (152) and "is the summ of what I either saw my self, or did receive Information from persons of undoubted Reputation and Credit" (161). Cotton Mather scrupulously introduces each anecdote in his *Memorable Providences* with attestations of truth, describing them as events that are "credibly Related and Attested" (*MP* 135), "*which many were Eye-witnesses of*" (*MP* 137) and who therefore "express . . . Attestation to the Truth of it" (*MP* 126). When he calls these events "so undoubted and so wonderful" (*MP* 141), he sounds like Christopher Columbus characterizing New World marvels as at once unbelievable and true. He presents himself as "an Eye-witness" to his account of the possessed Goodwin children, which includes "nothing but what I judge to be true," and he "challenge[s] all men to detect so much as one designed Falshood, yea, or so much as one important Mistake," for he has "Writ as plainly as becomes an Historian, as truly as becomes a Christian, tho perhaps not so profitably as became a Divine" (*MP* 123). Mather criticizes those "sensual Sadducees" who would "credit nothing but what they see and feel" (*MP* 95), yet as a historian he observes a Baconian and Boylean scientific practice of repeating "Experiments" in order to verify their truth in front of "Witnesses not a few" (*MP* 113), and more than once insists that he "carefully caus[ed] the Repetition of the Experiment" (*MP* 104) in order to assure its accuracy.[22]

Writers spent an equal amount of time challenging the truth of their critics as they did defending their own. Everyone maintained that they were telling the truth and everyone accused others of lying. These cross-accusations surely reached their height in Robert Calef's *More Wonders of the Invisible World* (1700), a collection of letters and documents that challenged Cotton Mather and the trials he had defended in his own *Wonders*. Calef's title parodies Mather's by investing the word "wonder" with the kind of skepticism that followed early travel reports by Columbus or Ralegh, and by suggesting that it is the words of Mather rather than the works of witches that are wondrous. But the form of the two books, *Wonders* and *More Wonders*, is nevertheless essentially the same: both are documentary collections of evidence gathered from a variety of sources and organized to support their central, though contrasting, claims. At the center of both books are the trial records of five accused and convicted witches, abstracted by Mather and repeated by Calef, and offered by both as the central documentary evidence for their cases. Mather concludes the presentation of these trials and the introduction of additional evidence with the reassurance that he "shall Report nothing but with Good Authority, and what I would invite all my Readers to examine, while 'tis yet Fresh and New, that if there be found any mistake, it may be as willingly *Retracted*, as it was unwillingly *Committed*" (*W* 201). Calef, as if taking up this very invitation, re-presents Mather's own words and evidence—framed by different documentary materials—to argue that *Wonders of the Invisible World* and other writings by Mather are themselves spectral creations that cannot be trusted as an accurate representation of reality.

More Wonders is in some ways constructed like a scientific experiment. It begins by inviting in those readers who are "*willing to Distinguish between Truth and Error*" (2:3). The first half of the book, which includes Cotton Mather's account of the possession of Margaret Rule and correspondence between Mather and others, ends with an epistolary debate about witchcraft between Calef and an unnamed gentleman, after which Calef admits that "*the great question in these controverted points still is, what is truth*" (2:187). That admission is followed by a section titled "*An Impartial Account of the most Memorable Matters of Fact, touching the supposed Witchcraft in* New-England" (3:3), which narrates the trials through a collection of letters and declarations as well as by reprinting the trial summaries from Mather's own *Wonders of the Invisible World*. But this half of the book suggests instead that what appears to be "matters of fact" and "impartial accounts" may not be either. After reprinting Mather's trial narratives from *Wonders* in his own *More Wonders*, Calef isolates selected passages from Mather's language to suggest that the divine's claims to impartiality are suspect. Quoting Mather's text, Calef notes that he describes Susanna Martin as "[']one of the most impudent, scurrilous, wicked Creatures in the World[']" and that he calls Martha Carrier "[']a *Rampant Hag*[']"—textual evidence that for Calef reveals that Mather "wrote more like an Advocate than an Historian" (3:122). Elsewhere in this section, Calef suggests that a similar problem beset the trials themselves, where words were often endowed with a premature certainty of meaning. He includes, for instance, a declaration by convicted witch Rebecca Nurse arguing that the court incorrectly "*took up my words*" (3:37) when she gave her testimony. This declaration is joined by one from a member of the jury who retrospectively admits that he accepted her words as evidence against her by too quickly determining their meaning, admitting now that he "*could not tell how to take her words . . . till she had a further opportunity to put her Sense upon them*" (3:36).

The last part of *More Wonders* is an extended critique of Cotton Mather's biography of William Phips, which Calef characterizes as hyperbolic and self-promotional. He accuses the divine of writing about Phips with "Rhetorical flourishes, and affected strains" at the expense of "*Integrity, Prudence*, and *Veracity*" (3:139). The result of such exaggeration is what Calef calls "a multitude of Misrepresentations," which he lists in direct quotations cited by particular page numbers from Mather's volume (3:139–40). Written language can itself be spectral, Calef suggests. He refuses to accept spectral evidence as legal currency, and indeed once such currency was no longer permitted to circulate in the courtroom, the trials and the Salem witchcraft affair were over.

Mather's support for paper money, like his support for the material individualist success of William Phips or his interest in science and scientific method, have seemed to many incongruent with his commitment to an older covenantal Puritanism. Jennifer Jordan Baker maintains that both Phips and paper money presupposed for Mather a kind of hopeful "economic commonwealth" that demanded "mutual obligation" and "binding relationships between parties" ("'It'" 7) that were consistent with Mather's disposition toward spiritual affairs.[23] Breitwieser argues that Mather's support for Phips and paper money functioned as a form of inoculation against the greater dangers of individualism and modernity. Both explanations work to suggest the ways in which paper money—much like spectral evidence—offered a paradoxically uncertain means to arrive at certainty, to promise the restoration of a "bottom" to the phantasmic political, legal, and economic status of New England in 1692.

It has often been said that no early American event has been subject to quite as many scholarly interpretations as the Salem witchcraft affair. But this critical legacy of Salem in many ways repeats the central terms of the original event itself: just as accusations of witchcraft and experiences of affliction seemed to multiply furiously over the months of 1692, theories aiming to understand what those accusations and experiences really meant have consistently multiplied since then. The witchcraft scare prompted contemporaries to explain a series of curious and inexplicable effects that had no apparent or visible causes, and a long train of Salem scholars have largely repeated this same hermeneutic enterprise. By linking Salem's witchcraft scare with the fears associated with the contemporary circulation of paper money, I have sought not to provide an economic basis for the events of 1692 but rather to understand these two events as paired responses to the paradigm shift that

Michel Foucault has described as a transition from a Renaissance episteme of resemblance to a Classical one of representation, a shift that he locates in the seventeenth century. It is not that writers like Cotton Mather are worrying about money by worrying about witches, but rather, as Marc Shell has argued in another context, that "the new forms of metaphorization or exchanges of meaning that accompanied . . . new forms of economic symbolization and production were changing the meaning of meaning itself. This participation of economic form in literature and philosophy, even in the discourse about truth, is defined . . . by the tropic interaction between economic and linguistic symbolization and production" (4). Spectral evidence and paper money posed the same representational dilemmas even as they promised to restore inviolable borders and certain foundations to a colony whose semiperipheral location in the capitalist world-system made it continuously penetrated by travelers and traders and their languages of credit. The language of the witchcraft documents reveals a set of concerns—with violated borders, invisible shapes, credibility, deception, and credit—that express a deep anxiety about witches, about commerce, and about lying, but above all about the terrifying possibility that all representation has become spectral.

Philip Gura suggests that the witches in Salem (like the Indians in Metacom's—or King Philip's—War) took the place of those religious radicals earlier in the century whose dissenting ideas and behavior were disciplined through "periodic rituals through which the population was brought to understand its communal purpose" (*Glimpse* 228). Gura posits here a transition from religious to more generically cultural and secular forms of dissent as the seventeenth century neared its end. I have argued in *Folded Selves* that expressions of dissent in New England, whether explicitly religious or not, maintain an economic dimension that persists throughout the seventeenth century, and that reflects the uneasy complicity of colonial subjects with a developing world-economy. Although the economic is never the only element to such dissent, it has repeatedly been the element most obscured in American literary and cultural histories.

In this light, what perhaps most distinguishes 1692 Salem from such earlier episodes as Ma-re Mount, the Antinomian Controversy, or the Cotton-Williams debates is not the evaporation of a definitively religious dimension to dissent but rather the demonstrated difficulty colonists experienced in identifying and disciplining a single source and figure of dissent. The spread of witchcraft accusations indicates a failed and anxious effort to locate a definitive site of disagreement, to fix an individual source of transgression. I have argued here that this accusatory circulation is evidence of the extent to which New England subjects had become embedded within a consolidating world-economy of mercantile capitalism that they also distrusted. This implication was given a dimension of public commitment by the 1690 issue of paper money in Massachusetts, and was likely experienced with particular distress in a colonial port town such as Salem, so dependent on transatlantic trade and its mysteriously uncertain credit instruments. The crisis at Salem is therefore evidence as well of the extent to which colonial subjects were dissenting, not only against others, but against unwelcome investments within themselves.

EPILOGUE: ECONOMIES OF POSSESSION AND DISSENT

> Roger Williams set foot in what would become Providence, Rhode Island in 1636. Because he saw water on all sides he wrongly assumed the land to be island. Although the native he saw standing before him was certainly isolated in isolated surroundings, he did not call him island. (Stevens/Aronhiòtas 3)

> [T]he forms and aesthetics that have currency in a given national literary space can be properly understood only if they are related to the precise position of this space in the world system. (Casanova 39)

IN *FOLDED SELVES* I have adopted from the world-systems theory of Immanuel Wallerstein and others a geoeconomic framework that positions the American colonies and colonial writing as crucial to the development and consolidation of the early modern world-economy. That framework has allowed me to identify in colonial New England writing episodes of resistance to and discomfort with the complex and often fearful terms of that emerging world-economy, episodes that have traditionally been read in isolated geographical terms as predominantly theological conflicts or disagreements. By positioning seventeenth-century New England writing within a transcontinental spatiality rather than a protonational temporality, the world-systems model has shaped the argument throughout this book that colonial New England dissent must be reconceived in a number of ways: so that it registers the socioeconomic as much as the theological roots and aims of radical disagreement; so that it registers the structural as well as individual location of resistance and critique; and so that it is conceptualized in terms of the spatial expanses of a transcontinental economy rather than in terms of the temporal anticipation of a national identity.

Sacvan Bercovitch has argued that rituals of consensus are fundamental to American political and cultural identity, a model in which dissent erupts on the ideological periphery only to become disciplined into an accommodation with the center.[1] Andrew Delbanco has suggested that Bercovitch's consensus argument offers "a powerful new explanation for the old problem of why America has no 'left' "; Bercovitch creates a "genealogical explanation for American arrogance" ("Puritan" 352) as well as an explanation for the attendant poverty of contemporary American dissent. Delbanco recasts the Puritans emigrating to New England in what seems to be less retrospective terms when he describes them as seeking escape from "what they were becoming in England—a people fully involved in the pursuit of economic advantage, playing by the new capitalist rules" ("Puritan" 355). But by positioning American Puritans as a committed "outgroup" in an isolated location where they had to invent new enemies to replace the one they had left behind, Delbanco is overlooking, as much as Bercovitch did, the participation of North America in the complexities and inequalities of global economics—in the relations of transoceanic investment, exchange, and credit that characterized the colonial project from the very beginning.

Read in this context, colonial writing exposes the ways in which dissent marks moments of resistance to America's participation in the spectral terms of a global economy.[2] In this view, dissent is not constituent to a protonational "American" identity but the outline of a troubling fold within the modern/colonial world-system and its subjects. Dissent erupts as a symptom of anxiety over the ongoing development of a credit economy and the attendant epistemic shift from a semiotic regime of resemblance to one of representation. Although dissent was often projected onto—and its discipline performed on—particular individuals characterized by their ideological marginality, in fact dissent registers a complex resistance not just from the edges but from the very center of the colony and its dominant ideology.

In her recent study *The World Republic of Letters*, Pascale Casanova offers the insight that although literary value has been positioned largely in terms of national literary histories, it is in fact generated and measured within a world economy of letters and "can be properly understood only if [it is] related to the precise position of this [national] space in the world system" (39). Casanova's study adopts the world-systems model from Fernand Braudel's work on the history of capitalism, which shares much with the Wallersteinian model adopted and adapted here. In many ways, *The World Republic of Letters* borrows the language of economic relations in order to reflect on the production of aesthetic value in what has always been a globalized literary world, more than it brings the materiality of global economic relations to bear on the production and reception of literary language. *Folded Selves*, by contrast, has been less concerned with the history or the measure of aesthetic valuation than with the possibility of developing a more materialist understanding of aesthetics. I return to the seventeenth century and the poetry of Edward Taylor in order to reflect on what elements of colonial experience we might recover and engage by adopting such an approach to colonial writing.

In one of over two hundred poetic meditations he wrote in preparation for delivering the Lord's Supper to his congregation in Westfield, Massachusetts, Edward Taylor begins by asking:

> Am I thy Gold? Or Purse, Lord, for thy Wealth;
> Whether in mine, or mint refinde for thee?
> I'me counted So, but count me o're thyselfe,
> Lest gold washt face, and brass in Heart I bee.
> I Feare my Touchstone touches when I try
> Mee, and my Counted Gold too overly. (Taylor 138)

This 1682 poem expresses Taylor's anxiety about determining his own spiritual value, a worry that the ability of himself or others to measure that value is compromised by humans' unavoidable depravity, their unacknowledged self-interest, and their attendant blindness to counterfeit piety. In place of such uncertainties, Taylor expresses a desire to have God deliver assurance by doing the reckoning, the reading, and the stamping of the currency that is the poet's soul. In the subsequent stanza, for instance, Taylor continues to present himself as a coin and urges God to read the "Image, and Inscription stampt on mee" since he is unable to trust his own "dim" eyes. The final stanza asks that the poet's "Soule" be made the Lord's "plate" on which He might set his seal and stamp his grace, for "Then I shall be thy Money, thou my Hord; / Let me thy Angell bee, bee thou my Lord." The concluding reference to "Angell" here recalls the poet's hope, at the end of the second, middle stanza to be "a Golden Angell" in the "hand" of God—a reference to an English coin that circulated until the early seventeenth century. Thus Taylor's final line expresses a simultaneous desire to be an ethereal, heavenly being and to be a weighty, earthly coin—to have both spiritual and material value.

A firm believer that the Lord's Supper should be administered only to God's elect, Taylor clearly uses the imagery of minting, stamping, and exchanging money in the poem as a way of preparing for and reflecting on the sacrament. Beyond its engaged reflections on Puritan spirituality, however, the poem raises a host of fascinating questions about the material local, regional, and global contexts in which it was produced. How might our reading of the poem be modified or enhanced, for example, by an understanding of Massachusetts coinage, colonial currency, transcontinental commerce, and socioeconomic identity in Westfield—an economically peripheral colonial town? By the time Taylor wrote this poem, Massachusetts had been operating a mint in Boston for thirty years; that mint was established sixteen years before Taylor arrived in the colony. But when Taylor arrived, in 1668, he lived for several weeks in the home of John Hull, the colony's mint master.

Much is made by scholars of Taylor's longing for the intellectual community he left behind in Boston, though few note that when he left for Westfield he left behind the colony's economic as well as its literary and cultural center. He traded the relative pleasures and ease of Boston for the daily labor of life in a small and remote frontier town, where one might seldom see currency that took the form of coin rather than corn, and where a clergyman's salary was subject to constant economic fluctuations. Indeed, in the late 1690s, Taylor threatened to leave Westfield after a number of salary disputes and repeated trouble collecting his salary (Peterson 123, 145). And as Peterson notes, Westfield lacked the mercantile infrastructure and economic outreach that helped stabilize and support Boston's Third Church, and that were especially critical to creating growth in the context of Taylor's high standards for church membership. What kinds of material anxieties and desires, then, might be embedded within Taylor's worry about spiritual overvaluation, within his fantasy of circulating and counting as a legitimate piece of gold?

The word "rustic" has become almost an obligatory adjective to describe Taylor's idiosyncratic imagery and its supposed evocation of the late seventeenth-century town of Westfield, where he lived and wrote. But the word "rustic" can also be seen as a way to describe poverty from the perspective of the economically entitled. And in fact, colonial Westfield was a relatively impoverished town that experienced continued economic hardship. Westfield began as a trading post on a stream that fed into the Connecticut River, but experienced significant underdevelopment in relation to the dramatic growth and wealth of the town of Springfield, founded and developed on the Connecticut River by the wealthy fur trader William Pynchon. Under these circumstances, when Taylor describes the fantasy of being transformed into a piece of gold safely held in the Lord's purse or hand, we must consider not only how the poem uses the vehicle of material gold to express spiritual value but also how the poem might exploit the topic of spiritual value to express a material want.

Writing over three hundred years later, the Mohawk poet James Thomas Stevens (Aronhiòtas) incorporates into his 1994 poem *Tokinish* the language of several seventeenth-century writers, including the colonial New Englanders Roger Williams and Edward Winslow, and the English poet and divine John Donne. *Tokinish* (Narragansett for "wake up") repeatedly engages the language of these early modern writers to reflect on the establishment and identification of borders, a practice that has made the definition of island—and so often of truth—possible. "Is the naked-eye observance of a border / in every direction, the thing we call true?" (3), Stevens asks. The poem invokes the visual theater of colonial geography in order to meditate on the constitution of the self and the body in relation to others and other bodies—but also to reflect on language as a tool for the performance and possession of truth, "as if knowing implies its ownership" (9). Stevens' observation about Roger Williams' differing perceptions of the colonial land and its Native inhabitant—who, though "certainly isolated in isolated surroundings, he did not call . . . island" (3)—might serve on the one hand as a reminder of the global connectedness rather than the regional isolation of colonial America: "Island. / Look to a map to prove the concept mute. All waters have a source and this connection renders earth / island" (3). But Stevens' poem reminds readers as well of the material economic struggle for possession that characterized the continental colonial encounter between indigenous natives and settling Europeans. The inequalities and injustices of that continental struggle for possession emerge too, along with the folded dynamics of transcontinental commerce, in the language of colonial New England dissent.

Notes

Introduction: Colonial Folds and the Space of Dissent

1. This illustrated title page—with its supporting columns and departing ship—immediately evokes the famous illustration from the title page of Francis Bacon's 1620 *Great Instauration*, long recognized as an image of the paired pursuit of knowledge and empire.
2. Although my focus here is on the region of New England, the framework I employ develops out of recognizing that region's place within a circumatlantic and translinguistic literary and cultural field. See Burnham ("Textual") for examples of how such an economic and spatial framework might impact readings of literature from regions other than New England or North America, and in languages other than English.
3. Virginia DeJohn Anderson notes that it cost approximately £25 for supplies and passage for a family of four to New England, which was equivalent to the cost of yearly rent for a family farm or upwards of a quarter of the personal property value of most urban artisans (33–34).
4. Everett Emerson indicates that Cotton composed the sermons in *Christ the Fountaine of Life; or Sundry Choyce Sermons on part of the fifth Chapter of the first Epistle of St. John*, between 1624 and 1632, and that it was published in London twice in 1651 (*John Cotton* 138). Cotton himself emigrated to New England in 1633.
5. This point is overlooked in most anthology selections of the text, which by excluding the pointedly economic sections of the sermon leave students and readers with a biased sense of Winthrop's central concerns and, in turn, a biased sense of American literature's ideological origins. For fine readings of the economic dimensions of Winthrop's "Modell," see Dawson ("'Christian'") and Schweitzer ("'John'").
6. Dawson's reading of Winthrop's text is founded on his own insightful argument that the sermon was neither written nor delivered on the ship as it traveled to Massachusetts, but rather in England before departing (see Dawson, "John").
7. Edmund S. Morgan reviews and recounts the controversy over religious versus economic motivations. Virginia Anderson more recently reasserts the predominance of religious motives for the New England migration (8, 44–45).
8. As Elizabeth Maddock Dillon notes, positioning colonial New England "within this imperial schema, rather than seeing it standing securely at the origin of a new American history, effects something of a Copernican revolution

in our understanding of the New England Puritans' location in the seventeenth-century colonial universe" (80).

9. There are widely varying views on the question of whether, or just how, orthodox John Cotton was. See, for example, Knight.
10. For more on Cotton's aesthetics, see Grabo, "John" and Toulouse, "'The Art.'"
11. Scholarship on the English seventeenth century has, of course, a long tradition of examining the interpenetration of religious and economic identities and debates, most particularly in the significant work of Christopher Hill. The more recent work of Sharpe and Zwicker is also relevant, who argue that "there is no history of literary forms outside of social and political history" (Sharpe and Zwicker 11).
12. For another discussion of the historical relationship of markets and churches in Europe and colonial America, see Robert Blair St. George (382–88)—a book I read as I was finishing my own, and whose project of materializing metaphysics and metaphorizing markets in colonial New England I greatly admire.
13. One earlier exception to this is Agnew's fascinating study of theater and the market. Recent books that pave the way for a colonial literary economics include those by Sweet, St. George, Bauer, and Jennifer J. Baker—all of which take seriously the relations between colonial economics and colonial literature.
14. Wallerstein rejects Weber's thesis that "Protestant theology is somehow more consonant with capitalism than Catholic theology" since Catholicism could be as adaptable to capitalism as Protestantism could be to anticapitalism. Wallerstein sees the alignment of industrialization with Protestantism instead as "a series of intellectually accidental historical developments" (*Modern* 1:152).
15. Various English settler colonies in the Americas served as sources of raw materials and agricultural products such as sugar, cotton, and tobacco as well as markets for "manufactures and reexports," and the usefulness of these colonies became especially enhanced with the development of triangular trade (*Modern* 2:103). See Bauer for a suggestive use of the uneven development paradigm to understand the uneven development of colonial literary forms (4).
16. See, for example, Canny and Pagden, and Seed, who remarks that "underneath the subsequently layered-on regulations governing natives' access to natural resources can often be seen vestiges of the original colonizer's economic aims—a colonial pentimento" (11). I review this literature more extensively in Burnham ("Textual").
17. In his *Two Voyages*, published in 1674, travel writer John Josselyn explains that fishermen separate their good fish from their "refuse fish" and sell both at different rates "to the *Massachusetts* Merchants," who in turn send "the merchantable fish" to various cities in France while "the refuse fish they put off at the *Charib-Islands*, *Barbadoes*, *Jamaica*, &c. who feed their *Negroes* with it" (144).
18. See Peter Taylor 17. Amin aligns New England with other white settler colonies and attributes to them a kind of economic exceptionalism since they are neither peripheral, tributary, nor capitalist (*Unequal* 57) but instead "characterized by exceptionally widespread simple commodity production within its social formation" (*Class* 296). He is, however, significantly off the mark to characterize New England's colonists as "destitute emigrants" whose settlement was "a

by-product of the proletarianization process in England" (*Unequal* 365). Ellen Meiksins Wood, who shares Brenner's critique of world-systems theory, nevertheless suggests that the English colonies in the Americas fit into a unique model of white settler colonialism that—in following the model of Irish colonialism—in fact imports from the outset capitalist modes of appropriation and property relations (155).

19. See Stern for a critique that Wallerstein undermines the role of agency on the periphery; see also Bushnell and Greene (4–8). Brenner, in "Origins," criticizes Wallerstein and others for their "neo-Smithian Marxism" or what Wood, in a synopsis of this critique, terms the "commercialization model" (11–21). Denemark and Thomas clarify what is at stake in this debate when they explain that "[f]or Brenner, the nation-state is the proper level of analysis" whereas for Wallerstein "the world-system is the proper level of analysis" (48).
20. See Brenner, "Origins," for a sustained critique of Wallerstein and others on this score. See also Amin, who seeks to combine proletarianization with long-distance commerce in the transition into the capitalist mode of production. Amin explains that Atlantic trade created a periphery for the mercantilist system in which merchants were backed by monarchs. The incoming wealth in turn encouraged the breakup of feudal relations resulting in proletarianization and the gradual development of capitalist agriculture (*Unequal* 33–36).
21. The touchstone passage for the debate about mercantile capitalism is chapter 20 of Marx's *Capital* (323–37). For debates about this passage and the transition in England, see Sweezy, Dobb (in Hilton), Brenner, and a fine synthesis of these by Ellen Meiksins Wood. For the American debate see, among others, Rothenberg, Gilje, Clark, and Merrill.
22. Fox and Fox-Genovese, whose interest is in the Old South, describe it as "in but not of the capitalist world" (16), "a hybrid society in but not of the worldwide capitalist mode of production" (19) by virtue of "a special case of the general effect produced by merchant capital" (16).
23. Merchants did not necessarily become capitalists upon this transition, however. As Wallerstein notes, in the core countries "there were some merchants and landowners who stood to gain from retaining those forms of production associated with 'feudalism'" and "some merchants and some landowners who stood to gain from the rise of new forms of industrial production" (*Modern* 1:124).
24. The best-known alternative to Marxist formulations of class are those inspired by Weber (see Giddens, *Class*), but see also the collection by Dimock and Gilmore, especially the effort by Amy Schrager Lang to think about class as one of many kinds of "syntax" that structure "the language of social identity" (10). See also Lang's *Syntax of Class*.
25. See Holstun's section "Status and Class" (96–106) for a fuller discussion.
26. Thus such useful studies as Margaret Newell's *From Dependency to Independence* nevertheless rely, as the title suggests, on a progressive narrative in which the colonial period is asked to serve as anachronistic "handmaiden" to a nation that did not yet exist—a fate that, as literary critics have argued, has for long beset colonial American literary materials as well.

27. See also Chase-Dunn and Hall, who seek to revise Wallerstein to acknowledge that different modes of production may exist within the same system rather than assuming that a world system must be defined only by one mode of production (32).
28. See also Samir Amin, who argues that New England was the "model *par excellence* of the precapitalist commodity mode. . . . [which] is incomprehensible as an isolated case but completely understandable when its functions in the world system of the time are considered" (*Class* 57).
29. For an interesting discussion of the oral network of female accounting and exchange relations in early New England, see Ulrich, who notes that although "in the entire century between 1650 and 1750 there is not a single [account book] known to have been kept by a woman" (44), there was "an extensive, less systematic, and largely oral trade network in which women predominated" (45).
30. My formulation here is indebted to Laurence Tribe's fascinating extension of quantum physics to think about the law. By translating post-Newtonian physics into the realm of law, Tribe abandons conceiving of the law as an inert "backdrop" to a reified state and instead sees the state as "a set of rules, principles, and conceptions that interact with a background which is in part a product of prior political actions." Doing so requires understanding the law as a force that shapes and bends juridical space and recognizing that the law has a "*geometry*" (25).
31. Gura admits to the influence of Hill's work on his own project, which might be seen as an effort to exhume and examine the radical ideas that circulated in the New England Way. But Gura, unlike Hill, positions this radicalism not as an alternative vision to the Protestant/capitalist synthesis that came to define the modern world, but as disturbances whose suppression and ingestion made that synthesis possible.
32. I thank Ivy Schweitzer for this insight.

Chapter 1. Investment: Uncertain Certainty and the Economic Subject

1. George Peckham's 1583 *True Reporte* of Sir Humphrey Gilbert's Newfoundland expedition similarly proclaims that after Columbus' return from America, England "became a laughing stocke to the *Spaniardes* themselves." Lewes Roberts, too, notes in *The Treasure of Traffike* that Isabella "pawne[d] her owne wearing Jewels" to enable Columbus to sail after "*Henry* the seventh, accounted amongst the wisest of our English Kings, had unhappily refused *Columbus*" (82).
2. Roberts' book title clearly draws from earlier travel narrative titles like Smith's 1612 *Map of Virginia* and Sir William Alexander's 1630 edition of *The Mapp and Description of New England*, just as its structure appears modeled after famous travel collections like Peter Martyr's *Decades* and Richard Hakluyt's *Principal Navigations*, which are also divided into four sections corresponding to the four parts of the world. In his "Epistle to the Reader," Roberts

even represents his project using travel metaphors. Describing his book itself as a voyage, he explains that "the further I sailed in this *Ocean* . . . the fewer were my furtherances [a standard term used to describe the economic assistance supplied by merchant adventurers to colonial projects] to my wished *Port*." He goes on to note that he has "beene constrained oftentimes in this *Desert* to travell without a certain *guide*, and not seldome to navigate by anothers *Compasse*." Ultimately, however, he has "at least by due sounding of the *Channell*, safely sailed over the *Ocean* afore-mentioned, and brought my *Barke* to an Anchor in *her* desired *Harbour*."

3. For a discussion of the term "mercantile capitalism" and the place of the American colonies in the early modern world-system, see the preceding introduction.
4. See also Richard Kroll, who likewise challenges the long-influential theses by Jones and Croll about the "modern" character of scientific prose, by arguing for the constitutive impossibility of antifiguralism. Markley maintains that plain style promoted an aesthetics for civilized debate that aimed to repress and amend political and social instability.
5. The distinction between these two types of merchants may have had class/status implications, as Lewes Roberts indicates in his 1641 *Treasure of Traffike* when he argues that trade should be divided into two groups, including that which "should bee left to the poore and common people" (51) and foreign trade, which requires greater knowledge and risk and whose "adventuring Merchant[s]" should perhaps be allowed "to attaine unto Nobility" (55). On medieval merchants in London, see Thrupp, whose study emphasizes the indeterminate boundaries of the medieval merchant "class," which often overlapped with the yeoman as well as the gentry class/statuses, and which is perhaps better defined by its differing attitudes toward labor and gain than it is by wealth. Attempts to define merchants as a stable class or status category in any era inevitably set up distinctions that tend to break down more often than they hold up.
6. See Rabb for an account of merchant versus gentry investment in English colonial enterprises.
7. Solomon opposes the merchant-traveler to the earlier figure of the magician, and identifies Shakespeare's Prospero, who is both magician and traveler in *The Tempest*, as a transitional figure between these two alternatives (*Objectivity* 48).
8. The recent series of U.S. corporate scandals at Enron and elsewhere offers a perfect illustration of how the "truth" or "fiction" of the company report is inevitably determined retroactively, within the context of investment relations.
9. Mun at another point claims: "*To make this plain*, suppose a Kingdom to be so rich by nature and art, that it may supply it self of forraign wares by trade, and yet advance yearly 200000 *l.* in ready mony: Next suppose all the King's revenues to be 9000000 *l.* and his expences but 400000 *l.* whereby he may lay up 3000000 *l.* more in his Coffers yearly than the whole Kingdom gains from strangers by forraign trade." "[W]ho sees not then," asks Mun, "that the King will gain more power by enriching his subjects through foreign trade than by hoarding treasure for himself?" (68; emphasis added).
10. See, in addition to Greenblatt, the work of Hulme, Pratt, and Todorov.

11. Here I am arguing precisely the reverse of Wayne Franklin's claim that the New World encounter prompted a *closer* coherence between word and thing (10); it did prompt rhetorical attempts to mimic such coherence, but those attempts speak more to the impossibility of such linguistic stability than they do to its possibility.
12. Misselden's *Circle of Commerce* is no more plain in its style, however, than Malynes' text. Both writers integrate Latin phrases, refer to philosophical and poetic works as a way to demonstrate their learning, and play with rhyme, synonym, and alliteration. But as Poovey notes, the two battle through two competing sets of metaphors: Misselden's balancing scale is associated with mercantile expertise, while Malynes' whale is associated with sovereign power (78). While Misselden places uncertainty at the (empty) center of trade, Malynes desires fixed rates or par that would provide a fixed ground (Poovey 76).
13. For discussions of the mysterious subjectivity of the early modern merchant, see Fumerton (chap. 5), Fuller (8–9), and Appleby.
14. Attacks on and defenses of merchants generally took place through an analysis of their use of language. Like Mun, Misselden defends merchants at every turn and discredits Malynes' claims to possess mercantile expertise. But Misselden carries out this critique largely through an analysis of Malynes' language, which he accuses of being incomprehensible. Malynes' confusing and unreadable prose thus becomes evidence that he lacks the expert knowledge that honest, discreet, and "plain" merchants like Misselden possess.
15. Marius' book went through three subsequent editions and many more reprintings. But it was also appended to a large number of other seventeenth-century economic tracts, including ones by Malynes and Roberts.
16. Consider John Smith's frank admission in *A Description* that despite other motives for overseas ventures such as "Religion, Charity, and the Common good," "I am not so simple, to thinke, that ever any other motive then wealth, will ever erect there a Commonweale" (346).

Chapter 2. Merchants: William Bradford and Plain Style

1. Bradford, *Of Plymouth* 8. All subsequent quotations are from this edition and are cited parenthetically as *OPP*.
2. See, for example, Delbanco, *Puritan* 193–95; Francis Murphy; Wenska; Hovey; Rosenmeier ("With"); Daly; Levin; and Grabo ("William"). See Douglas Anderson for an entirely different reading, which sees Bradford's final list of *Mayflower* descendants as a celebration of Plymouth's increase rather than decline (24).
3. David Read recently argues that Bradford was attempting to create a genre that did not yet exist: the economic history.
4. Most important among these exceptions is Read, but see also Griffith, who attends to the pervasive economic concerns of the text but unconvincingly reads it as an epic that narrates "how the Pilgrims triumph by obtaining economic

sufficiency" (232). Likewise, Hovey describes the book as "a vindicatory account of a business venture" (51), yet Bradford's text is far more perplexed about the business matters it recounts than it is vindicatory or triumphant. Critics who see these business details as evidence of disarray include Daly and Sargent.

5. Reising 36. See also Schaub, and Porter 3–22.
6. See Wenska on Bradford's version of "the American dream" (163); Grabo ("William") on the text's "American specialness" (5); Griffith on the text as an "American success story" that prefigures Franklin's *Autobiography* (233); Francis Murphy on Bradford's version of an "essential American myth" (xxiv); Laurence on the book as "too 'American' too soon" (56); and Fritscher on its development of a "native style" in which to tell of "the proto-American experience" (90). Wayne Franklin's caution against imposing such inaugural and unifying demands on early American texts like Bradford's represents an important countervoice within this tradition (179).
7. I have adapted here a remark by Bradford Smith on the three contracts supporting Plymouth plantation (217).
8. On the Puritan plain style as an attempt to have language conform to "the simple vividness of Scripture," see Bozeman 37; and Bercovitch, *Puritan* 29.
9. Although I agree with Douglas Anderson's description of Bradford's fundamentally transnational consciousness, I part here with his argument that Bradford's book "embraces transformation rather than stasis" (108).
10. For more on merchants during this period, see Kriedte, Ball, and, on New England merchants in particular, Bailyn.
11. Rutman insists that seventeenth-century English artisans would nevertheless have come from an agricultural society (*Husbandmen* 4).
12. For more on merchant involvement with colonial ventures, see Rabb, whose study makes clear that the English gentry also invested in colonial ventures. Rabb indicates that the gentry, however, consistently favored those projects that promised national glory, while merchants consistently chose those that promised profit from trade.
13. The critical connection between Bradford's use of plain style and his Puritanism has a long history. For example, see E. F. Bradford 138–39; Murdock 83; Gay 48; and Howard 257.
14. See Jones, "Science and English" and "Science and Language." As Mary B. Campbell notes, scientific "description and commercial empire were to burgeon together" (*Witness* 261). On the scientific method and changing notions of truth, see Shapin, *Scientific*, chap. 2; and *Social History*. For a useful challenge to both the Croll and Jones assumption that plain prose was antifigurative, see Kroll, who insists, following Foucault, that this style "is conscious of its own artificiality" and its writers "fully aware that to excise figuration from representation altogether amounts to abolishing language itself" (4, 66). This view is in fact supported by those many critics who have noted the stylistic sophistication of *Of Plymouth Plantation,* despite its proclaimed plainness; see Westbrook, Howard, Fritscher, and Ogburn.
15. Montgomery further notes that Royal Society writers compared excessive prose to women, rich foods, and secrecy (87).

16. See also Murdock, and Fritscher. While this explanation for Bradford's plain style is certainly too simple and limited, it does acknowledge the conventional seventeenth-century alignment of plain speech and writing with a common status.
17. See Cornelius 5–22.
18. See Spengemann, *New*; Campbell, *Witness*; Montgomery; and Fuller.
19. These particulars were not admitted to political citizenship at Plymouth and were not permitted to take part in Indian trade (see Langdon 19).
20. Of course, the differences between Bradford and Weston are not nearly as absolute as Bradford claims, since the Pilgrims themselves periodically emerge as participants in similar practices of self-interest and fraud. Cushman's letter condemning Weston and his group, for example, was deceptively sent "as the letter of a wife to her husband" (*OPP* 118).
21. Again, this episode reveals the same kind of slippage evident in Bradford's account of the Weston affair, since the governor and planters are able to detect and bring Lyford and Oldham to justice only by engaging in precisely the same practices of sneaky interception and surreptitious copying of which they accuse them. Yet here, too, Bradford defends his practices on the basis of a linguistic plainness that, unlike the "scurrilous and flouting annotations" of Lyford (*OPP* 166), he equates with truthfulness.
22. Bradford apparently wrote three dialogues, but the second one has been lost. For more on the dialogues, see Sargent.
23. For Bozeman, Puritan intellectuals' interest in Hebrew is consistent with their antimodern "primitivism" (15). Bradford's last known writings—the 1652 dialogue and the 1654 verses—both include passages written in Hebrew.

Chapter 3. Inflation: Thomas Morton and Trading-Post Pastoral

1. In adopting Morton's own spelling of Ma-re Mount—which preserves the name's playful allusions to the sea as well as to merriment—I follow the suggestion of Kupperman and the practice of Salisbury.
2. Bradford, *Of Plymouth* 226, 227. Further references to this text are cited parenthetically as *OPP*.
3. Zuckerman offers a more psychoanalytic reading of Bradford's response to the two plantations, suggesting that "Merry Mount provoked the saints precisely because they themselves were not immune to its appeal, precisely because they struggled ambivalently with the heady desires its indiscipline epitomized" (275).
4. For this reading of Morton, see Round, who positions *New English Canaan* within this and other transatlantic contexts (49–51). For more on maypoles and other countryside revelry in the seventeenth century, see Underdown and Marcus.
5. Philip Round has convincingly argued that the two writers were essentially participating in competing forms of truth telling, with Bradford operating in an emergent mode of civility associated with the new discourses of commerce and science, and Morton in an older, "knightly" (48) mode of discourse designed to exclude readers who might hail from a lower social order.

6. I take the term "public mirth" from Leah Marcus' fine study.
7. Karen Kupperman argues that "control of the fur trade" (663) was the central issue at stake in the conflict between the two settlements. See also Salisbury, and Demos, "Maypole."
8. John Demos remarks that at Plymouth—as at Boston, Hartford, New Haven, and Providence—the economic principle organizing the community was "*self*-provision" and therefore "trade was secondary to agriculture and artisanship." The same was not, however, true of Morton's Ma-re Mount ("Maypole" 85). This broader debate about colonial economic ideology also helps to explain why Morton continued to be prosecuted by Puritan New England colonists years later, even after his claims to the fur trade would have been minimal.
9. See, for example, Salisbury, who remarks that Bradford's "spelling [of Ma-re Mount], like his entire perspective, has prevailed among the partisans of both sides" (157) and notes also that Plymouth's victory over Ma-re Mount has seemed, for writers and scholars since, "to have set the course of New England's and America's history" (159).
10. Richard Drinnon, for example, characterizes Morton as an incipient communalist in the line of the English Ranters and Gerrard Winstanley (notes on 409); Michael Zuckerman celebrates the "casual democracy" of his antihierarchical vision (276); Robert Arner depicts him as developing a pagan culture that is in harmony with nature (162); John Demos attributes to him a protoenvironmentalism ("Maypole" 87); and Dempsey (124), Zuckerman (263), and Slotkin (64) all portray him as a multiculturalist, eager to share and integrate with the native Indians. Dempsey does also significantly account for Morton's occasional abuse of the Indians or the land. While it is worth applauding Morton's genuine affection for and willingness to cohabit and trade with the Indians, celebrating such attitudes as integrationist or multiculturalist assumes a mutual compliance in both economic and sexual relations for which there is no evidence. To admit as much is not, of course, to suggest that Bradford's xenophobia was any less harmful or exploitative.
11. Salisbury also usefully complicates this critical dichotomy, arguing that the conflict between Morton and Bradford represented "two approaches to the colonization of the continent and its inhabitants"—Morton's use of friendship, and Bradford's of fear (162). My analysis explores the economic frameworks that supported these two different approaches. Murphy aligns her own reading with both Salisbury's and Kupperman's, insisting on Morton as "a typical Englishman who wanted to grow rich off New World bounty and to help his countrymen do the same" (757).
12. Indeed, Daniel Shea would seem to speak for many critics when he suggests that Book III is the text's center, on which the previous books depend (62). Richard Drinnon reads the three books of *New English Canaan* as having three entirely separate agendas (395) yoked into a single volume.
13. Bradford's section on Morton, of course, was written nearly two decades after the events it records, considerably after Morton wrote his own volume.
14. See both Arner and Connors for discussions of Morton's hybrid and backward-looking style, which they situate in the context of earlier literary and

cultural traditions, from Renaissance drama to Ancient Greek comedy and mythology to pagan fertility rituals.

15. I share here Arner's view that Morton mixes "pastoral and promotional modes" (217).
16. For more on whether or not Morton had a legitimate claim to land in New England as early as 1620, see Dempsey 69–72. Dempsey also explains that Morton came from the "middling gentry" (22) and that his family, like Gorges', probably attained that status through his father's military service for the Crown.
17. The Plymouth patent was in fact revoked in 1635, but the revocation was never put into effect.
18. By 1658, when he published the *Briefe Narration*, Gorges could offer only a lament about his own economic efforts and financial martyrdom in New England. The description of the Virginia colonization plans of Gilbert and Grenville as "so many fruitlesse attempts and endlesse charge" (4) that begins his 1658 *Briefe Narration* aptly summarizes the narrative that follows of his own plantation efforts in New England. One after another of Gorges' investments yields "nothing to my private profit" (19) and results largely in "an accompt of the failings and disasters as what hath past in those my former and forreigne undertakings" (32). Gorges defends his new patent to New England against charges that "it was a Monopoly, and the colour of planting a Colony put upon it for particular ends, and private gaine" (37), and maintains his commitment to the principles of the public good, national glory and wealth, and missionary Christianity. He paints himself as a financial martyr, one who never traveled to America himself but whose unrequited economic support "opened the way for others, to make their gaine" (69).
19. Patterson suggests that in the seventeenth century the genres of pastoral and georgic became necessarily intertwined around the crucial issue of landownership (134). Among critics of Morton, only McWilliams recognizes the centrality of "legal land title" to the Ma-re Mount conflict (45).
20. Gorges himself nominated King James II as "another *Salomon*, for wisedome and justice" (4) in his 1658 *Briefe Narration*. Orgel notes that King James I was often represented as Solomon (73) and that he was portrayed as Neptune in Jonson's January 1625 masque *Neptune's Triumph for the Return of Albion* (71).
21. Alpers insists that country-house poems are not pastoral but another form altogether, since they lack the figure of the herdsman who is the "representative anecdote" that determines pastoral. Although I find much of value in Alpers' formidable study, his formalist approach sidelines the important materialist dimensions of pastoral that are foregrounded so compellingly by Raymond Williams.
22. Salisbury astutely recognizes that Morton's "admiration of the Indians' lifestyle was largely a shrewd recognition of their skills in efficiently extracting and utilizing the region's natural resources" (161).
23. Patterson records the appearance of this new translation of Virgil (164). See Shea (65) on Morton's allusion to Virgil, and Dempsey (199 n.687).
24. Unlike Williams, Paul Alpers suggests that pastoral does not deny but instead naturalizes and aestheticizes such painful realities as suffering or death or error (59)—or, he might have added, labor.

25. Consider the examples of Francis West and David Thompson. West, captain of Robert Gorges' ship, which arrived in 1623 in a failed attempt to stop interloper trading, raised the price of peas in hopes of gaining additional profits from Plymouth's desperate settlers, insisting that "under £8 he would not take, and yet would have beaver at an under rate" (*OPP* 140). That same year, David Thompson also arrived in Massachusetts Bay with a grant from the Council. He settled at Piscataqua and in 1626 raised Bradford's ire when his competition with Plymouth for goods being sold from Abraham Jenness' failed plantation at Monhegan raised the prices for those goods (*OPP* 202).
26. Patterson notes the failure of Francis Bacon's attempt in his 1605 *Advancement of Learning* to yoke together the pastoral with the georgic, the figures of the shepherd and the farmer, "as a program for the intellectual development of the seventeenth century" (138). Her assessment of pastoral's early modern fate builds on the work of Low and of Orgel 49–52.
27. As Richard Helgerson notes, Hakluyt's list of reasons to travel begins with conversion but is followed by twenty-eight subsequent reasons that all concern commerce (167).
28. Dempsey observes this elision of Morton's servants' labor (148).
29. I am indebted to Tim Sweet's fine reading of Johnson in his *American Georgics* for this understanding of moles.
30. See Sayre for other examples of descriptions of beaver in colonial travel narratives.

Chapter 4. Vent: Anne Hutchinson and Antinomian Selfhood

1. For critiques of the continuist, exceptionalist, ecclesiastical, and regional biases of American literary histories, see, for example, Gura, "Study"; Spengemann, *Mirror*; DeProspo; and Houston Baker.
2. Hall 206. All further references to materials collected in Hall's volume appear parenthetically as *AC*.
3. As Edmund Morgan notes, when pushed too far the emphasis on preparation came dangerously close to the heresy of Arminianism, which held that individuals could by force of will invite salvation (*Puritan* 136–37). For analyses that interpret the controversy as a debate over preparationism, see Miller, *New England Mind* 57–67; and Andrew Delbanco, *Puritan* 118–48.
4. Cotton insisted, for example, in his *Treatise of the Covenant of Grace*, that there "is more than the Letter of the Word that is required . . . [for] spiritual grace [to be] revealed to the soul" (qtd. in Delbanco, *Puritan* 135).
5. The antinomians refused also to attend the new governor with due ceremonial conventions, requiring Winthrop to hire his own servants to attend him to public meetings and to signal his arrival into town (Winthrop, *History* 1:224–25). Considering that, as Larzer Ziff notes, the success of trade in New England relied on sustaining political alliances with Native American tribes (74), one might read a suppressed economic incentive within the antinomians' Pequot War resistance effort.

6. Other commentaries focus on the relationship between the merchant class and antinomianism, including both Ziff and Bailyn, *New England*. Like Battis, however, these studies all read this relationship as a causal one that enabled merchants to legitimize their pecuniary interests. I argue instead that mercantile capitalism and antinomianism provided shared discourses within which a modern subjectivity became articulated.
7. See also Bailyn, who notes that William Hutchinson's brother Richard exported manufactured goods from London to members of his family living in Boston, who not only sold those goods in the Bay Colony and farther inland but also exported them to the West Indies, where another member of the Hutchinson family exchanged them for sugar and cotton (*New England* 88–89). Emery Battis notes that William Hutchinson left the mercer shop in the charge of his sons while he pursued other investment opportunities and fulfilled public responsibilities (75).
8. For John Winthrop Jr.'s account of the not very lucrative sale of the Groton estate, see R. C. Winthrop 169–74.
9. For a survey of Winthrop's landholdings, see Rutman, *Winthrop's* 87–89. Winthrop's "Modell of Christian Charity" is one central source for his economic ideas, particularly concerning how the rules of mercy and justice govern loans and debts.
10. I agree with Elizabeth Dillon's argument that Winthrop was, like Hutchinson, "embedded in the financial relations of mercantile-capitalism" (270 n.47), and have come to see them as economic subjects who bore a more anxiously uncanny than flatly oppositional relationship to each other. I am indebted to Dillon's chapter, as well as to conversations with Ivy Schweitzer and correspondence with Jim Holstun, for this view. I also maintain, however, that Winthrop was aggressively resistant to his implication in these economic relations and their effects, and one of the ways in which he expressed such resistance was through his hostility to Hutchinson.
11. For a discussion of the exclusion of merchants from direct involvement in governing institutions, and the political conflicts between gentlemen and merchants in the context of the inflationary prices during the 1630s, see Bailyn, *New England* 19–40. Rutman refers to the group of wealthy Boston merchants—including the antinomian supporters William Hutchinson, Coggshall, Colborne, Aspinwall, Baulston, Keayne, and others—as "lesser members of the gentry" (*Winthrop's* 75) or a "new breed of gentry" (246). Such classifications, however, by blurring the distinctions between material wealth and economic ideology that I am emphasizing, risk confusing such men with Winthrop and other gentlemen. Robert Brenner's category of "new merchants" better describes these wealthy colonial citizens who were never members of England's landed gentry; for Brenner, these new merchants emerged during the seventeenth century in distinction both to the colonizing aristocracy and to London company merchants (*Merchants* 111–12, 159).
12. I concur with Louise A. Breen's assessment of Battis' reading as an "unsatisfying" explanation for the class conflicts that underlay the antinomian crisis (15 n.26). Furthermore, Battis' interpretation fails to accommodate Cotton's

consistent denunciations of profiteering and his support of fixed prices, as well as Hutchinson's own declarations condemning the association her examiners made between her religious beliefs and the sanction of lawlessness.

13. In describing Hutchinson's subjectivity as "monstrous," I deliberately invoke the word used by Winthrop, Cotton, Weld, and Johnson to describe the deformed fetuses of Hutchinson and Mary Dyer. For a consideration of this aspect of the controversy, see Schutte.
14. For a good discussion of subjectivity, language, and violence in the Antinomian Controversy, see Pudaloff, who locates the event, *pace* Foucault, in the historical moment of shift from Renaissance organicism to Classical contractualism.
15. See Bailyn, *Apologia*, in which Keayne's insistence that his possessions and estate be assessed "according to the common worth and value that such goods and lands shall bear at that time in this country" (4) reads as deathbed support for the antimercantilist notion of just price.
16. Michael Winship, who convincingly makes the case that Henry Vane was a more central and threatening figure in the Antinomian (or Free Grace) Controversy than historians have recognized, also argues that Hutchinson's gender was less relevant than many have assumed (*Times* 116)—thereby disregarding, however, the significance of the language her opponents use to describe her during and after her trials. In their otherwise admirable efforts to emphasize the centrality of theological and scriptural debates to the controversy, Winship (76) and Michael Ditmore (356–57) both reject or sideline economic analyses of the events. My argument here and throughout this book is that these two realms must be seen as integrated, not separated.
17. According to the *OED*, the verb "to vent" also signified the discharge or evacuation of organs from a body, while the noun "vent" referred to an opening by which blood issues from the body, or to the anus or vulva of an animal.
18. For other studies of representations of the body politic and its metonymic links with the bodies of women and Indians during the antinomian crisis, see Schramer and Sweet, and Kibbey.
19. The first use of "venter" is clearly synonymous with "venture" or "adventure," but the idiosyncratic spelling and usage of words in *Good news* make it difficult to determine unequivocally the precise meaning of the second use of "venter." My interpretation, that it is used to suggest a division of goods, perhaps for sale, relies on context as well as on the assumption that the preceding verb "to divide" is employed in a conventional sense.

Chapter 5. Equivalence: Roger Williams and the Typology of Trade

1. Williams was formally banished from Massachusetts in October 1635, and finally fled to Narragansett Bay in January 1635/36 in order to escape being deported to England.
2. Williams' texts are cited parenthetically according to the following abbreviations: *BT* (*The Bloudy Tenent of Persecution*); *K* (*A Key into the Language of America*); *MC* (*Mr. Cottons Letter*); *HM* (*A Hireling Ministry None of*

Christs); *C* (*Correspondence of Roger Williams*); *CM* (*Christenings Make Not Christians*).

3. Of course, Williams' point here is not that members of churches function like merchant-traders or investors but that the divisions and disputes within a church should not disturb the peace of the state, much as disagreements within a company of merchants or a college of physicians would not affect the state's peace. It is nevertheless significant that of all the societies or companies he might have mentioned, he specifies only the mercantile and medical professions (both being the repeated source of his dominant metaphors of exchange and infection).
4. By the nineteenth century, the word along with the office of the alnager was obsolete, whereas the meaning of garbling had changed completely. Its new meaning was in many ways the inverse of its old meaning, as it came to signify not the maintenance of quality or purity but "The action or process of making selections with a view to misrepresentation," "The refuse or remainder of a staple commodity after selection of the best," or "the mixing of rubbish with a cargo stowed in bulk" ("Garbling"). What had once meant the determination of purity came to signify its corruption. The verb "to garble," which used to mean to select or sift out the best or most valuable items from the waste, came instead to mean a selection or reorganization of language for the purpose, or with the effect, of misrepresenting the truth ("Garble").
5. Williams' earlier courtship of Jane Whalley had been denied on financial grounds, and his letters indicate his acceptance and acknowledgment that his lack of money disqualified him as a suitor.
6. Chapin, *Trading* 19. Chapin speculates that Williams may have established the post as early as 1636, when he perhaps sought to take advantage of the opportunities for Indian trade opened up in the wake of John Oldham's murder in the summer of that year.
7. LaFantasie also maintains that Williams refused to trade in either firearms or liquor ("Day" 101).
8. Williams turns nearly as frequently to the language of medicine in *The Bloudy Tenent*; he continues this comparison by adding, "or *poyson* hurt the *body* when it is not touched or taken, yea and *antidotes* are received against it" (*BT* 198).
9. See, for example, Murray 239; Teunissen and Hinz 6.
10. Williams argues that, in scripture, the term "Heathen" is analogous to "Nation" and the term "Christian" is reserved for those who conform to the pure form of the original church. Thus, those calling themselves Christian would better be called Heathen. As Murray is quick to point out, Williams is no deconstructionist *avant la lettre*, despite the ways in which his positions teeter on the precipice of a kind of cultural relativism (240–41). But because he holds linguistic meaning as well as other truth to such a high standard (and a standard that ultimately cannot be registered in the present terms of the world), he is constantly exposing the misuse of words like Christendom, which functions within English patents as a term legitimating English claims to Native land.

11. See also Keary 265. Keary perceptively argues that although Williams conducted early land exchanges with the Narragansetts in their cultural terms, he interpreted those exchanges and his plantation-building practice "within an English framework of meaning" (267). After 1638, she discovers a gradual shift from speech to writing and English terms of understanding in Williams' land purchases (276–77).
12. On "hard word" dictionaries and their audiences, see Hayashi 33–41 and Landau 41.
13. On Withals' and similar manuals, see Starnes and Noyes 2–3, and Hayashi 25.
14. For other references to Williams' interest in methods for teaching a foreign language, see Chelline 40.
15. Such a typology is clearly at work in *The Bloudy Tenent*, where Williams refuses to align the "garden," or the true and perfect church of Israel, with "wilderness," or the imperfect institutions of the world. The national church of Israel was, for Williams, inimitable; no church in the world was equivalent to it or would be until God ushered in the new millennium. As Gordis and others explain, once this temporal continuity between the past and the present was severed, it became illegitimate (and the result of imperfect human understanding) to base present New England laws on past Israelite law (see Gordis 125).
16. Smolinski maintains that Williams "was far less willing to take the risk of spelling out his vision of the New Heavens and the New Earth" (89), though I am inclined to see this not as a reluctance to describe what he believes but as an admission of the fundamental imperfection and uncertainty of his belief.
17. Williams frequently replaces corn for wheat, as in *The Bloudy Tenent* (102–3).
18. See Gordis 127–32 for a lucid analysis of Williams' images of the wilderness and the garden.
19. Here, again, Williams equates the field with the world, or at least positions it firmly within the world, rather than as anticipatory of a future garden. And here, too, Williams turns to the language not only of trade but of medicine.
20. LaFantasie suggests that Harris was not aligned with any particular religious group, but that he did deny that heaven and hell exist anywhere outside the present world and self.
21. This response echoes Williams' earlier concern, expressed in a May 1664 letter to John Winthrop, Jr., that "the Common Trinitie of the World (profit, praeferment[,] pleasure) wil here be the Tria omnia, as in all the World beside" and that "God Land will be (as now it is) as great a God with us English as God Gould was with the Spaniards etc." (*C* 528). This lament appeared in the context of Richard Smith's efforts to organize his Cocumscussoc neighborhood into the township of Wickford, and to become part of Connecticut.
22. Williams repeats the phrase "without Lymmits" three times in little over a page in his description of Harris and his land claims in the 1677 letter to the court (*C* 742–43), clearly outraged at the boundless quality to his opponent's possessiveness.

Chapter 6. Debt: Salem Witchcraft and Paper Money

1. As Gildrie notes, the New England Company was refinanced out of the failed settlement at Cape Ann through investments by merchants and gentry from the West Country, by members of the London financial community, and by aristocrats from East Anglia (1).
2. Newman clarifies that this early paper money was intended not as a circulating medium, as it is today, but instead as "a borrowing for a specific public expenditure," and that it should accordingly be referred to as "bill of credit" rather than "money" (8). In this chapter, however, I follow the practice of those colonial New Englanders who in the 1690s called it paper money.
3. For other significant studies of Salem witchcraft not mentioned here, see Rosenthal; Demos, *Entertaining*; and especially Norton, whose study I engage more directly later in this chapter.
4. For Boyer and Nissenbaum, of course, these economic tensions were complexly interwoven with a variety of influences and motives that combined to trigger the 1692 accusations, including antagonisms within and between families, conflicts between neighbors and between residents of the town center and the village outskirts, and disputes over the establishment of a church and appointment of a minister. By situating witchcraft in the broader context of the pressures resulting from the growth of a market economy, Boyer and Nissenbaum build on the thesis of Keith Thomas, whose earlier study of witchcraft in early modern England similarly positioned it within the context of an emergent market economy. In further citations I use *SP* to refer to Boyer and Nissenbaum's *Salem Possessed* and *SVW* to refer to their documentary collection, *Salem-Village Witchcraft*.
5. Hunter's thesis relies on a long scholarly tradition that has distinguished the economic, religious, and cultural differences between West Country and East Anglian immigrants to New England. In his study of early Salem, for instance, Richard Gildrie notes that most of Salem's early population came from England's West Country, where manorial, closed-field farming was practiced and where most espoused a hybrid of the Anglican and Puritan faiths. A wave of immigrants arrived from East Anglia in the early 1630s, however, who practiced a more commercial, open-field agriculture and who mostly—like their minister Roger Williams—favored a far more radical form of Puritanism. See also Allen (especially 82–160) and Fischer. Gildrie is careful to note, however, that the West Country and East Anglian immigrants, in Salem at least, cannot be easily distinguished from one another in terms of economic class/status.
6. Those who debate whether spectral evidence really was the basis of conviction, or who debate the Mathers' positions on spectral evidence, provide useful historical analyses but also somehow miss what was most at stake in the Salem event: the dangers, seductions, and limits of spectral representation. For another analysis of Salem that highlights the centrality of spectral evidence in relation to selfhood, see Ruttenburg 31–82.

7. Paper money practices in colonial America were, in fact, based on credit practices among merchants. As Curtis P. Nettels explains, the issue of paper money in North America was "derived originally from the experience of the colonists with private instruments of credit. The first public paper in America grew naturally out of the use of private credit at a time when paper money issued by governments was unknown to the colonists. Accordingly, they applied to public bills the same principles to which they were accustomed in dealing with the notes and bills of individuals" (275–76).
8. Daniel Defoe would describe the fantastic elements of the treasure-seeking project when he characterized it as "a lottery of a hundred thousand to one odds; a hazard, which if it had failed everybody would have been ashamed to have owned themselves concerned in it; a voyage that would have been as much ridiculed as Don Quixot's adventure upon the windmill" (qtd. in Barnes 283).
9. I refer to selected works of Cotton Mather in subsequent citations according to the following abbreviations: *W (Wonders of the Invisible World), D (Diary of Cotton Mather), MP (Memorable Providences),* and *MCA (Magnalia Christi Americana).*
10. See Godbeer for another analysis of the fear of invasion in the Salem witchcraft accusations (179–204).
11. Although Norton's study does not concern economic matters in any central way, her book's details offer stunning insight into the ways in which transregional trade relations may well have contributed significantly to Salem's witchcraft events.
12. See Norton, who notes that "some prominent accused men had regularly traded with or fought against the Indians" (12).
13. I owe my awareness of this passage to Mary Beth Norton, who quotes from it in her study (83).
14. Indeed, because the sermons and practice of Salem's pastor Samuel Parris so deeply inscribed the division between church members and nonmembers, it is likely the church covenant book had an especially inflated and vexed status.
15. I also thank Jane Kamensky for sharing with me her unpublished paper.
16. Among these books (whose form and use were described in considerable detail in a number of seventeenth-century mercantile manuals) were the journal, which recorded economic transactions by the day on which they transpired, and the ledger, which grouped credits and debits by account (whether it be client or customer, shop or business, venture or partnership). Others included the petty expense book, the specie book, the factor book, and the memorial.
17. As the younger Mather notes, money is only one of several means by which the devil tempts humans: "One mans Condition makes him *Hunger* for Preferments, or Employments, another mans makes him *Hunger* for Cash or Land, or Trade; another mans makes him *Hunger* for Merriments, or Diversions" (*W* 221).
18. For more on these forfeitures, including the destitution to which this often reduced the families of felons, see David C. Brown.

19. For some documentary accounts of these petitions, see *SVW* 17, 35, 66, 90.
20. Later, in 1706, during his quarrel with Joseph Dudley, Mather rebuked traders who engaged in allegedly illicit trade with the French. Among those traders was John Phillips, the brother of Mather's then-deceased wife Abigail. As a result, Mather's former father-in-law, John Phillips, Sr., reputedly cut Mather and his children out of his will (Silverman 212–13, 283). This is likely the same John Phillips to whom Mather addressed his 1691 pamphlet on paper money. Mather's subsequent marriage to Lydia George was preceded by a prenuptial contract in which Mather would face a stiff penalty in the event that he intervened in his new wife's considerable estate, despite the fact that he was made responsible for the estate of her late son-in-law. See Silverman for fuller discussions of Mather's marriage and later experiences with debt (283–90, 310–21).
21. Mather's own position on spectral evidence was more subtle than many recognized: he argued that it provided a justified occasion for further inquiry though not for conviction (*W* 34–35).
22. In doing so, Mather was following the suggestion of his father who wished, in his earlier *Essay*, that "the Natural History of New-England might be written and published to the World; the Rules and method described by that Learned and excellent person Robert Boyle Esq. being duely observed" (16). For more on Cotton Mather's relationship to scientific discourse, see Jeske, and Winship ("Prodigies").
23. See also Baker's *Securing the Commonwealth* 27–42.

Epilogue: Economies of Possession and Dissent

1. As A. J. R. Russell-Wood explains, the concepts of center and periphery are "parallax—the apparent change in the position of what constitutes *center* and what *periphery* resulting from a change in the viewer's position—be this in spatial or chronological terms, or even of social or financial circumstances" (106). Wallerstein remarks of the phenomenon of uneven development that "[i]t is not only that, within this world-economy, towns were unevenly distributed, but that within towns, ethnic groups were probably unevenly distributed. We must not forget here the concept of layers within layers" (*Modern* 1:119). We might import these parallax and layered formulations into our understanding of the category of dissent and its relation to consensus. Depending on where one stands geographically as well as ideologically, such colonial figures as William Bradford, Thomas Morton, Anne Hutchinson, Roger Williams, and Cotton Mather take on very different identities in relation to dissent, to consensus, and to each other.
2. Perhaps the most recent example of resistance to such spectrality is the outrage with which citizens and investors have responded to the Enron and WorldCom corporate scandals, in which top executives were accused of falsely inflating stock prices—only a few months after the September 2001 attack on the World Trade Center, a symbol identified by its attackers as the geographical heart of global capitalism. The detail repeatedly lost in the critiques

of the indicted corporate leaders, however, is the fact that their acts of hiding corporate debt and inflating value depended on the spectral effects of standard stock rhetoric and its practice of folding investment time. The sudden exposure of this uncertain certainty might explain how Enron went from being "celebrated from boardrooms to business schools as a lodestar for the future of the corporate world, the embodiment of a company that got everything right" to becoming "emblematic of everything wrong in corporate America." When Sherron Watkins worried in her famous letter to Enron Chairman Kenneth Lay that Enron's "past successes" would be perceived by the public as "nothing more than an elaborate accounting hoax" (Eichenwald), she came close to unfolding the distinction between success and hoax as little more than a matter of perception.

Works Cited

Adams, Charles Francis, Jr. "Morton of Merry-Mount." In *A New English Canaan*. By Thomas Morton. 1883. New York: Burt Franklin, 1967. 1–105.

Agnew, Jean-Christophe. *Worlds Apart: The Market and the Theater in Anglo-American Thought, 1550–1750*. Cambridge: Cambridge UP, 1986.

Alexander, William. *The Mapp and Description of New England*. London, 1630.

Allen, David Grayson. *In English Ways: The Movement of Societies and the Transferal of English Local Law and Custom to Massachusetts Bay in the Seventeenth Century*. Chapel Hill: U of North Carolina P, 1981.

Alpers, Paul. *What Is Pastoral?* Chicago: U of Chicago P, 1996.

Amin, Samir. *Class and Nation: Historically and in the Current Crisis*. Trans. Susan Kaplow. New York: Monthly Review P, 1980.

——. *Unequal Development: An Essay on the Social Formations of Peripheral Capitalism*. Trans. Brian Pearce. New York: Monthly Review P, 1976.

Anderson, Douglas. *William Bradford's Books:* Of Plimmoth Plantation *and the Printed Word*. Baltimore: Johns Hopkins UP, 2003.

Anderson, Virginia DeJohn. *New England's Generation: The Great Migration and the Formation of Society and Culture in the Seventeenth Century*. Cambridge: Cambridge UP, 1991.

Appleby, Joyce Oldham. *Economic Thought and Ideology in Seventeenth-Century England*. Princeton: Princeton UP, 1978.

Arner, Robert D. "Pastoral Celebrations and Satire in Thomas Morton's 'New English Canaan.'" *Criticism* 16.3 (1974): 217–31.

Bacon, Francis. *The Advancement of Learning*. Ed. G. W. Kitchin. London: J. M. Dent, 1973.

——. *Novum Organum*. Trans. and ed. Peter Urbach and John Gibson. Chicago: Open Court, 1994.

——. "Of Plantations." *The Complete Essays of Francis Bacon*. New York: Washington Square, 1963. 90–92.

——. "Of Truth." In *The Moral and Historical Works of Francis Bacon*. Ed. Joseph Devey. London: Henry G. Bohn, 1852.

Bailyn, Bernard, ed. *The Apologia of Robert Keayne: The Self-Portrait of a Puritan Merchant*. New York: Harper, 1964.

——. *The New England Merchants in the Seventeenth Century*. Cambridge: Harvard UP, 1955.

Baker, Houston A., Jr. *Blues, Ideology, and Afro-American Literature: A Vernacular Theory*. Chicago: U of Chicago P, 1984.

Baker, Jennifer Jordan. "'It is uncertain where the Fates will carry me': Cotton Mather's Theology of Finance." *Arizona Quarterly* 56.4 (2000): 1–23.

——. *Securing the Commonwealth: Debt, Speculation, and Writing in the Making of Early America*. Baltimore: Johns Hopkins UP, 2005.

Ball, J. N. *Merchants and Merchandise: The Expansion of Trade in Europe, 1500–1630*. New York: St. Martin's, 1977.

Barbour, Philip L., ed. *The Complete Works of Captain John Smith*. 3 vols. Chapel Hill: North Carolina UP, 1986.

Barnes, Viola. "The Rise of William Phips." *New England Quarterly* 1.3 (1928): 271–94.

Battis, Emery John. *Saints and Sectaries: Anne Hutchinson and the Antinomian Controversy in the Massachusetts Bay Colony*. Chapel Hill: North Carolina UP, 1962.

Bauer, Ralph. *The Cultural Geography of Colonial American Literature: Empire, Travel, Modernity*. Cambridge: Cambridge UP, 2003.

Bercovitch, Sacvan. *The American Jeremiad*. Madison: U of Wisconsin P, 1978.

——. *The Puritan Origins of the American Self*. New Haven: Yale UP, 1975.

——. *The Rites of Assent: Transformations in the Symbolic Construction of America*. New York: Routledge, 1993.

——. "Typology in Puritan New England: The Williams-Cotton Controversy Reassessed." *American Quarterly* 19.2 (1967): 166–91.

Blackwell, John. *Some Additional Considerations*. 1691. In Davis 197–208.

Boyer, Paul, and Stephen Nissenbaum. *Salem Possessed: The Social Origins of Witchcraft*. Cambridge: Harvard UP, 1974.

——, eds. *Salem-Village Witchcraft: A Documentary Record of Local Conflict in Colonial New England*. Belmont, CA: Wadsworth Pub. Co., 1972.

Bozeman, Theodore Dwight. *To Live Ancient Lives: The Primitivist Dimension in Puritanism*. Chapel Hill: U of North Carolina P, 1988.

Bradford, E. F. "Conscious Art in Bradford's *History of Plymouth Plantation*." *New England Quarterly* 1 (April 1928): 133–57.

Bradford, William. "A Dialogue, or the Sum of a Conference. . . ." In Young 414–58.

——. *Letter Book*. Boston: Massachusetts Society of Mayflower Descendants, 1906.

——. *Of Plymouth Plantation, 1620–1647*. New York: Random, 1981.

——. "Verses." *Proceedings of the Massachusetts Historical Society* 2 (October 1870): 465–82.

Brattle, Thomas. "Letter of Thomas Brattle, F.R.S., 1692." In Burr 169–90.

Braudel, Fernand. *The Perspective of the World*. Vol. 3 of *Civilization and Capitalism, 15th–18th Century*. Trans. Siân Reynolds. 3 vols. New York: Harper & Row, 1984.

——. *The Wheels of Commerce*. Vol. 2 of *Civilization and Capitalism, 15th–18th Century*. Trans. Siân Reynolds. 3 vols. New York: Harper & Row, 1979.

Breen, Louise A. "Religious Radicalism in the Puritan Officer Corps: Heterodoxy, the Artillery Company, and Cultural Integration in Seventeenth-Century Boston." *New England Quarterly* 68.1 (1995): 3–43.

Breen, T. H. "Right Man, Wrong Place." *New York Review of Books* 33.18 (November 20, 1986): 48–50.

Breen, T. H., and Stephen Foster. "Moving to the New World: The Character of Early Massachusetts Immigration." In *Puritans and Adventurers: Change and Persistence in Early America*. By T. H. Breen. New York: Oxford UP, 1980. 46–67.

Breitwieser, Mitchell Robert. *Cotton Mather and Benjamin Franklin: The Price of Representative Personality*. Cambridge: Cambridge UP, 1984.

Brenner, Robert. *Merchants and Revolution: Commercial Change, Political Conflict, and London's Overseas Traders, 1550–1653*. Princeton: Princeton UP, 1993.

——. "The Origins of Capitalist Development: A Critique of Neo-Smithian Marxism." *New Left Review* 104 (1997): 25–92.

Brockunier, Samuel Hugh. *The Irrepressible Democrat, Roger Williams*. New York: Ronald P, 1940.

Brown, David C. "The Forfeitures at Salem, 1692." *William and Mary Quarterly* 3rd ser. 50.1 (1993): 85–111.

Burr, George Lincoln, ed. *Narratives of the New England Witchcraft Cases*. 1914. Repr. Mineola, NY: Dover, 2002.

Burnham, Michelle. "Textual Investments: Economics and Colonial American Literatures." In *Companion to the Literatures of Colonial America*. Ed. Susan Castillo and Ivy Schweitzer. London: Blackwell, 2005. 60–77.

Bushnell, Amy, and Jack P. Greene. "Peripheries, Centers, and the Construction of Early Modern American Empires: An Introduction." In *Negotiated Empires: Centers and Peripheries in the Americas, 1500–1820*. Ed. Christine Daniels and Michael V. Kennedy. New York: Routledge, 2002. 1–14.

Caldwell, Patricia. "The Antinomian Language Controversy." *Harvard Theological Review* 69 (1976): 345–67.

Calef, Robert. *More Wonders of the Invisible World*. Vols. 2and 3. *The Witchcraft Delusion in New England*. Ed. Samuel G. Drake. 1866. 3 vols. Repr. New York: Burt Franklin, 1970.

Campbell, Mary Baine. *The Witness and the Other World: Exotic European Travel Writing, 400–1600*. Ithaca: Cornell UP, 1988.

——. *Wonder & Science: Imagining Worlds in Early Modern Europe*. Ithaca: Cornell UP, 1999.

Canny, Nicholas, and Anthony Pagden, eds. *Colonial Identity in the Atlantic World, 1500–1800*. Princeton: Princeton UP, 1987.

Casanova, Pascale. *The World Republic of Letters*. Trans. M. B. DeBevoise. Cambridge: Harvard UP, 2004.

Ceci, Lynn. "Native Wampum as a Peripheral Resource in the Seventeenth-Century World-System." In *The Pequots in Southern New England: The Rise and Fall of an American Indian Nation*. Ed. Laurence M. Hauptman and James D. Wherry. Norman: U of Oklahoma P, 1990. 48–63.

Chapin, Howard M. *Documentary History of Rhode Island*. Providence: Preston and Rounds, 1916–19.

——. *The Trading Post of Roger Williams with Those of John Wilcox and Richard Smith*. Providence: E. L. Freeman, 1933.

Chase-Dunn, Christopher, and Thomas D. Hall. *Rise and Demise: Comparing World-Systems*. Boulder, CO: Westview, 1997.

Chelline, Warren H. "John Milton's American Friend." *Publications of the Missouri Philological Association* 6 (1981): 39–42.

Clark, Christopher, ed. "The Transition to Capitalism in America: A Panel Discussion." *The History Teacher* 27.3 (May 1994): 263–88.

Cohen, Matt. "Morton's Maypole and the Indians: Publishing in Early New England." *Book History* 5 (2002): 1–18.

Cohen, Murray. *Sensible Words: Linguistic Practice in England, 1640–1785*. Baltimore: Johns Hopkins UP, 1977.

Columbus, Christopher. *The "Diario" of Christopher Columbus's First Voyage to America, 1492–1493*. Trans. Oliver Dunn and James E. Kelley, Jr. Norman: Oklahoma UP, 1989.

Connors, Donald. *Thomas Morton*. New York: Twayne, 1969.

Cornelius, Paul. *Languages in Seventeenth- and Early Eighteenth-Century Imaginary Voyages*. Geneva: Librairie Droz, 1965.

Cotton, John. *Christ the Fountaine of Life*. 1651. New York: Arno, 1972.

——. *Gods Promise to His Plantation*. London, 1630.

——. *A Letter of Mr. John Cottons*. 1643. In *The Complete Writings of Roger Williams*. Vol. 1. New York: Russell & Russell, 1963. 13–27.

Croll, Morris W. *"Attic" and Baroque Prose Style: The Anti-Ciceronian Movement: Essays by Morris W. Croll*. Ed. J. Max Patrick and Robert O. Evans. Princeton: Princeton UP, 1966.

Cushman, Robert. "Cushman's Discourse." In *Chronicles of the Pilgrim Fathers of the Colony of Plymouth, from 1602 to 1625*. Ed. Alexander Young. 2nd ed. Boston: Little, Brown, 1844. 255–68.

Dafforne, Richard. *The Merchants Mirrour*. 2nd ed. London, 1651.

Daly, Robert. "William Bradford's Vision of History." *American Literature* 44.4 (January 1973): 557–69.

Davis, Andrew McFarland, ed. *Colonial Currency Reprints, 1682–1751*. New York: Augustus M. Kelley, 1964.

Dawson, Hugh. "'Christian Charitie' as Colonial Discourse: Rereading Winthrop's Sermon in Its English Context." *Early American Literature* 33.2 (1998): 117–48.

——. "John Winthrop's Rite of Passage: The Origins of the 'Christian Charitie' Discourse." *Early American Literature* 26.3 (1991): 219–31.

Delbanco, Andrew. "The Puritan Errand Re-Viewed." *Journal of American Studies* 18.3 (1984): 343–60.

——. *The Puritan Ordeal*. Cambridge: Harvard UP, 1989.

Deleuze, Gilles. *The Fold: Leibniz and the Baroque*. Trans. Tom Conley. Minneapolis: U of Minnesota P, 1993.

Demos, John Putnam. *Entertaining Satan: Witchcraft and the Culture of Early New England*. New York: Oxford UP, 1982.

——. "The Maypole of Merry Mount." *American Heritage* (October–November 1986): 83–87.

Dempsey, Jack. "Thomas Morton: The Life and Renaissance of an Early American Poet." In Morton 1–354.

Denemark, Robert A., and Kenneth P. Thomas. "The Brenner-Wallerstein Debate." *International Studies Quarterly* 32 (1988): 47–65.

DePaoli, Neill. "Beaver, Blankets, Liquor, and Politics: Pemaquid's Fur Trade, 1614–1760." *Maine Historical Society Quarterly* 33.3–4 (1993–94): 166–201.

DeProspo, R. C. "Marginalizing Early American Literature." *New Literary History* 23.2 (1992): 233–65.

Derrida, Jacques. *Specters of Marx: The State of the Debt, the Work of Mourning, and the New International*. Trans. Peggy Kamuf. New York: Routledge, 1994.

Dillon, Elizabeth Maddock. *The Gender of Freedom: Fictions of Liberalism and the Literary Public Sphere*. Stanford: Stanford UP, 2004.

Dimock, Wai Chee, and Michael T. Gilmore, eds. *Rethinking Class: Literary Studies and Social Formations*. New York: Columbia UP, 1994.

Discourses upon Trade. 1691. In *Early English Tracts on Commerce*. Ed. J. R. McCulloch. Cambridge: Cambridge UP, 1954. 505–40.

Ditmore, Michael G. "A Prophetess in Her Own Country: An Exegesis of Anne Hutchinson's 'Immediate Revelation.'" *William and Mary Quarterly* 3rd ser. 57.2 (2000): 349–92.

Drinnon, Richard. "The Maypole of Merry Mount: Thomas Morton and the Plantation Patriarchs." *Massachusetts Review* 21 (1980): 382–410.

Eichenwald, Kurt. "News Analysis: Stakes High in Final Chapter of Enron Saga." 26 January 2006. *International Herald Tribune*. 5 February 2006. <http://www.iht.com>

Emerson, Everett. *John Cotton*. Rev. ed. Boston: Twayne, 1990.

Ernst, James. *Roger Williams: New England Firebrand*. 1932. Repr. New York: AMS, 1969.

Fischer, David Hackett. *Albion's Seed: Four British Folkways in America*. New York: Oxford UP, 1989.

Fish, Stanley E., ed. *Seventeenth-Century Prose: Modern Essays in Criticism*. New York: Oxford UP, 1971.

Foster, Stephen. *The Long Argument: English Puritanism and the Shaping of New England Culture, 1570–1700*. Chapel Hill: North Carolina UP, 1991.

Foucault, Michel. *The Order of Things: An Archaeology of the Human Sciences*. New York: Vintage, 1970.

Fox-Genovese, Elizabeth, and Eugene D. Genovese. *Fruits of Merchant Capital: Slavery and Bourgeois Property in the Rise and Expansion of Capitalism*. New York: Oxford UP, 1983.

Franklin, Wayne. *Discovers, Explorers, Settlers: The Diligent Writers of Early America*. Chicago: U of Chicago P, 1979.

Fritscher, John J. "The Sensibility and Conscious Style of William Bradford." *Bucknell Review* 17.3 (1969): 80–90.

Fuller, Mary C. *Voyages in Print: English Travel to America, 1576–1624*. Cambridge: Cambridge UP, 1995.

Fumerton, Patricia. *Cultural Aesthetics: Renaissance Literature and the Practice of Social Ornament*. Chicago: U of Chicago P, 1991.

"Garble." *Oxford English Dictionary Online*. 2nd ed. Oxford UP, 1989. Santa Clara U. July 2003. <http://www.oed.com>

"Garbling." *Oxford English Dictionary Online*. 2nd ed. Oxford UP, 1989. Santa Clara U. July 2003. <http://www.oed.com>

Garrett, John. *Roger Williams: Witness beyond Christendom, 1603–1683*. New York: Macmillan, 1970.

Gay, Peter. *A Loss of Mastery: Puritan Historians in Colonial America*. Berkeley: California UP, 1996.

Gentleman, Tobias. *England's way to win wealth*. 1614. Delmar: Scholars' Facsimilies and Reprints, 1992.

Giddens, Anthony. *The Class Structure of the Advanced Societies*. London: Hutchinson U Library, 1973.

Gildrie, Richard P. *Salem, Massachusetts, 1626–1683: A Covenant Community*. Charlottesville: UP of Virginia, 1975.

Gilje, Paul A., ed. *Wages of Independence: Capitalism in the Early Republic*. Madison, WI: Madison House, 1997.

Gilpin, W. Clark. *The Millenarian Piety of Roger Williams*. Chicago: U of Chicago P, 1979.

Godbeer, Richard. *The Devil's Dominion: Magic and Religion in Early New England*. Cambridge: Cambridge UP, 1992.

Good news from New-England with An exact relation of the first Planting that Countrey. London, 1648.

Gordis, Lisa M. *Opening Scripture: Bible Reading and Interpretive Authority in Puritan New England*. Chicago: U of Chicago P, 2003.

Gorges, Sir Ferdinando. *Briefe Narration of the Originall Undertakings of the Advancement of Plantations Into the parts of America*. London, 1658.

——. *A Briefe Relation of the Discovery and Plantation of New England*. London, 1622.

Grabo, Norman S. "John Cotton's Aesthetic: A Sketch." *Early American Literature* 3.1 (1968): 4–10.

——. "William Bradford: *Of Plymouth Plantation*." In *Landmarks of American Writing*. Ed. Hennig Cohen. New York: Basic, 1969. 3–19.

Gragg, Larry. *A Quest for Security: The Life of Samuel Parris, 1653–1720*. New York: Greenwood P, 1990.

Greenblatt, Stephen. *Marvelous Possessions: The Wonder of the New World*. Chicago: U of Chicago P, 1991.

Griffith, John. "*Of Plymouth Plantation* as a Mercantile Epic." *Arizona Quarterly* 28 (1972): 231–42.

Gura, Philip. *A Glimpse of Sion's Glory: Puritan Radicalism in New England, 1620–1660*. Middletown, CT: Wesleyan UP, 1984.

——. "John *Who*?: Captain John Smith and Early American Literature." *Early American Literature* 21.3 (1986/87): 260–67.

——. "The Study of Colonial American Literature, 1966–1987: A Vade Mecum." *William and Mary Quarterly* 3rd ser. 45.2 (1988): 305–51.

Gyles, John. *Memoirs of Odd Adventures, Strange Deliverances, etc.* 1736. In *Puritans among the Indians: Accounts of Captivity and Redemption, 1676–1724*. Ed. Alden T. Vaughan and Edward W. Clark. Cambridge: Belknap P of Harvard UP, 1981. 93–131.

Hakluyt, Richard. *The Principal Navigations, Voyages, Traffiques and Discoveries of the English Nation*. 1598–1600. 12 vols. Glasgow: J. MacLehose, 1903–5.

Hall, David D., ed. *The Antinomian Controversy, 1636–1638: A Documentary History*. 2nd ed. Durham: Duke UP, 1990.

Hatton, Edward. *The Merchant's Magazine; or, Trades-Man's Treasury*. London, 1697.

Hayashi, Tetsuro. *The Theory of English Lexicography, 1530–1791*. Amsterdam: John Benjamins B.V., 1978.

Helgerson, Richard. *Forms of Nationhood: Elizabethan Writing of England*. Chicago: U of Chicago P, 1992.

Heyrman, Christine Leigh. *Commerce and Culture: The Maritime Communities of Colonial Massachusetts, 1690–1750*. New York: Norton, 1984.

Hill, Christopher. *The World Turned Upside Down: Radical Ideas during the English Revolution*. London: Penguin, 1972.

Hilton, R. H., ed. *The Transition from Feudalism to Capitalism*. London: Verso, 1976.

Holstun, James. *Ehud's Dagger: Class Struggle in the English Revolution*. London: Verso, 2000.

Hovey, Kenneth Alan. "The Theology of History in *Of Plymouth Plantation* and Its Predecessors." *Early American Literature* 10.1 (1975): 47–66.

Howard, Alan B. "Art and History in Bradford's *Of Plymouth Plantation*." *William and Mary Quarterly* 3rd ser. 28.2 (April 1971): 237–66.

Howell, A. C. "*Res et Verba*: Words and Things." In Fish 187–99.

Hull, John. *Diaries of John Hull*. In *Puritan Personal Writings: Diaries*. Ed. Sacvan Bercovitch. New York: AMS, 1982.

Hulme, Peter. *Colonial Encounters: Europe and the Native Caribbean, 1492–1797*. London: Methuen, 1986.

Hunter, Phyllis Whitman. *Purchasing Identity in the Atlantic World: Massachusetts Merchants, 1670–1780*. Ithaca: Cornell UP, 2001.

Innes, Stephen. *Creating the Commonwealth: The Economic Culture of Puritan New England*. New York: Norton, 1995.

——. *Labor in a New Land: Economy and Society in Seventeenth-Century Springfield*. Princeton: Princeton UP, 1983.

Jed, Stephanie. *Chaste Thinking: The Rape of Lucretia and the Birth of Humanism*. Bloomington: Indiana UP, 1989.

Jeske, Jeffrey. "Cotton Mather: Physico-Theologian." *Journal of the History of Ideas* 47.4 (1986): 583–94.

Johnson, Edward. *Wonder-Working Providence of Sions Saviour in New England*. 1654. Ed. J. Franklin Jameson. New York: Charles Scribner's Sons, 1910.

Jones, R. F. "Science and English Prose Style, 1650–75." In Fish 53–89.

——. "Science and Language in England of the Mid-Seventeenth Century." In Fish 94–111.

Jonson, Ben. *Neptune's Triumph for the Return of Albion*. 1624. In *Ben Jonson: The Complete Masques*. Ed. Stephen Orgel. New Haven, CT: Yale UP, 1969. 409–24.

Jordan, Louis. *John Hull, the Mint and the Economics of Massachusetts Coinage*. Hanover, NH: UP of New England, 2002.

Josselyn, John. *Two Voyages to New-England*. 1674. In *John Josselyn, Colonial Traveler: A Critical Edition of Two Voyages to New-England*. Ed. Paul J. Lindholdt. Hanover, NH: UP of New England, 1988.

Kamensky, Jane. "The Devil's Book: The Material Culture of Witchcraft in Early New England." Paper delivered at American Historical Association, Seattle, January 1998.

Karlsen, Carol F. *The Devil in the Shape of a Woman: Witchcraft in Colonial New England*. New York: Vintage Books, 1987.

Kaufmann, Michael. *Institutional Individualism: Conversion, Exile, and Nostalgia in Puritan New England*. Hanover, NH: UP of New England / Wesleyan UP, 1998.

Kayll, Robert. *The Trades Increase*. London, 1615.

Keary, Anne. "Retelling the History of the Settlement of Providence: Speech, Writing, and Cultural Interaction on Narragansett Bay." *New England Quarterly* 69.2 (1996): 250–86.

Kemys, Lawrence. *A Relation of the second Voyage to Guiana*. London, 1596.

Kibbey, Anne. *The Interpretation of Material Shapes in Puritanism*. Cambridge: Cambridge UP, 1986.

Knight, Janice. *Orthodoxies in Massachusetts: Rereading American Puritanism*. Cambridge: Harvard UP, 1994.

Kriedte, Peter. *Peasants, Landlords, and Merchant Capitalists: Europe and the World Economy, 1500–1800*. Cambridge: Cambridge UP, 1980.

Kroll, Richard. *The Material World: Literate Culture in the Restoration and Early 18th Century*. Baltimore: Johns Hopkins UP, 1991.

Kulikoff, Allan. *The Agrarian Origins of American Capitalism*. Charlottesville: UP of Virginia, 1992.

——. *From British Peasants to Colonial American Farmers*. Chapel Hill: U of North Carolina P, 2000.

Kupperman, Karen Ordahl. "Thomas Morton, Historian." *New England Quarterly* 50.4 (1977): 660–64.

LaFantasie, Glenn W. "A Day in the Life of Roger Williams." *Rhode Island History* 46.3 (1987): 95–111.

——. "Introduction." In *The Correspondence of Roger Williams*. Vol. 1. Ed. Glenn LaFantasie. 2 vols. Hanover, NH: UP of New England, 1988. xxv–xlv.

Landau, Sidney I. *Dictionaries: The Art and Craft of Lexicography*. New York: Scribners, 1984.

Lang, Amy Schrager. *Prophetic Woman: Anne Hutchinson and the Problem of Dissent in the Literature of New England*. Berkeley: U of California P, 1987.

——. *The Syntax of Class: Writing Inequality in Nineteenth-Century America*. Princeton: Princeton UP, 2003.

Langdon, George D., Jr. *Pilgrim Colony: A History of New Plymouth, 1620–1691*. New Haven: Yale UP, 1966.

Laurence, David. "William Bradford's American Sublime." *PMLA* 102 (January 1987): 55–65.

Lawson, Deodat. *A Brief and True Narrative of Witchcraft at Salem Village*. 1692. In Burr 152–64.

Leverenz, David. *The Language of Puritan Feeling: An Exploration in Literature, Psychology, and Social History*. New Brunswick: Rutgers UP, 1980.

Levett, Christopher. *Voyage into New England*. London, 1628.

Levin, David. "William Bradford: The Value of Puritan Historiography." In *Major Writers of Early American Literature*. Ed. Everett Emerson. Madison: Wisconsin UP, 1972. 11–31.

Linebaugh, Peter, and Marcus Rediker. *The Many-Headed Hydra: Sailors, Slaves, Commoners, and the Hidden History of the Revolutionary Atlantic*. Boston: Beacon, 2000.

Low, Anthony. *The Georgic Revolution*. Princeton: Princeton UP, 1985.

Malynes, Gerald de. *The Maintenance of Free Trade*. 1622. New York: Augustus M. Kelley, 1971.

Marcus, Leah S. *The Politics of Mirth: Jonson, Herrick, Milton, Marvell and the Defense of Old Holiday Pastimes*. Chicago: U of Chicago P, 1986.

Marius, John. *Advice concerning Bills of Exchange*. London, 1651.

Markley, Robert. *Fallen Languages: Crisis of Representation in Newtonian England, 1660–1740*. Ithaca: Cornell UP, 1993.

Martin, John Frederick. *Profits in the Wilderness: Entrepreneurship and the Founding of New England Towns in the Seventeenth Century*. Chapel Hill: U of North Carolina P, 1991.

Marx, Karl. *Capital*. Vol. 3. Ed. Frederick Engels. New York: International, 1976.

Mason, John. *A Briefe Discourse of the New-found-land*. Edinburgh, 1620.

Mather, Cotton. "A Brand Pluck'd Out of the Burning." 1693. In Burr 259–87.

——. *Diary of Cotton Mather*. Vol. 1. New York: Frederick Ungar Publishing, 1911.

——. *Magnalia Christi Americana; or, The Ecclesiastical History of New-England*. New York: Russell & Russell, 1967.

——. *Memorable Providences*. 1689. In Burr 93–143.

[——]. *Some Considerations on the Bills of Credit Now passing in New-England*. 1691. In Davis 189–96.

——. *The Wonders of the Invisible World*. In *The Witchcraft Delusion in New England*. Vol. 1. Ed. Samuel G. Drake. 1866. 3 vols. Repr. New York: Burt Franklin, 1970.

Mather, Increase. *An Essay for the Recording of Illustrious Providences*. 1684. In Burr 8–38.

McCarron, Robert. "Some Considerations of Style and Rhetoric in the Writings of Roger Williams." Diss. Indiana U, 1980.

McCusker, John J. *Money and Exchange in Europe and America, 1600–1775*. Chapel Hill: U of North Carolina P, 1978.

McCusker, John J., and Russell R. Menard. *The Economy of British America, 1607–1789*. Chapel Hill: U of North Carolina P, 1985.

McIntyre, Ruth A. *Debts Hopeful and Desperate: Financing the Plymouth Colony*. Plymouth: Plimoth Plantation, 1963.

McWilliams, John. *New England's Crises and Cultural Memory: Literature, Politics, History, Religion, 1620–1860*. Cambridge: Cambridge UP, 2004.

Merrill, Michael. "Putting 'Capitalism' in Its Place: A Review of Recent Literature." *William and Mary Quarterly* 3rd ser. 52.2 (1995): 315–26.

Mignolo, Walter D. *Local Histories/Global Designs: Coloniality, Subaltern Knowledges, and Border Thinking*. Princeton: Princeton UP, 2000.

Miller, Perry. *The New England Mind: The Seventeenth Century*. New York: Macmillan, 1939.

——. "The Plain Style." In Fish 147–86.

Miller, Perry, and Thomas H. Johnson, eds. *The Puritans: A Sourcebook of Their Writings*. Vol. 1 of 2 vols. New York: Harper, 1963.

Misselden, Edward. *The Circle of Commerce*. 1623. New York: Augustus M. Kelley, 1971.

Moloney, Francis T. *The Fur Trade in New England, 1620–1676*. Hamden, CT: Archon, 1967.

Montgomery, Scott L. *The Scientific Voice*. New York: Guilford, 1996.

Morgan, Edmund S. "The Historians of Early New England." In *The Reinterpretation of Early American History: Essays in Honor of John Edwin Pomfret*. Ed. Ray Allen Billington. San Marino, CA: Huntington Library, 1966. 45–52.

——. *The Puritan Dilemma: The Story of John Winthrop*. Ed. Oscar Handlin. Boston: Little, Brown, 1958.

Morton, Thomas. *New English Canaan*. 1637. Ed. Jack Dempsey. Scituate, MA: Digital Scanning, 1999.

Mourt, G. *A Relation . . . of the Beginning and Proceedings of the English Plantation*. 1622. Amsterdam: Theatrum Orbis Terrarum, 1974.

Mun, Thomas. *England's Treasure by Forraign-Trade*. 1664. Oxford: Basil Blackwell, 1959.

Murdock, Kenneth. *Literature and Theology in Colonial New England*. Westport: Greenwood, 1949.

Murphy, Edith. "'A Rich Widow, Now to Be Tane Up or Laid Downe': Solving the Riddle of Thomas Morton's 'Rise Oedipeus.'" *William and Mary Quarterly* 3rd ser. 53.4 (1996): 755–68.

Murphy, Francis. "Introduction." In *Of Plymouth Plantation, 1620–1647*. By William Bradford. New York: Random, 1981. vii–xxiv.

Murray, David. "Using Roger Williams' Key into America." *Symbiosis: A Journal of Anglo-American Literary Relations* 1.2 (1997): 237–53.

Myles, Anne G. "Arguments in Milk, Arguments in Blood: Roger Williams, Persecution, and the Discourse of the Witness." *Modern Philology* 91.2 (1993): 133–60.

"Mystery." *Oxford English Dictionary Online*. 2nd ed. Oxford UP, 1989. Santa Clara U. August 2004. <http://www.oed.com>

Nettels, Curtis P. *The Money Supply of the American Colonies Before 1720*. 1934. Repr. Clifton, NJ: Augustus M. Kelley, 1973.

Newell, Margaret Ellen. *From Dependency to Independence: Economic Revolution in Colonial New England*. Ithaca: Cornell UP, 1998.

Newman, Eric P. *The Early Paper Money of America*. Racine, WI: Whitman Pub. Co., 1967.

Norton, Mary Beth. *In the Snare of the Devil: The Salem Witchcraft Crisis of 1692*. New York: Knopf, 2002.

Ogburn, Floyd, Jr. *Style as Structure and Meaning: William Bradford's "Of Plymouth Plantation."* Washington, DC: UP of America, 1981.

Orgel, Stephen. *The Illusion of Power: Political Theater in the English Renaissance*. Berkeley: U of California P, 1975.

Parris, Samuel. *The Sermon Notebook of Samuel Parris, 1689–1694*. Ed. James F. Cooper, Jr. and Kenneth P. Minkema. Boston: Colonial Society of Massachusetts, 1993.

Patterson, Annabel. *Pastoral and Ideology: Virgil to Valery*. Berkeley: U of California P, 1987.

Peckham, George. *True Reporte, of the late discoveries, and possession, taken in the Right of the Crowne of Englande, of the New-found Landes*. London, 1583.

Peterson, Mark. *The Price of Redemption: The Spiritual Economy of Puritan New England*. Stanford: Stanford UP, 1997.

"Plain." *Oxford English Dictionary Online*. 2nd ed. Oxford UP, 1989. Santa Clara U. August 2005. <http://www.oed.com>

Pooley, Roger. "Anglicans, Puritans and Plain Style." In *1642: Literature and Power in the Seventeenth Century*. Ed. Francis Barker et al. Colchester: Dept. of Literature, U of Essex, 1981. 187–200.

Poovey, Mary. *The History of the Modern Fact: Problems of Knowledge in the Sciences of Wealth and Society*. Chicago: U of Chicago P, 1998.

Porter, Carolyn. *Seeing and Being: The Plight of the Participant Observer in Emerson, James, Adams, and Faulkner*. Middletown, CT: Wesleyan UP, 1981.

Pratt, Mary Louise. *Imperial Eyes: Travel Writing and Transculturation*. London: Routledge, 1992.

Pudaloff, Ross. "Sign and Subject: Antinomianism in Massachusetts Bay." *Semiotica* 54 (1985): 147–63.

Purchas, Samuel. *Hakluytus Posthumous; or, Purchas His Pilgrimes*. 1625. Glasgow: J. MacLehose, 1905–7.

Quijano, Aníbal, and Immanuel Wallerstein. "Americanity as a Concept, or the Americas in the Modern World-System." *ISSJ* 134 (1992): 549–57.

Rabb, Theodore K. *Enterprise and Empire: Merchant and Gentry Investment in the Expansion of England, 1575–1630*. Cambridge: Harvard UP, 1967.

Ralegh, Walter. *The Discoverie of the Large, Rich and Bewtiful Empire of Guiana*. 1596. Repr. ed. Sir Robert H. Schomburgh. London: Hakluyt Society, 1848.

Read, David. "Silent Partners: Historical Representation in William Bradford's *Of Plymouth Plantation*." *Early American Literature* 33.3 (1998): 291–314.

Reising, Russell. *The Unusable Past: Theory and the Study of American Literature*. New York: Methuen, 1986.

Roberts, Lewes. *The Merchants Mappe of Commerce*. London, 1638.

——. *The Merchants Map of Commerce, Second Edition Corrected and much Enlarged*. London, 1671.

——. *The Treasure of Traffike*. London, 1641.

Roberts, William I., III. *The Fur Trade of New England in the Seventeenth Century*. Diss. U of Pennsylvania, 1958.

Rosenmeier, Jesper. "The Teacher and the Witness: John Cotton and Roger Williams." *William and Mary Quarterly* 3rd ser. 25.3 (1968): 408–31.

——. "'With my owne eyes': William Bradford's *Of Plymouth Plantation*." In *The American Puritan Imagination*. Ed. Sacvan Bercovitch. New York: Cambridge UP, 1974. 77–106.

Rosenthal, Bernard. *Salem Story: Reading the Witch Trials of 1692*. Cambridge: Cambridge UP, 1993.

Rosier, James. *A True Relation of the most prosperous voyage made this present yeere 1605*. London, 1605.

Rothenberg, Winifred Barr. *From Market-Places to Market-Economy: The Transformation of Rural Massachusetts, 1750–1850*. Chicago: U of Chicago P, 1992.

Round, Philip H. *By Nature and By Custom Cursed: Transatlantic Civil Discourse and New England Cultural Production, 1620–1660*. Hanover, NH: UP of New England, 1999.

Russell-Wood, A. J. "Centers and Peripheries in the Luso-Brazilian World, 1500–1808." In *Negotiated Empires: Centers and Peripheries in the Americas, 1500–1820*. Ed. Christine Daniels and Michael V. Kennedy. New York: Routledge, 2002. 105–42.

Rutman, Darrett B. *Husbandmen of Plymouth: Farms and Villages in the Old Colony, 1620–1692*. Boston: Beacon, 1967.

——. *Winthrop's Boston: A Portrait of a Puritan Town, 1630–1649*. New York: Norton, 1972.

Ruttenburg, Nancy. *Democratic Personality: Popular Voice and the Trial of American Authorship*. Stanford: Stanford UP, 1998.

Sacks, David Harris. *Trade, Society, and Politics in Bristol, 1500–1640*. 2 vols. New York: Garland, 1985.

Salisbury, Neal. *Manitou and Providence: Indians, Europeans, and the Making of New England, 1500–1643*. Oxford: Oxford UP, 1982.

Salutati, Coluccio. *De Seculo et Religione*. Ed. B. L. Ullman. Firenze, Italy: Olschki, 1957.

Sargent, Mark L. "William Bradford's 'Dialogue' with History." *New England Quarterly* 65 (September 1992): 389–421.

Sayre, Gordon M. *Les Sauvages Américains: Representations of Native Americans in French and English Colonial Literature*. Chapel Hill: U of North Carolina P, 1997.

Schama, Simon. *The Embarrassment of Riches: An Interpretation of Dutch Culture in the Golden Age*. London: William Collins, 1987.

Schaub, Thomas Hill. *American Fiction in the Cold War*. Madison: Wisconsin UP, 1991.

Schramer, James, and Timothy Sweet. "Violence and the Body Politic in Seventeenth-Century New England." *Arizona Quarterly* 48.2 (Summer 1992): 1–32.

Schutte, Anne Jacobson. "'Such Monstrous Births': A Neglected Aspect of the Antinomian Controversy." *Renaissance Quarterly* 38 (1985): 85–106.

Schweitzer, Ivy. "John Winthrop's 'Model' of American Affiliation." *Early American Literature* 40.3 (2005): 441–69.

——. "Salutary Decouplings: The Newest New England Studies." *American Literary History* 13.3 (Fall 2001): 578–91.

——. *The Work of Self-Representation: Lyrical Poetry in Colonial New England*. Chapel Hill: U of North Carolina P, 1991.

Seed, Patricia. *American Pentimento: The Invention of Indians and the Pursuit of Riches*. Minneapolis: U of Minnesota P, 2001.

Severals Relating to the Fund. 1682. In Davis 109–19.

Shapin, Steven. *The Scientific Revolution*. Chicago: U of Chicago P, 1996.

———. *A Social History of Truth: Civility and Science in 17th- Century England*. Chicago: U of Chicago P, 1994.

Sharpe, Kevin, and Steven N. Zwicker, eds. *Refiguring Revolutions: Aesthetics and Politics from the English Revolution to the Romantic Revolution*. Berkeley: U of California P, 1998.

Shea, Daniel B. "'Our Professed Old Adversary': Thomas Morton and the Naming of New England." *Early American Literature* 23.1 (1988): 52–69.

Shell, Marc. *Money, Language, and Thought*. Baltimore: Johns Hopkins UP, 1982.

Silverman, Kenneth. *The Life and Times of Cotton Mather*. 1984. Repr. New York: Welcome Rain Publishers, 2002.

Slotkin, Richard. *Regeneration through Violence: The Mythology of the American Frontier, 1600–1860*. Middletown, CT: Wesleyan UP, 1973.

Smith, Bradford. *Bradford of Plymouth*. Philadelphia: J. B. Lippincott, 1951.

Smith, John. *A Description of New England*. 1616. In Barbour 1:298–363.

———. *Map of Virginia*. 1612. In Barbour 1:121–77.

———. *New Englands Trials*. 1620. In Barbour 1:387–441.

Smolinski, Reiner. "'The Way to Lost Zion': The Cotton-Williams Debate on the Separation of Church and State in Millenarian Perspective." In *Millennial Thoughts in America: Historical and Intellectual Contexts, 1630–1860*. Ed. Bernd Engler, Joerg Fichte, and Oliver Scheiding. Trier: WVT, Wessenschaftler Verlag, 2002. 61–96.

Solomon, Julie. *Objectivity in the Making: Francis Bacon and the Politics of Inquiry*. Baltimore: Johns Hopkins UP, 1998.

———. "'To Know, To Fly, To Conjure': Situating Baconian Science at the Juncture of Early Modern Modes of Reading." *Renaissance Quarterly* 44.3 (1991): 513–58.

Spengemann, William C. *A Mirror for Americanists: Reflections on the Idea of American Literature*. Hanover, NH: UP of New England, 1989.

———. *A New World of Words: Redefining Early American Literature*. New Haven: Yale UP, 1994.

St. George, Robert Blair. *Conversing by Signs: Poetics of Implication in Colonial New England Culture*. Chapel Hill: U of North Carolina P, 1998.

Starnes, DeWitt T., and Gertrude E. Noyes. *The English Dictionary from Caudrey to Johnson, 1604–1775*. Chapel Hill: U of North Carolina P, 1946.

Stavely, Keith. "Roger Williams: Bible Politics and Bible Art." In *Pamphlet Wars: Prose in The English Revolution*. Ed. James Holstun. London: Frank Cass, 1992. 76–91.

Steele, Ian K. *The English Atlantic, 1675–1740: An Exploration of Communication and Community*. New York: Oxford UP, 1986.

Stern, Steve J. "Feudalism, Capitalism, and the World-System in the Perspective of Latin America and the Caribbean." *American Historical Review* 93.4 (1988): 829–72.

Stevens, James Thomas (Aronhiòtas). *Tokinish*. 1994. In *Visit Teepee Town: Native Writings after the Detours*. Ed. Diane Glancy and Mark Nowak. Minneapolis: Coffee House P, 1994. 1–19.

Sweet, Timothy. *American Georgics: Economy and Environment in Early American Literature*. Philadelphia: U of Pennsylvania P, 2002.

Sweezy, Paul Marlor, et al. *The Transition from Feudalism to Capitalism*. London: NLB, 1976.

Taylor, Edward. *God's Determinations* and *Preparatory Meditations*. Ed. Daniel Patterson. Kent, OH: Kent State UP, 2003.

Taylor, Peter J. *Political Geography: World-Economy, Nation-State and Locality*. London: Longan, 1985.

Teunissen, John J., and Evelyn J. Hinz. "Anti-Colonial Satire in Roger Williams' *A Key into the Language of America*." *Ariel* 7.3 (1976): 5–26.

Thirsk, Joan, and J. P. Cooper, eds. *Seventeenth-Century Economic Documents*. Oxford: Clarendon, 1972.

Thomas, Keith. *Religion and the Decline of Magic*. New York: Scribners, 1971.

Thrupp, Sylvia L. *The Merchant Class of Medieval London, 1300–1500*. Chicago: U of Chicago P, 1948.

Todorov, Tzvetan. *The Conquest of America: The Question of the Other*. Trans. Richard Howard. New York: Harper, 1984.

Toulouse, Teresa. "'The Art of Prophesying': John Cotton and the Rhetoric of Election." *Early American Literature* 19.3 (1985): 279–99.

Tribe, Laurence H. "The Curvature of Constitutional Space: What Lawyers Can Learn from Modern Physics." *Harvard Law Review* 103.1 (November 1989): 1–39.

Ulrich, Laurel Thatcher. *Good Wives: Image and Reality in the Lives of Women in Northern New England, 1650–1750*. New York: Knopf, 1982.

Underdown, David. *Revel, Riot, and Rebellion: Popular Politics and Culture in England, 1603–1660*. Oxford: Clarendon, 1985.

Wallerstein, Immanuel. *The Capitalist World-Economy*. Cambridge: Cambridge UP, 1979.

———. "Comments on Stern's Critical Tests." *American Historical Review* 93.4 (1988): 873–85.

———. *The Modern World-System: Capitalist Agriculture and the Origins of the European World-Economy in the Sixteenth Century*. New York: Academic, 1974.

———. *The Modern World-System II: Mercantilism and the Consolidation of the European World-Economy, 1600–1750*. New York: Academic, 1980.

Walton, Gary M., and James F. Shepherd. *The Economic Rise of Early America*. London: Cambridge UP, 1979.

Weber, Max. *The Protestant Ethic and the Spirit of Capitalism*. Trans. Talcott Parsons. London: Unwin, 1930.

Wenska, Walter P. "Bradford's Two Histories: Pattern and Paradigm in *Of Plymouth Plantation*." *Early American Literature* 13 (Fall 1978): 151–64.

Westbrook, Perry D. *William Bradford*. Boston: Twayne, 1978.

White, John. *The Planters Plea*. 1630. In *Tracts and Other Papers*. Coll. Peter Force. Vol. 3. Item 3. New York: Peter Smith, 1947.

———. "To John Winthrop." 16 Nov. 1636. In *Winthrop Papers*. Vol. 3 of 5 vols. Boston: Massachusetts Historical Society, 1943–47. 3:321–23.

Williams, Raymond. *The Country and the City*. New York: Oxford UP, 1973.

Williams, Roger. *The Bloudy Tenent of Persecution*. Ed. Samuel L. Caldwell. In *The Complete Writings of Roger Williams*. Vol. 3.

——. *Christenings Make Not Christians*. Ed. Perry Miller. In *The Complete Writings of Roger Williams*. Vol. 7.

——. *The Complete Writings of Roger Williams*. 7 vols. New York: Russell & Russell, 1963.

——. *The Correspondence of Roger Williams*. 2 vols. Ed. Glenn W. LaFantasie. Hanover, NH: UP of New England, 1988.

——. *A Hireling Ministry None of Christs*. Ed. Perry Miller. In *The Complete Writings of Roger Williams*. Vol. 7.

——. *A Key into the Language of America*. Ed. John J. Teunissen and Evelyn J. Hinz. Detroit: Wayne State UP, 1973.

——. *Mr. Cottons Letter Lately Printed, Examined and Answered*. Ed. Reuben Aldridge Guild. In *The Complete Writings of Roger Williams*. Vol. 1.

Winship, Michael P. "Prodigies, Puritanism, and the Perils of Natural Philosophy: The Example of Cotton Mather." *William and Mary Quarterly* 3rd ser. 51.1 (1994): 92–105.

——. *The Times and Trials of Anne Hutchinson: Puritans Divided*. Lawrence: UP of Kansas, 2005.

Winslow, Edward. *Hypocrisie Unmasked*. 1646. New York: Burt Franklin, 1968.

Winthrop, John. *The History of New England from 1630 to 1649*. Ed. James Savage. 2 vols. Boston: Little, Brown, 1853.

——. "John Winthrop to John Endecott." 3 Jan. 1633/34. In *Winthrop Papers*. Vol. 3 of 5 vols. Boston: Massachusetts Historical Society, 1943–47. 3:146–49.

——. "A Modell of Christian Charity." In *Winthrop Papers*. Vol. 2 of 5 vols. Boston: Massachusetts Historical Society, 1943–47. 2:282–94.

Winthrop, Robert Charles. *Life and Letters of John Winthrop*. Boston: Little, Brown, 1866.

Wood, Ellen Meiksins. *The Origin of Capitalism: A Longer View*. Rev. ed. London: Verso, 2000.

Wood, William. *New England's Prospect*. 1634. Ed. Alden T. Vaughan. Amherst: U of Massachusetts P, 1977.

Young, Alexander, ed. *Chronicles of the Pilgrim Fathers of the Colony of Plymouth, from 1602 to 1625*. 2nd ed. Boston: Little, Brown, 1844.

Ziff, Larzer. *Puritanism in America: New Culture in a New World*. New York: Viking, 1973.

Zuckerman, Michael. "Pilgrims in the Wilderness: Community, Modernity, and the Maypole at Merry Mount." *New England Quarterly* 50.2 (1977): 255–77.

Zwicker, Steven N. *Lines of Authority: Politics and English Literary Culture, 1649–1689*. Ithaca: Cornell UP, 1993.

Index